BERLITZ®

Thai
PHRASE BOOK
& DICTIONARY

✓ W9-BFD-041

Easy to use features

- Handy thematic colour coding
- Quick Reference Guide—opposite page
- Tipping Guide—inside back cover
- Quick reply panels throughout

How best to use this phrase book

● We suggest that you start with the **Guide to pronunciation** (pp. 6-9), then go on to **Some basic expressions** (pp. 10-16). This gives you not only a minimum vocabulary, but also helps you get used to pronouncing the language. The phonetic transcription throughout the book enables you to pronounce every word correctly.

● Consult the **Contents** pages (3-5) for the section you need. In each chapter you'll find travel facts, hints and useful information. Simple phrases are followed by a list of words applicable to the situation.

● Separate, detailed contents lists are included at the beginning of the extensive **Eating out** and **Shopping guide** sections (Menus, p. 39, Shops and services, p. 97).

● If you want to find out how to say something in Thai, your fastest look-up is via the **Dictionary** section (pp. 164-189). This not only gives you the word and phonetic transcription, but is also cross-referenced to its use in a phrase on a specific page.

● If you wish to learn more about constructing sentences, check the **Basic grammar** (pp. 160-163).

● Note the **colour margins** are indexed in Thai and English to help both listener and speaker. And, in addition, there is also an index in Thai for the use of your listener.

● Throughout the book, this symbol ☛ suggests phrases your listener can use to answer you. If you still can't understand, hand this phrase book to the Thai-speaker to encourage pointing to an appropriate answer. The English translation for you is just alongside the Thai.

First edition — 1994   Printed in Switzerland

Contents

4

Travelling around 65

Sightseeing 80

Relaxing 86

Making friends 92

Shopping guide 97

Acknowledgements
We are particularly grateful to Wasant Paileeklee and Rachel
Harrison for their help in the preparation of this book.

Guide to Pronunciation

This chapter is intended to make you familiar with the phonetic transcription we have devised and to help you get used to the sounds of Thai. If you follow carefully the indications supplied below, you will have no difficulty in making yourself understood.

The Thai Script

The Thai script dates back to stone inscriptions of the 13th century and is written from left to right, as in English. The marked difference, however, is the absence of spaces between words, so that words are joined together in one long phrase.

There are 44 consonants in the Thai script and 48 different vowels producing sounds not usually found in Western languages. Vowels take one of four possible positions in relation to the consonant; they can appear to its right, its left, above it or below it. Some of the more complex "vowel clusters" are made up of two or three components surrounding the vowel on two or three sides. There are no punctuation marks in the Thai script, although spaces are left between the end of one sentence and the beginning of the next. There are no capital letters either.

Tones

Thai is a tonal language and the script has five different tones represented by four different tone marks. In the phonetic transcriptions devised in this phrase book, the tonal system is represented by the following tone marks above the first vowel of each syllable:

Tone	Pitch	Symbol
Mid tone:	normal speaking with the voice at a steady pitch	no mark
High tone	pitched slightly higher than normal	´
Low tone	pitched slightly lower than normal	`
Falling tone	pitched high and falling sharply	^
Rising tone	pitched low and rising sharply	ˇ

Every syllable in Thai has a definite tone, and therefore tones play an integral part in the meaning of words. The syllable *kar* provides a good example of this:

kar	mid tone	to dangle
kàr	low tone	galanga (a spice used in cooking)
kár	high tone	to trade
kâr	falling tone	to kill
kǎr	rising tone	a leg

Consonants

Consonants are considerably easier to pronounce in Thai than vowels since all but a few have English equivalents. The sounds you will find as **intial consonants** of syllables are as follows:

Aspirated sounds—consonants with a "huh" sound in them

b	like b as in banana	k	like k as in kiss
ch	like ch as in cheese	p	like p as in pinch
d	like d as in door	s	like s as in sit
f	like f as in free	t	like t as in take
h	like h as in happy		

It is important to recognize the above sounds as aspirates, because some Thai letters also have an unaspirated version, which is not the case in English. These are:

(b)p	pronounced like a sharp p with the "uh" sound removed.
(d)t	pronounced like sharp t with the "uh" sound removed
g	like g as in gas
j	like j as in jump
l	like l in letter
n	like n in new
ng	like ng as in sing it
r	like r in red
w	like w in win
y	like y in yellow

The range of consonant sounds **at the end** of Thai syllables are much fewer than the group above. They are the unaspirated sounds **p**, **t**, and **k** which should ideally be pronounced **(b)p**, **(d)t** and **g** but have not been written as such for simplicity sake.

PRONUNCIATION

Also **y**, **n**, **r**, **w** and **ng** occur as final consonant sounds, as do long and short vowels.

Vowels

Many Thai vowels have a long and a short version. For example:

aih/air	a/ar
euh/eur	i/ee
eh/ey	u/oo
oh/oe	o/or

There are a very large number of vowel sounds in Thai. You will need to persevere with pronunciation practice here, using the full list of vowel sounds below:

a	like **a** in t**a**n
ar	like **ar** in c**a**rt, without pronouncing the **r**
ai	like **y** in tr**y**
i	like **i** in sp**i**t
ee	like **ee** in fr**ee**
eh	like a short, sharp exclamation "**eh?**"
er	like **er** in p**er**k, without pronouncing the **r**
ey	a long version of the above, as in pr**ey**
o	like **o** in sp**o**t
oe	like **oe** in t**oe**
oo	like **oo** in sh**oo**t
or	like **or** in w**or**n, without pronouncing the **r**
u	like **u** in p**u**t

Diphthongs

Other vowel sounds are made by combining two vowels. For example:

i + a gives **ia**, written here as **ear**
u + a gives **ua**, written here as **ua**
eur + a gives **eura**, written here as **eua**

air	like **air** in f**air**, without pronouncing the **r**
aih	a shortened version of **air** above
ear	like **ear** in d**ear**, without pronouncing the **r**

eua	no comparable sound in English except "**Eugha**! How horrible."
euh	as we might say in English "**uh**? What's that? I didn't hear"
eur	the closest sound in English is an exclamation of revulsion: "**Eugh**? What's that horrible thing?'
ia	a shortened version of **ear** above
oey	like **oeil** in the French "trompe l'**oeil**"
ow	like **ow** in c**ow**
ua	like **ure** in mat**ure**

Thai alphabet

The full Thai alphabet in order is given below:

Consonants					
ก	g	ต	t	ฝ	f
ข	k	น	n	พ	p
ค	k	ด	d	ย	y
ฆ	k	ต	(d)t	ร	r
ง	ng	ถ	t	ฤ	ri
จ	j	ท	t	ล	l
ฉ	ch	ธ	t	ว	w
ช	ch	น	n	ศ	s
ซ	s	บ	b	ษ	s
ย	y	ป	(b)p	ส	s
ฎ	(d)t	ผ	p	ห	h
ฏ	t	ฝ	f	ฬ	l
ฐ	t	พ	p	อ	h

Vowels*					
◌ั	an	◌ึ	eur	เ◌ีย	ear
◌ะ	a	◌ุ	u	เ◌ีย	ia
◌ัว	ua	◌ู	oo	เ◌ือ	eua
◌อ	or	เ◌	ey	แ◌	air
ไ◌	ai	เ◌ะ	eh	แ◌ะ	aih
◌า	ar	เ◌ย	oey	โ◌	oe
◌ำ	am	เ◌อ	er	โ◌ะ	oh
◌ิ	i	เ◌อะ	erh	ไ◌	ai
◌ี	ee	เ◌า	ow		
◌ึ	euh	เ◌าะ	o		

* – indicates the position of the consonant in relation to the vowel or vowel cluster.

Some basic expressions

Yes*.	ครับ (ค่ะ)	kráp (kâ)
No.	ไม่	mâi
Please.	กรุณา	ga run ar
Thank you.	ขอบคุณ	kòrp kun
Thank you very much.	ขอบคุณมาก	kòrp kun mârk
That's all right/ You're welcome.	ไม่เป็นไร	mâi pehn rai

Greetings   สวัสดี

Good morning/ afternoon.	สวัสดี	sa wàt dee
Good evening.	สวัสดี	sa wàt dee
Good night.	ราตรีสวัสดี	rar tree sa wàt
Goodbye.	สวัสดี	sa wàt dee
See you later.	แล้วเจอกัน	láiw jer gan
Hello/Hi!	สวัสดี	sa wàt dee
This is Mr./Mrs./ Miss...	นี่คุณ...	nêe kun
How do you do? (Pleased to meet you.)	ยินดีที่รู้จัก	yin dee têe róo jàk
How are you?	เป็นยังไง?	pehn yang ngai
Very well, thanks. And you?	สบายดี ขอบคุณ แล้วคุณละ?	sa bai dee kòrp kun. láiw kun lâ
How's life?	เป็นไง?	(b)pehn ngai
Fine.	สบายดี	sa bai dee
I beg your pardon?	อะไรนะ?	arai ná
Excuse me. (May I get past?)	ขอโทษ	kòr tôet
Sorry!	ขอโทษ	kòr tôet

---

* In Thai there is no exact word meaning yes and no. Instead, to affirm something the polite word is used; a man would say **kráp** and a woman **kâ**. For more information see the GRAMMAR section.

Questions   คำถาม

Where?	ที่ไหน?	têe năi
How?	ยังไง?	yang ngai
When?	เมื่อไหร่?	mêua rài
What?	อะไร?	arai
Why?	ทำไม?	tam mai
Who?	ใคร?	krai
Which?	อันไหน?	an năi
Where is/are ...?	...อยู่ที่ไหน?	... yòo têe năi
Where can I find/ get ...?*	ผม(ดิฉัน)จะหา ...ได้ที่ไหน?	pŏm (di chán) ja hăr...dâi têe năi
How far?	ไกลไหม?	glai măi
How long?	นานไหม?	narn măi
How much/ How many?	เท่าไหร่?	tôw rài
How much does this cost?	อันนี้เท่าไหร่?	an née tôw rài
When does ... open/ close?	....เปิด/ ปิดเมื่อไหร่?	...(b)pèrt/(b)pìt mêua rài
What do you call this/that in Thai?	...นี่/ นั่นภาษาไทย เรียกว่าอะไร?	nêe/nân par săr tai rêarg wâr arai
What does this/that mean?	นี่/ นั่นมีความหมาย ว่ายังไง?	nêe/nân mee kwarm măi wâr yang ngai

Do you speak ...?   คุณพูด...ได้ไหม?

Do you speak English?	คุณพูดภาษา อังกฤษได้ไหม?	kun pôot par săr ang grit dâi măi
Does anyone here speak English?	ที่นี่มีใครพูดภาษา อังกฤษได้บ้าง?	têe nêe mee krai pôot par săr ang grit dâi bârng
I don't speak (much) Thai.	ผม(ดิฉัน)พูดภาษาไทย ได้นิดหน่อย	pŏm (di chán) pôot par săr tai dâi nít nòy
Could you speak more slowly?	พูดช้าลงหน่อยได้ไหม?	pôot chár long nòy dâi măi

---

* The man would refer to himself as **pŏm**, a female speaker would say **di chan**.

Could you repeat that?	พูดอีกทีได้ไหม?	pôot èek tee dâi mǎi
Could you spell it?	ช่วยสะกดให้ดูหน่อย?	chûay sa gòt hâi doo nòy
How do you pronounce this?	อันนี้ออกเสียงยังไง?	an née òrk sěarng yang ngai
Could you write it down, please?	เขียนให้ดูหน่อย?	kěarn hâi doo nòy
Can you translate this for me?	ช่วยแปลอันนี้ให้ผม(ดิฉัน)หน่อย?	chûay (b)plair an née hâi pǒm (di chán) nòy
Can you translate this for us?	ช่วยแปลอันนี้ให้เราหน่อย?	chûay (b)plair an née hâi row nòy
Could you point to the... in the book, please?	ช่วยชี้...นั้นในหนังสือให้ดูหน่อย?	chûay chée... nân nai náng sěur hâi doo nòy
word	คำ	kam
phrase	วลี	wa lee
sentence	ประโยค	(b)pra yôek
Just a moment.	สักครู่	sàk krôo
I'll see if I can find it in this book.	ผม(ดิฉัน)จะลองดูว่าจะหามันเจอไหมในหนังสือเล่มนี้	pǒm (di chán) ja lorng doo wâr ja hǎr man jer mǎi nai náng sěur lêhm née
I understand.	ผม(ดิฉัน)เข้าใจ	pǒm (di chán) kôw jai
I don't understand.	ผม(ดิฉัน)ไม่เข้าใจ	pǒm (di chán) mâi kôw jai
Do you understand?	คุณเข้าใจไหม?	kun kôw jai mǎi

Can/May...? *ขอ/ช่วย... ?*

Can I have...?	ขอ...ได้ไหม?	kǒr...dâi mǎi
Can we have...?	ขอ...ได้ไหม?	kǒr...dâi mǎi
Can you show me...?	ช่วยบอกผม(ดิฉัน)หน่อย...?	chûay bòrk pom (di chán) nòy
I can't...	ผม...ไม่ได้	pǒm...mâi dâi
Can you tell me...?	ช่วยบอกผม(ดิฉัน)หน่อย...?	chûay doo pǒm (di chán) nòy
Can you help me?	ช่วยผม(ดิฉัน)หน่อยได้ไหม?	chûay pǒm (di chán) nòy dâi mǎi

| Can I help you? | มีอะไรให้ช่วยไหม? | mee arai hâi chûay măi |
| Can you direct me to...? | ช่วยบอกทางไป...ให้ผม(ดิฉัน)หน่อย? | chûay bòrk tarng pai...hâi pŏm (di chán) nòy |

Do you want...? *คุณอยาก...ไหม?*

I'd like...	ผมอยาก...	pŏm yàrk
We'd like...	เราอยาก...	row yàrk
What do you want?	คุณต้องการอะไร?	kun (d)tông garn arai
Could you give me...?	ให้...ผม(ดิฉัน)ได้ไหม?	hâi...pŏm (di chán) dâi măi
Could you bring me...?	เอา...มาให้ผม(ดิฉัน)หน่อยได้ไหม?	ow...mar hâi pŏm (di chán) nòy dâi măi
Could you show me...?	ช่วยบอกผม(ดิฉัน)หน่อย...?	chûay bòrk pŏm (di chán) nòy
I'm looking for...	ผม(ดิฉัน)กำลังหา...	pŏm (di chán) gam lang hăr
I'm searching for...	ผม(ดิฉัน)กำลังค้นหา...	pŏm (di chán) gam lang kón hăr
I'm hungry.	ผม(ดิฉัน)หิว	pŏm (di chán) hĭw
I'm thirsty.	ผม(ดิฉัน)หิวน้ำ	pŏm (di chán) hĭw nárm
I'm tired.	ผม(ดิฉัน)เหนื่อย	pŏm (di chán) nèuay
I'm lost.	ผม(ดิฉัน)หลงทาง	pŏm (di chán) lŏng tarng
It's important.	มันสำคัญ	man săm kan
It's urgent.	มันด่วนมาก	man dùan mârk

It is/There is... *มัน/มี...*

It is...	มัน(คือ/เป็น)...	man (keur/pehn)
Is it...?	มัน...ไหม?	man...măi
It isn't...	มันไม่...	man mâi
Here it is.	นี่อยู่ที่นี่	nêe yòo têe nêe
Here they are.	นี่อยู่ที่นี่	nêe yòo têe nêe
There it is.	นั่นไงอยู่ที่นั่น	nân ngai yòo têe nân

| There they are. | นั่นไงอยู่ที่นั่น | nân ngai yòo têe nân |

There is/There are ...	มี...	mee
Is there/Are there ...?	มี...	mee
There isn't/aren't ...	ไม่มี...	mâi mee
There isn't/aren't any.	ไม่มี	mâi mee

It's ...   มัน...

beautiful/ugly	สวย/น่าเกลียด	sŭay/nâr glèart
better/worse	ดีกว่า/เลวกว่า	dee gwàr/leyw gwàr
big/small	ใหญ่/เล็ก	yài/léhk
cheap/expensive	ถูก/แพง	tòok/pairng
early/late	เช้า/สาย	chów/săi
easy/difficult	ง่าย/ยาก	ngâi/yârk
free (vacant)/ occupied	ว่าง/ไม่ว่าง	wârng/mâi wârng
full/empty	เต็ม/ว่าง	(d)tehm/wârng
good/bad	ดี/เลว	dee/lehw
heavy/light	หนัก/เบา	nàk/bow
here/there	ที่นี่/ที่นั่น	têe nêe/têe nân
hot/cold	ร้อน/เย็น	rórn/yehn
near/far	ใกล้/ไกล	glâi/glai
next/last	หน้า/ที่แล้ว	nâr/têe láiw
old/new	เก่า/ใหม่	gòw/mài
old/young	แก่/เด็ก	kàir/dèhk
open/shut	เปิด/ปิด	(b)pèrt/(b)pìt
quick/slow	เร็ว/ช้า	rehw/chár
right/wrong	ถูก/ผิด	tòot/pìt

Quantities   ปริมาณ

a little/a lot	น้อย/มาก	nóy/mârk
few/a few	น้อย/ไม่กี่	nóy/mâi gèe
much	มาก	mârk
many	หลาย	lăi

| more/less than | มากกว่า/น้อยกว่า | mârk gwàr/nóy gwàr |

| enough/too | พอ/เกินไป | por/gern (b)pai |
| some/any | บาง/ใด | barng/dai |

A few more useful words คำที่เป็นประโยชน์อีกจำนวนหนึ่ง

above	บน	bon
after	หลังจาก	lăng jàrk
and	และ	láih
at	ที่	têe
before (time)	ก่อน	gòrn
behind	หลัง	lăng
below	ต่ำกว่า/ใต้	(d)tàm gwàr/(d)tâi
between	ระหว่าง	ra wàrng
but	แต่	tàir
down	ลง	long
downstairs	ชั้นล่าง	chán lârng
during	ระหว่าง	ra wàrng
for	เพื่อ/ สำหรับ	pêua/săm ràp
from	จาก	jàrk
in	ใน	nai
inside	ข้างใน	kârng nai
near	ใกล้	glâi
never	ไม่เคย	mâi koey
next to	ติดกับ	(d)tìt gàp
none	ไม่เลย	mâi loey
not	ไม่	mâi
nothing	ไม่มีอะไร	mâi mee arai
now	ตอนนี้	(d)torn née
on	บน	bon
only	เท่านั้น	tôw nán
or	หรือ	rĕua
outside	ข้างนอก	kârng nôrk
perhaps	บางที	barng tee
since	ตั้งแต่	(d)tâng (d)tàir
soon	ในไม่ช้า	nai mâi chár
then	แล้วก็	láiw gò
through	ผ่าน	pàrn
to	ถึง	tĕuhng
too (also)	เหมือนกัน	mĕuan gan
towards	ตรงไปที่	(d)trong (b)pai têe
under	ใต้	(d)tâi
until	กระทั่ง	gra tâng
up	ขึ้น	kêuhn
upstairs	ชั้นบน	chán bon
very	มาก	mârk
with	กับ/ ด้วย	gàp/dûay
without	ไม่มี	mâi mee
yet	ยัง	yang

Arrival

Passport Control *ที่ตรวจหนังสือเดินทาง*

Before arrival you will be asked to fill out an immigration card and a customs declaration form asking for details of valuables, electrical equipment and amounts of money in excess of $10,000 being taken into the country. When you leave Thailand you may be asked to prove that you are taking with you the items you have listed.

For most foreign nationals a visa is not required to enter Thailand for a stay of under 15 days. Transit visas are valid for 30 days, tourist visas for 60 and non-immigrant visas for 90 days.

Visitors may be asked to prove their solvency by producing the equivalent of 10,000 baht (per person) or 20,000 baht (per family) in currency, traveller's cheques or credit cards.

You may be asked to show a vaccination certificate if you are travelling from an area infected with yellow fever. Vaccinations against cholera are no longer required but those for typhoid fever and hepatitis A are strongly recommended.

Here's my passport.	นี่หนังสือ เดินทางของผม(ดิฉัน)	née náng sĕur dern tarng kŏrng pŏm (di chán)
I'll be staying...	ผม(ดิฉัน)จะอยู่...	pŏm (di chán) ja yòo
a few days	สองสามวัน,	sŏrng sărm wan
a week	หนึ่งอาทิตย์	nèuhng ar tìt
2 weeks	สองอาทิตย์	sŏrng ar tìt
a month	หนึ่งเดือน	nèuhng deuan
I don't know yet.	ผม(ดิฉัน)ยังไม่รู้	pŏm (di chán) yang mâi róo
I'm here on holiday.	ผม(ดิฉัน)มาเที่ยว	pŏm (di chán) mar têaw
I'm here on business.	ผม(ดิฉัน)มาธุระ	pŏm (di chán) mar tu rá
I'm just passing through.	ผม(ดิฉัน)แคแวะ ผ่านเทาน้ัน	pŏm (di chán) kâir wáih pàrn tôw nán

If things become difficult:

I'm sorry, I don't understand.	ขอโทษ ผม (ดิฉัน)ไม่เข้าใจ	kŏr tôet pŏm (di chán) mâi kôw jai
Does anyone here speak English?	ที่นี่ มีใครพูดภาษา อังกฤษได้ไหม?	têe nêe mee krai pôot pa săr ang krìt dâi măi

ศุลกากร
CUSTOMS

After collecting your baggage at the airport you have a choice: use the green exit if you have nothing to declare. Or leave via the red exit if you have items to declare (in excess of those allowed).

มีรายการสิ่งของต้องแสดง	ไม่มีรายการสิ่งของต้องแสดง
goods to declare	**nothing to declare**

The chart below shows what you can bring in duty-free

	Cigarettes	Cigars	Tobacco	Spirits (Liquor)	Wine
Into Thailand:	200	or 200	or 250g.	1 l. or 1 l.	

I have nothing to declare.	ผม(ดิฉัน) ไม่มีรายการสิ่งของ ต้องแสดง	pŏm (di chán) mâi mee rai garn sìng kŏrng (d)tôrng sa dairng
I have ...	ผม(ดิฉัน)มี...	pŏm (di chán) mee
a carton of cigarettes	บุหรี่หอหนึ่ง	bu rèe hòr nèuhng
a bottle of whisky	วิสกี้ขวดหนึ่ง	wít sa gêe kùat nèuhng
It's for my personal use.	อันนี้สำหรับใช้ส่วนตัว	an née săm ràp chái sùan (d)tua
It's a gift.	อันนี้เป็นของฝาก	an née (b)pehn kŏrng fàrk

ขอดูหนังสือ เดินทาง (พาสปอร์ต)หน่อย	Your passport, please.
คุณมีรายการสิ่งของต้องแสดงไหม?	Do you have anything to declare?
ช่วยเปิดถุงใบนี้หน่อย	Please open this bag.
คุณจะ ต้องจ่ายภาษีสำหรับสิ่งนี้	You'll have to pay duty on this.
คุณมีกระเป๋าอีกไหม?	Do you have any more luggage?

Baggage—Porter กระเป๋า คนยกกระเป๋า

Porters are readily available in the airport arrival hall, as well as at the mainline railway station and coach terminals.

Porter!	คนยกกระเป๋า	kon yók gra (b)pŏw
Please take (this/my)...	ช่วยยก...	chûay yók
luggage	กระเป๋า	gra (b)pŏw
suitcase	กระเป๋า	gra (b)pŏw
(travelling) bag	กระเป๋า(เดินทาง)	gra (b)pŏw (dern tarng)
Take this luggage...	ยกกระเป๋า ใบนี้...ให้หน่อย	yók gra (b)pŏw bai née...hâi nòy
to the bus	ไปที่รถบัส	(b)pai têe rót bàt
to the luggage lockers	ไปที่ฝากกระเป๋า	(b)pai têe fàrk gra (b)pŏw
to the taxi	ไปที่รถแท็กซี่	(b)pai têe rót táihk sêe
How much is that?	เท่าไหร่?	tôw rài
There's one piece missing.	มีของหายไปชิ้นหนึ่ง	mee kŏrng hăi (b)pai chín nèuhng
Where are the luggage trolleys (carts)?	รถเข็นกระเป๋าอยู่ที่ไหน?	rót kĕhn gra (b)pŏw yòo têe năi

Changing money แลกเงิน

Banks are open between 8.30am and 3.30pm, Monday to Friday. In tourist areas most banks operate a foreign exchange service until 8pm or later, seven days a week, including public holidays.

BANK—CURRENCY, see page 129

Where's the nearest currency exchange office?	กแงินที่ใกล้ ที่สุดอยู่ที่ไหน?	têe lâirk ngern têe glai têe sùt yòo têe nǎi
Can you change these traveller's cheques (checks)?	รับแลกเช็คเดินทางไหม?	ráp lâirk chéhk dern tarng mǎi
I want to change some dollars/pounds.	ผม(ดิฉัน)อยาก แลกเงินดอลลาร์/ ปอนด์หนอย	pǒm (di chán) yàrk lâirk ngern dorn lar/(b)porn nòy
Can you change this into baht?	ขอแลกอันนี้ เป็นเงินบาทได้ไหม?	kǒr lâirk an née (b)pehn ngern bàrt dâi mǎi
What's the exchange rate?	อัตราแลกเปลี่ยนเป็น ยังไง?	a (d)trar lâirk (b)plèarn/ (b)pehn yang ngai

Where is...? ...อยู่ที่ไหน?

Where is the...?	...อยู่ที่ไหน?	...yòo têe nǎi
booking office	ที่จองตั๋ว	têe jorng (d)tǔa
duty (tax)-free shop	ร้านขายของปลอดภาษี	rárn kǎi kǒrng (b)plòrt par sěe
newsstand	ร้านขายหนังสือพิมพ์	rárn kǎi nǎng sěur pim

How do I get to..?	จะไป...ไปยังไง?	ja (b)pai...(b)pai yang ngai
Is there a bus into town?	มีรถบัสเข้าไปในเมืองไหม?	mee rót bàt kôw (b)pai nai meuang mǎi
Where can I get a taxi?	ผม(ดิฉัน)จะ เรียกแท็กซี่ได้ที่ไหน?	pǒm (di chán) ja rêark táihk sêe dâi têe nǎi
Where can I hire (rent) a car?	ผม(ดิฉัน)จะ เช่ารถได้ที่ไหน?	pǒm (di chán) ja chôw rót dâi têe nǎi

Hotel reservation ของโรงแรม

Do you have a hotel guide (directory)?	คุณมีสมุดรายชื่อ โรงแรมไหม?	kun mee sa mùt rai chêur roeng rairm mǎi
Could you reserve a room for me?	ช่วยจองห้องพักให้ผม (ดิฉัน)ห้องหนึ่งได้ไหม?	chúay jorng hôrng pák hâi pǒm (di chán) hôrng nèuhng dâi mǎi

in the centre	ที่ใจกลางเมือง	têe jai glarng meuang
near the railway station	ใกล้กับสถานีรถไฟ	glai gàp sa tǎr nee rót fai
a single room	ห้องเดี่ยว	hôrng dèaw
a double room	ห้องคู่	hôrng kôo
not too expensive	ไม่แพงนัก	mâi pairng nák

HOTEL/ACCOMMODATION, see page 22

| Where is the hotel/ guesthouse? | โรงแรม/ เกสต์เฮาส์อยู่ที่ไหน? | roeng rairm/gèyt hôwt yòo têe năi |
| Do you have a street map? | คุณมีแผนที่ถนนไหม? | kun mee păirn têe ta nŏn măi |

Car hire (rental) รถเช่า

To rent a car you must be over 21 and hold a valid International Driving Licence. You may be asked to pay a deposit equal to the estimated cost of the rental. Larger companies, however, waive this deposit for credit-card holders.

I'd like to hire (rent) a car.	ผม(ดิฉัน)อยากเช่ารถ สักคัน	pŏm (di chán) yàrk chôw rót sàk kan
small	เล็ก	léhk
medium-sized	ขนาดกลาง	ka nàrt glarng
large	ใหญ่	yài
automatic	อัตโนมัติ	àt a noe mát
I'd like it for a day/ a week.	ผมอยากเช่าวันหนึ่ง/ อาทิตย์หนึ่ง	pŏm yàrk chôw wan nèuhng/ar tìt nèuhng
Do you have any special rates?	มีราคาพิเศษไหม?	mee rar kar pi sèyt măi
What's the charge per day/week?	ค่าเช่าเท่าไหร่ต่อวัน/ อาทิตย์?	kâr chôw tôw rài (d)tòr wan/ar tìt
Is mileage included?	บวกระยะทางแล้วยัง?	bùak rá yá tarng láiw yang
What's the charge per kilometre?	คิดค่าเช่าต่อ กิโลเมตรเท่าไหร่?	kít kâr chôw (d)tòr gi loe mét tôw rài
I'd like to leave the car in...	ผม(ดิฉัน) ต้องการทิ้งรถไว้ที่...	pŏm (di chán) (d)tôrng garn tíng rót wái têe
I'd like full insurance.	ผม(ดิฉัน)อยากได้ที่มี ประกันเต็มที่	pŏm (di chán) yàrk dâi têe mee (b)pra gan (d)tehm têe
How much is the deposit?	ค่ามัดจำเท่าไหร่?	kâr mát jam tôw rài
I have a credit card.	ผม(ดิฉัน)มีบัตรเครดิต	pŏm (di chán) mee bàt krey dìt
Here's my driving licence.	นี่ใบขับขี่ของผม(ดิฉัน)	née bai kàp kèe kŏrng pŏm (di chán)

CAR, see page 75

Taxi แท็กซี่

You shouldn't have any difficulty finding a taxi as every time you venture outside you will probably be hailed by a number of over-enthusiastic taxi drivers. Only those with the official yellow registration plates and signs on the roof should be used. Although a small number of Bangkok taxis have meters, the majority do not and a price must be agreed with the driver before the journey begins. In addition to taxis there are three-wheeled tuk tuks which are slightly cheaper. Outside Bangkok, their equivalent is the pedal-powered *samlor* or rickshaw.

Where can I get a taxi/tuk tuk?	ผม(ดิฉัน)จะเรียกแท็กซี่/ ตุ๊กตุ๊กได้ที่ไหน?	pŏm (di chán) ja rêark táih/ sêe/(d)túk (d)túk dâi têe nái
Where is the taxi rank (stand)?	ที่จอดรถแท็กซี่อยู่ที่ไหน?	têe jòrt rót táihk sêe yòo têe nái
Could you get me a taxi?	เรียกแท็กซี่ให้ผม(ดิฉัน) คันหนึ่งได้ไหม?	rêark táihk sêe hâi pŏm (di chán) kan nèuhng dâi mái
What's the fare to…?	ไป...คิดเท่าไหร่?	(b)pai…kìt tôw rài
That's too expensive. How about…baht?	แพงไป ...บาทได้ไหม	pairng (b)pai…bàrt dâi mái
How far is it to…?	ไป...ไกลไหม?	(b)pai…glai mái
Take me to…	พาผม(ดิฉัน) ไปส่งที่...ด้วย	par pŏm (di chán) (b)pai sòng têe…dûay
this address	ที่อยู่นี้	têe yòo née
the airport	สนามบิน	sa nărm bin
the town centre	ใจกลางเมือง	jai glarng meuang
the… Hotel	โรงแรม...	roeng rairm
the railway station	สถานีรถไฟ	sa tăr nee rót fai
Turn… at the next corner.	เลี้ยว...ที่หัวมุมข้างหน้า	léaw ..têe hŭa mum kârng nâr
left/right	ซ้าย/ ขวา	sái/kwâr
Go straight ahead.	ตรงไป	(d)trong (b)pai
Please stop here.	จอดที่นี่	jòrt têe nêe
Could you wait for me?	รอเดี๋ยวนะ?	ror dĕaw ná
I'll be back in 10 minutes.	ผม(ดิฉัน)จะกลับมา ในอีกสิบนาที	pŏm (di chán) ja glàp mar nai èek sìp nar tee

TIPPING, see inside back-cover

Hotel—Other accommodation

Information on some of the larger hotels can be obtained from international branches of the Tourism Authority of Thailand (TAT) and booking made direct. A booking service is also available at the Thai Hotels Association desk in the arrival hall of Bangkok airport. Most large provincial towns in Thailand have TAT branches which can provide names and addresses of hotels in the area.

Most large hotels add 11% government tax and 8-10% service charges to the bill.

โรงแรม (roeng rairm)	Hotel. It is a good idea to book a hotel in Bangkok before you arrive as the majority of its 30,000 rooms are often full. Prices vary from the very cheapest guest houses in the Khao Sarn Road (*ta nǒn kòw sǎrn*) to some of the most luxurious first class hotels in the world. Among the middle range hotels, many offer a choice of air conditioning or a simple ceiling fan. The latter are cheaper. Most hotels have a swimming pool. Outside Bangkok, hotel accommodation may be more basic but prices are cheap.
โรงแรมม่านรูด (roeng rairm mârn rôot)	Motels are known in Thai as "hotels with curtains" (the curtains are to hide the car so the guests retain their anonymity) and are usually rented out by the hour. While people can stay for several days at a time this would probably not be the best type of tourist accommodation.
บังกาโล (bang ga loe)	Beach resorts not only have a full range of hotel accommodation but also offer bamboo bungalows built on the beach which are clean, simple and very good value for money.
บ้านพักชายทะเล (bârn pák chai ta ley)	A beach bungalow is a complex of huts on the beach, with a central bungalow which acts as a reception area and restaurant.
กระท่อม (gra tôm)	In jungle and hill resorts (in Kanchanaburi and Northern Thailand) cottages that are part of a larger complex are also available.

แพ		
(pair)	For the adventurous, there are rafts on the River Kwai (*mâir nárm kwair*).	
Can you recommend a hotel/guest house?	ช่วยแนะนำโรงแรม/ เกสเฮ้าส์ให้ผม (ดิฉัน)หน่อย?	chûay náih nam roeng rairm/gèyt hôwt hâi pŏm (di chán) nòy
Are there any self-catering flats (apartments) vacant?	มีแฟลต/ อพาร์ตเมนท์ที่ทำอาหาร กินเองได้ว่างไหม?	mee fláiht/ar pârt méyn têe tam ar hǎrn gin eyng dâi wârng mǎi

Checking in—Reception เช็คอิน แผนกต้อนรับ

My name is...	ผม(ดิฉัน)ชื่อ...	pŏm (di chán) chêur
I have a reservation.	ผม(ดิฉัน)จองห้องไว้	pŏm (di chán) jorng hôrng wái
We've reserved 2 rooms/ an apartment.	เราจองห้องเอาไว้สองห้อง /อพาร์ตเมนท์เอาไว้ หลังหนึ่ง	row jorng hôrng ow wái sŏrng hôrng/ar pârt méyn ow wái lǎng nèuhng
Here's the confirmation.	นี่คือคำยืนยัน	nêe keur kam yeurn yan
Do you have any vacancies?	คุณมีห้องว่างไหม?	kun mee hôrng wârng mǎi
I'd like a...	ผม(ดิฉัน)อยากได้...	pŏm (di chán) yàrk dâi
single room	ห้องเดี่ยว	hôrng dèaw
double room	ห้องคู่	hôrng kôo
We'd like a room...	เราอยากได้ห้องๆหนึ่ง...	row yàrk dâi hôrng hôrng nèuhng
with twin beds	ที่มีเตียงเดี่ยวสองเตียง	têe mee (d)teang dèaw sŏrng (d)teang
with a double bed	ที่มีเตียงคู่	têe mee (d)teang kôo
with a bath	ที่มีห้องน้ำด้วย	têe mee hôrng nárm dûay
with a shower	ที่มีฝักบัว	têe mee fàk bua
with a balcony	ที่มีระเบียง	têe mee ra beang
with a view	ที่มีวิวข้างนอก	têe mee wiw kârng nôrk
at the front	ด้านหน้า	dârn nâr
at the back	ด้านหลัง	dârn lǎng
It must be quiet.	มันจะต้องเงียบ	man ja (d)tôrng ngêarp
Is there ...?	มี...ไหม?	mee...mǎi
air conditioning	แอร์	air
a conference room	ห้องประชุม	hôrng (b)pra chum

CHECKING OUT, see page 31

24

a laundry service	บริการซักรีด	bo ri garn sák rêet
a private toilet	ห้องน้ำส่วนตัว	hôrng nárm sùan (d)tua
a radio/television in the room	วิทยุ/โทรทัศน์ในห้อง	wít ta yú/to ra tát nai hôrng
a swimming pool	สระว่ายน้ำ	sà wâi nárm
hot water	น้ำร้อน	nárm rórn
room service	บริการรูมเซอร์วิส	bo ri garn room ser wít
running water	น้ำประปา	nárm (b)pra (b)par
Could you put an extra bed/a cot in the room?	ช่วยใส่เตียงอีกเตียง/ อุ่นอนเข้าไปในห้องด้วย?	chûay sài (d)tearng èek (d)teang/òo norn kôw (b)pai nai hôrng dûay

How much? เท่าไหร่?

What's the price...?	...เท่าไหร่?	...tôw rài
per day	วันละ	wan lá
per week	อาทิตย์ละ	ar tìt lá
for bed and breakfast	ค่าที่พักและอาหารเช้า	kâr têe pák láih ar hărn chów
excluding meals	ไม่รวมอาหาร	mâi ruam ar hărn
for full board (A.P.)	รวมอาหารทุกมื้อ	ruam ar hărn túk méur

| Does that include...? | นั่นรวม...ด้วยไหม? | nân ruam...dûay măi |

breakfast	อาหารเช้า	ar hărn chów
service	ค่าบริการ	kâr bo ri garn
Is there any reduction for children?	มีส่วนลดสำหรับเด็กไหม?	mee sùan lót săm ràp dèhk măi
Do you charge for the baby?	คิดค่าเด็กอ่อนด้วย หรือเปล่า?	kít kâr dèhk òrn dûay rěua (b)plôw
That's too expensive.	แพงเกินไป	pairng gern (b)pai
Do you have anything cheaper?	มีอะไรที่ถูกกว่านั้นไหม?	mee arai têe tòok gwàr nán măi

| Is electricity included in the rental? | ค่าไฟฟ้ารวมอยู่ในค่าเช่า ด้วยหรือเปล่า? | kâr fai fár ruam yòo nai kâr chôw dûay rěua (b)plôw |

How long? นานไหม?

We'll be staying...	เราจะอยู่...	row ja yòo
overnight only	แค่คืนเดียว	kâir keurn deaw
a few days	สองสามวัน	sŏrng sărm wan
a week (at least)	(อย่างน้อย)อาทิตย์หนึ่ง	(yàrng nói) ar tìt nèuhng

NUMBERS, see page 147

| I don't know yet. | ผม/(ดิฉัน)ยังไม่รู้เลย | pŏm (di chán) yang mâi róo loey |

Decision ตัดสินใจ

May I see the room?	ขอดูห้องก่อนได้ไหม?	kŏr doo hôrng gòrn dâi măi
That's fine. I'll take it.	ตกลง ผม/(ดิฉัน)เอาห้องนี้	(d)tòk long. pŏm (di chán) ow hôrng née
No. I don't like it.	ไม่ ผม/(ดิฉัน)ไม่ชอบห้องนี้	mâi. pŏm (di chán) mâi chôrp hôrng née
It's too...	มัน...เกินไป	man...gern (t)pai
cold/hot	หนาว/ร้อน	nŏw/rórn
dark/small	มืด/เล็ก	mêurt/léhk
noisy	เสียงดัง	sĕarng dang
I asked for a room with a bath.	ผม/(ดิฉัน)ขอห้อง ที่มีอ่างอาบน้ำ	pŏm (di chán) kŏr hôrng têe mee àrng àrp nárm
Do you have anything...?	คุณมีอะไร...ไหม?	kun mee arai...măi
better	ดีกว่านั้น	dee gwàr nán
bigger	ใหญ่กว่านั้น	yài gwàr nán
cheaper	ถูกกว่านั้น	tòok gwàr nán
quieter	เงียบกว่านั้น	ngêab gwàr nán
Do you have a room with a better view?	คุณมีห้องที่มีวิว ดีกว่านี้ไหม?	kun mee hôrng têe mee wiw dee gwàr née măi

Registration ลงทะเบียน

Upon arrival at a hotel or guesthouse you may be asked to fill in a registration form (ใบลงทะเบียน —*bai long ta biarn*).

นามสกุล/ชื่อ	Name/First name
เมือง/ถนน/เลขที่	Home town/Street/Number
สัญชาติ/อาชีพ	Nationality/Occupation
วัน/สถานที่เกิด	Date/Place of birth
มาจาก/จะไปที่	Coming from.../ Going to...
เลขที่หนังสือเดินทาง	Passport number
สถานที่/วันที่	Place/Date
ลายมือชื่อ	Signature

TELLING THE TIME, see page 143

What does this mean?	อันนี้มีความหมายยังไง?	an née mee kwarm măi yang ngai

ขอดูหนังสือเดินทาง (พาสปอร์ต)หน่อย?	May I see your passport, please?
ช่วยกรอกแบบฟอร์ม ลงทะเบียนนี้ด้วย?	Would you mind filling in this registration form?
ช่วยเซ็นชื่อตรงนี้ด้วย	Please sign here.
จะอยู่ที่นี่นานไหม?	How long will you be staying?

What's my room number?	ห้องผม(ดิฉัน) หมายเลขเท่าไหร่?	hông pŏm (di chán) măi lêyg tôw rài
Will you have our luggage sent up?	ช่วยขนกระเป๋าของเรา ขึ้นไปให้ด้วย?	chûay kŏn gra (b)pŏw kôrng row kêuhn (b)pai hâi dûay
Where can I park my car?	ผม(ดิฉัน)จะ จอดรถได้ที่ไหน?	pŏm (di chán) ja jòrt rót dâi têe năi
Does the hotel have a garage?	ที่โรงแรมมีโรงรถไหม?	têe roeng rairm mee roeng rót măi
I'd like to leave this in the hotel safe.	ผม(ดิฉัน)อยากจะฝาก อันนี้เอาไว้ในตู้เซฟของ โรงแรม	pŏm (di chán) yàrk ja fàrk an née ow wái nai (d)tôo seyf kŏrng roeng rairm

Hotel staff พนักงานโรงแรม

hall porter	พนักงานยกกระเป๋า	pa nák ngarn yók gra (b)pŏw
maid	พนักงานดูแลห้อง	sŏw chái
manager	ผู้จัดการ	pôo jàt garn
porter	คนยกกระเป๋า	kon yók gra (b)pŏw
receptionist	พนักงานต้อนรับ	pa nák ngarn (d)tôrn ráp
switchboard operator	พนักงานรับโทรศัพท์/ โอเปอเรเตอร์	pa nák ngarn ráp toe ra sàp/oer (b)per rey (d)têr
waiter	พนักงานเสริฟ/บ๋อย	pa nák ngarn sèrp/bŏy
waitress	พนักงานเสริฟ	pa nák ngarn sèrp

Hotel staff may be addressed as *kun kráp* if you are a male speaker or *kun kâ* if you are female.

TELLING THE TIME, see page 153

General requirements ความต้องการทั่วไป

The key to room..., please.	ขอกุญแจห้อง...ด้วย	kŏr gun jair hôrng...dûay
Could you wake me at... please?	ช่วยปลุกผม(ดิฉัน) เวลา...ด้วย?	chûay (b)plùk pŏm (di chán) wey lar...dûay
When is breakfast/ lunch/dinner served?	อาหารเช้า/เที่ยง/ เย็นเสิร์ฟตอนกี่โมง?	ar hărn chów/têang/yehn sèrp (d)torn gèe moeng
May we have breakfast in our room, please?	ขออาหารเช้าที่ห้องได้ไหม?	kŏr ar hărn chów têe hôrng dâi mái
Is there a bath on this floor?	ชั้นนี้มีอ่างอาบน้ำไหม?	chán née mee àrng àrp nárm măi
What's the voltage?	ที่นี่ใช้ไฟฟ้ากี่โวลท์?	têe nêe chái fai fár gèe woel
Where's the shaver socket (outlet)?	ปลั๊กเสียบเครื่อง โกนหนวดไฟฟ้า อยู่ที่ไหน?	(b)plák sèarp krèuang goen nùat fai fár yòo têe năi
Can you find me a...?	ช่วยหา...ให้ผม (ดิฉัน)หน่อย?	chûay hăr...hâi pŏm (di chán) nòy
babysitter	คนเลี้ยงเด็ก	kon léarng déhk
secretary	เลขานุการ	ley kăr nú garn
typewriter	เครื่องพิมพ์ดีด	krèuang pim dèet
May I have a/an/ some...?	ขอ...หน่อย?	kŏr...nòy
ashtray	ที่เขี่ยบุหรี่	têe kèar bu rèe
bath towel	ผ้าขนหนู	pâr kŏn nóo
(extra) blanket	ผ้าห่ม(อีกผืน)	pâr hòm (èek pěurn)
envelopes	ซองจดหมาย	sorng jòt măi
(more) hangers	ไม้แขวนเสื้อ(อีกหน่อย)	mái kwairn sêua (èek nòy)
hot-water bottle	ถุงน้ำร้อน	tŭng nárm rórn
ice cubes	น้ำแข็ง	nárm kăihng
needle and thread	เข็มกับด้าย	kĕhm gàp dâi
(extra) pillow	หมอน(เพิ่ม)	mŏrn (pêrm)
reading lamp	โคมไฟหัวเตียง	kŏem fai hŭa (d)teang
soap	สบู่	sa bòo
Where's the...?	...อยู่ที่ไหน?	yòo têe năi
bathroom	ห้องอาบน้ำ	hôrng àrp nárm
dining-room	ห้องทานอาหาร	hôrng tarn ar hărn
emergency exit	ทางออกฉุกเฉิน	tarng òrk chùk chĕrn
lift (elevator)	ลิฟท์	líf
Where are the toilets?	ห้องน้ำอยู่ที่ไหน?	hôrng nárm yòo têe năi

BREAKFAST, see page 40

Telephone—Post (mail) โทรศัพท์ ไปรษณีย์

Can you get me Pattaya 123-45-67?	ช่วยต่อทางไกลไป พัทยา หมายเลข ๑๒๓-๔๕-๖๗?	chûay (d)tòr tarng glai (b)pai pát a yar măi lêyk nèuhng sŏrng sărm-sèe hâr-hòk jèht
Do you have any stamps?	มีแสตมป์ไหม?	mee sa (d)tàirm măi
Would you post this for me, please?	ช่วยส่งอันนี้ทาง ไปรษณีย์ให้ด้วย?	chûay sòng an née tarng (b)prai sa nee hâi dûay
Are there any letters for me?	มีจดหมายมาถึงผม (ดิฉัน)บ้างไหม?	mee jòt măi mar tĕuhng pŏm (di chán) bârng măi
Are there any messages for me?	มีใครฝากขอความอะไรถึ งผม(ดิฉัน)บ้างไหม?	mee krai fàrk kôr kwarm arai tĕuhng pŏm (di chán) bârng măi
How much is my telephone bill?	ค่าโทรศัพท์ของผม (ดิฉัน)เท่าไหร่?	kâr toe ra sàp kŏrng pŏm (di chán) tôw rài

Difficulties ปัญหายุ่งยาก

The ... doesn't work.	...ไม่ทำงาน	... mâi tam ngarn
air conditioning	แอร์	air
fan	พัดลม	pát lom
heating	เครื่องทำความร้อน	krèuang tam kwarm rórn
light	ไฟฟ้า	fai fár
radio	วิทยุ	wít ta yú
television	โทรทัศน์	to ra tát
The tap (faucet) is dripping.	ก๊อกน้ำหยด	gòk nárm yòt
There's no hot water.	ไม่มีน้ำร้อน	mâi mee nárm rórn
The washbasin is blocked.	อ่างล้างหน้าอุดตัน	àrng lárng nâr ùt (d)tan
The window is jammed.	หน้าต่างเปิดไม่ได้	nâr (d)tàrng (b)pèrt mâi dâi
The mesh screen is broken.	มุ้งลวดขาด	múng lûat kàrt
The curtains are stuck.	ผ้าม่านเลื่อนไม่ได้	pâr mârn lêuan mâi dâi
The bulb is burned out.	หลอดไฟขาด	lòrt fai kàrt
My bed hasn't been made up.	เตียงของผม(ดิฉัน) ยังไม่มีคนปูให้เรียบร้อย	(d)teang kŏrng pŏm (di chán) yang mâi mee kon (b)poo hâi rêarp róy

POST OFFICE AND TELEPHONE, see page 132

The ... is broken.	...เสีย/ ชำรุด	... sĕar/cham rút
blind	มู่ลี่	môo lêe
lamp	หลอดไฟ	lòrt fai
plug	ปลั๊กไฟ	plák fai
shutter	หน้าตูงบานเกล็ด	nâr (d)tàrng barn glèht
switch	สวิทช์ไฟ	sa wìt fai
Can you get it repaired?	ช่วยซ่อมให้หน่อยได้ไหม?	chûay sôrm hâi nòy dâi mǎi
Can you spray the room, please?	ช่วยฉีดยากันยุง ในห้องให้ด้วย	chûay chèet yar gan yung nai hôrng hâi dûay

Laundry—Dry cleaner's ซักรีด ซักแห้ง

Thais are scrupulous about cleanliness and most hotels and guest houses have a laundry service. Although dry cleaning is rare in Thailand facilities are available in large hotels, department stores and tourist areas.

I'd like these clothes...	ช่วยเอาเสื้อผ้าพวกนี้ไป... ให้ด้วย	chûay ow sêua pâr pûak née (b)pai...hâi dûay
cleaned	ซักแห้ง	sák hâirng
ironed	รีด	rêet
washed	ซัก	sák
When will they be ready?	จะเสร็จเมื่อไหร่?	ja sèht mêua rài
I need them...	ผม(ดิฉัน)อยากได้...	pǒm (dì chán) yàrk dâi
today	วันนี้	wan née
tonight	คืนนี้	keurn née
tomorrow	พรุ่งนี้	prûng née
before Friday	ก่อนวันศุกร์	gòrn wan sùk
Can you ... this?	ช่วย...ตัวนี้หน่อยได้ไหม?	chûay...(d)tua née nòy dâi mǎi
mend	ซ่อม	sôrm
patch	ปะ	(b)pà
stitch	สอย	sǒy
Can you sew on this button?	ช่วยเย็บตรงกระดุม นี้หน่อยได้ไหม?	chûay yéhp (d)trong gra dum née nòy dâi mǎi
Can you get this stain out?	ช่วยจัดการกับ รอยคราบนี้ด้วย?	chûay jàt garn gàp roy krârp née dûay
Is my laundry ready?	เสื้อผ้าที่ผม(ดิฉัน)เอามา ซักเสร็จหรือยัง?	sêua pâr têe pǒm (dì chán) ow mar sák sèht rěua yang

| There's something missing. | มีอะไรหายไปบางอย่าง | mee arai hăi (b)pai barng yàrng |
| There's a hole in this. | อันนี้เป็นรู | an née (b)pehn roo |

Hairdresser—Barber ร้านเสริมสวย ร้านตัดผม

Is there a hairdresser/ beauty salon in the hotel?	ในโรงแรมนี้มีร้านเสริมสวยไหม?	nai roeng rairm née mee rárn sěrm sŭay mǎi
Can I make an appointment for Thursday?	ขอนัดวันพฤหัสฯได้ไหม?	kôr nát wan pa ru hàt dâi mǎi
I'd like a cut and blow dry.	อยากให้ตัดและเป่า	yàrk hâi (d)tàt láih (b)pòw
I'd like a haircut, please.	ผม(ดิฉัน)อยากตัดผม	pǒm (di chán) yàrk (d)tàt pǒm
bleach	กัดสีผม	gàt sěe pǒm
blow-dry	เป่า	(b)pòw
colour rinse	ทำสีผม	tam sěe pǒm
dye	ยอม	yórm
face pack	ฟอกหน้า	fôrk nâr
hair gel	เยลใส่ผม	yeyl sài pǒm
manicure	แตงเล็บ	(d)tàirng léhp
permanent wave	ดัดถาวร	dàt tǎr won
setting lotion	น้ำยาเซ็ทผม	nárm yar séht pǒm
shampoo and set	สระเซ็ท	sà séht
with a fringe (bangs)	ไว้ผมด้านหน้า(ผมม้า)	wái pǒm dârn nâr (pom már)
I'd like a shampoo for ... hair.	อยากได้แชมพูสำหรับผม...	yàrk dâi chairm poo sǎm ràp pǒm
normal/dry/ greasy (oily)	ธรรมดา/แห้ง/ มัน	ta ma dar/hâirng/man
Do you have a colour chart?	มีตารางสีไหม?	mee (d)tar rarng sěe mǎi
Don't cut it too short.	อย่าตัดสั้นเกินไปนะ	yàr (d)tàt sân gern (b)pai ná
A little more off the ...	เอา...ออกอีกนิด	ow...òrk èek nít
back	ด้านหลัง	dârn lǎng
neck	แถวคอ	tǎiw kor
sides	ด้านข้าง	dârn kârng
top	ข้างบน	kârng bon
I don't want any hairspray.	ไม่ต้องฉีดสเปรย์ให้นะ	mâi (d)tôrng chèet sa (b)prey hâi ná
I'd like a shave.	ช่วยโกนหนวดให้ด้วย	chûay goen nùat hâi dûay

DAYS OF THE WEEK, see page 151

Would you trim my .., please?	ช่วยเล็ม...ให้ด้วย?	chûay lehm...hâi dûay
beard	เครา	krow
moustache	หนวด	nùat
sideboards (sideburns)	จอน	jorn

Checking out เช็คเอ้าท์

May I have my bill, please?	ขอใบเสร็จด้วย?	kŏr bai sèht dûay
I'm leaving early in the morning.	ผม(ดิฉัน)จะ ออกจากนี้ตอนเช้า	pŏm (di chán) ja òrk jàrk née (d)torn chów
Please have my bill ready.	ช่วยเตรียมใบเสร็จให้ เรียบร้อยด้วย	chûay (d)trearm bai sèht hâi rêarp róy dûay
We'll be checking out around noon.	เราจะเช็คเอ้าท์ราวๆเที่ยง	row ja chéhk ôw row row têarng
Is everything included?	รวมทุกอย่างแล้วหรือยัง?	ruam túk yàrng láiw rěua yang
Can I pay by credit card?	จ่ายด้วย บัตรเครดิตได้ไหม?	jài dûay bàt krey dìt dâi mǎi
I think there's a mistake in the bill.	คิดว่ามีอะไรผิด ในใบเสร็จนี้	kit wâr mee arai (b)pìt nai bai sèht née
Can you get us a taxi?	ช่วยเรียกแท็กซี่ให้หน่อย ได้ไหม?	chûay rèark táihk sêe hâi nòy dâi mǎi
Could you have our luggage brought down?	ช่วยขนกระเป๋าลงไป ข้างล่างให้ด้วย	chûay kŏn gra (b)pŏw long (b)pai kârng lârng hâi dûay
Here's the forwarding address.	นี่คือที่อยู่ที่สามารถติดต่อ ผม(ดิฉัน)ได้หลังจากนี้	nêe keur têe yòo têe sǎr mârt (d)tìt tòr pŏm (di chán) dâi ̌lǎng jàrk née
You have my home address.	คุณมีที่อยู่ของผม(ดิฉัน) แลว	kun mee têe yòo kǔng pŏm (di chán) láiw
It's been a very enjoyable stay.	อยู่ที่นี่สนุกมาก	yòo têe née sa nùk mârk

TIPPING, see inside back-cover

Camping แค้มป์ปิ้ง

Several National Parks offer camping facilities, and tents can be hired out on a number of the islands. However, camping sites are not common in Thailand and camping out in the wilds is not recommended.

Is there a camp site near here?	แถวนี้มีที่ตั้งแค้มป์ไหม?	tǎiw née mee têe (d)tâng káirm mǎi
Can we camp here?	เราตั้งแค้มป์พัก ที่นี่ได้ไหม?	row (d)táng kâirm pák têe nêe dâi mǎi
Do you have room for a tent/caravan (trailer)?	คุณมีที่สำหรับกางเต้นท์/ จอดรถนอนไหม?	kun mee têe sǎm ràp garng (d)têyn/jòrt rót norn mǎi
What's the charge...?	คิดเท่าไหร่...?	kít tôw rài
per day	ต่อวัน	(d)tòr wan
per person	ต่อคน	(d)tòr kon
for a car	ต่อคัน	(d)tòr kan
for a tent	ต่อเต็นท์	(d)tòr têyn
Is tourist tax included?	รวมภาษีนักท่องเที่ยว ด้วยหรือเปล่า?	ruam par sěe nák tôrng têaw dûay rěua plòw
Is there/Are there (a)...?	มี...ไหม?	mee...mǎi
drinking water	น้ำดื่ม	nárm dèurm
electricity	ไฟฟ้า	fai fár
playground	สนามวิ่งเล่น	sa nǎrm wîng lêhn
restaurant	ร้านอาหาร	rárn ar hǎrn
shopping facilities	ที่ขอปปิ้ง/ร้านขายของ	têe chórp (b)pîng/rárn kǎi kǒrng
swimming pool	สระว่ายน้ำ	sà wâi nárm
Where are the showers/toilets?	ที่อาบน้ำฝักบัว/ ห้องน้ำอยู่ที่ไหน?	têe àrp nárm fàk bua/hôrng nárm yòo têe nǎi
Where can I get butane gas?	ผม(ดิฉัน)จะ หาก๊าซบิวเทนได้ที่ไหน?	pǒm (di chán) ja hǎr gárt biw teyn dâi têe nǎi
Is there a youth hostel near here?	แถวนี้มีที่พัก เยาวชนไหม?	tǎiw née mee têe pák sǎm ràp yow wa chon mǎi

CAMPING EQUIPMENT, see page 106

Eating out

Thai cuisine combines Indian and Chinese influences with its own distinctive blend of flavours and aromas: lemongrass and coconut milk, galangal and garlic, fresh coriander and sweet basil, lime leaves and fish paste. Thai food will normally use fresh ingredients, speedily cooked, with a healthy combination of firm vegetables, steamed rice and lean, trimmed meats, beautifully served in an array of colour and texture.

Thais are fond of eating out and dining is a social activity. You'll find numerous foodstalls, coffee shops, restaurants and bars. Pavements are often teeming with vendors selling snacks and appetizers from mobile trolleys or from a pair of wicker baskets carried on a pole over the shoulder. Both savoury and sweet foods are on offer.

You will also see mobile vendors with cabinets of fresh fruit, ready-peeled and sliced. This is sold in polythene bags, complete with wooden skewers and an explosive mixture of sugar, salt and chilli powder (*prík gà gleua*) which Thais use as a dip. Some vendors wheel barrows of dried squid pegged to rails and grill them to order. You may also see people deep frying locusts.

แผงลอย
(păirng loy)

The cheapest places to eat are roadside stalls selling noodles or rice dishes from a barrow surrounded by stools. Here you can eat fresh food, prepared while you wait: a skewer of spicy satay, rice with tasty fried chicken or pork in a rich coconut sauce, with a sweet pancake topped with fresh coconut to finish.

ศูนย์อาหาร
(sŏon arhărn)

These food plazas, often found in department stores, offer a full range of simple meals such as noodle soup, boiled chicken on rice, fried rice, curry or mussel omelettes. Most operate on a coupon system where coupons are bought from a central cash point and then used as currency at individual stalls. One of the busiest and best known food halls is in the Mahboonkhrong Centre in Bangkok's Siam Square, but there are many others.

ร้านข้าวแกง
(rárn kôw gairng)

These curry and rice bar restaurants have a display cabinet in the doorways with trays of different curries and soups. You can have one or two of these served on rice or served separately as a side dish with rice.

ร้านอาหาร ร้านอาหาร
(rárn ar hǎrn)

Cheap range roadside restaurants sell a variety of fried rice and noodle dishes which are ideal for lunch. These tend not to be air-conditioned and are largely open for day-time trade, closing in the early evening.

ภัตตาคาร ภัตตาคาร
(pát ta karn)

Grander establishments serve full Thai meals comprising numerous succulent dishes accompanied by rice. Most *pát ta karn* are air-conditioned, although some may have an open-air section. Look for the *Thai Shell Good Food Guide* signs: a rice-bowl with blue lettering signifying that the establishment serves the very best of authentic Thai food.

สวนอาหาร
(sǔan ar hǎrn)

Some restaurants are large, open-air complexes known as food gardens. While the atmosphere is relaxing and refreshing, the food tends to be similar to that in the *pát ta karn*. The biggest restaurant in the world is the Tamnak Thai (*(d)tàm nàk tai*) food garden complex on Bangkok's Ratchadapisek Road. It is divided into four different sectors, corresponding to the four different regions of Thailand, and serves the appropriate regional cuisine in each sector. The restaurant is so vast that waiters deliver food on roller skates.

ร้านอาหารทะเล
(rárn ar hǎrn ta ley)

These restaurants, usually open-air, specialize in seafood which is often on display pre-cooked, or which can be chosen and cooked to order. These are particularly popular at coastal resorts, where you will find a dazzling array of the day's catch: crabs and lobsters, squid, clams and giant prawns, and a tempting variety of fresh fish. Inland seafood restaurants can also be found in Bangkok and Chiang Mai.

ผับ
(pàp)

Western-style pubs have become popular in Bangkok and many provincial capitals, and they sell a wide range of foods. As an accompaniment to alcohol, Thais like to eat snacks called *gàp glâihm*.

Meal times *เวลาอาหาร*

Thai food is meant for sharing and Thais eat their main meal of the day in groups, each with their own individual plate of boiled rice and dipping into the shared savoury dishes that accompany it. The emphasis is on balance and variety, with hot and sour flavours soothed by rich and sweet, steamed dishes and fried, tender and crispy textures.

Thais eat rice at all times of the day, though for breakfast and lunch they may opt for noodles instead.

Breakfast (*ar hărn chów* or *kôw chów*) usually consists of a bowl of thick rice soup, flavoured with ground pork, chicken or prawns, pepper, garlic, fresh coriander and sometimes an egg.

Lunch (*ar hărn glarng wan* or *kôw têang*) is usually taken between 11.30am and 1pm and tends to consist of a single plate of food, either rice based or noodle based. A typical Thai lunch would involve both a "wet" and a "dry" noodle dish.

Dinner (*ar hărn kâm* or *kôw yehn*) can be long and protracted. Evening meals comprise two main parts, rice (*kôw*) and savoury dishes served with rice (*gàp kôw*).

Thai cuisine *อาหารไทย*

Thai food is heavily influenced by Chinese and Indian cuisine. The Chinese influence is mainly in the eating of noodles and the techniques of stir-frying and steaming, while the Indian influence is felt in the delicious blends of hot and aromatic spices. Others, such as Japanese, Malaysian, Arabian and Portuguese, have also added some of their flavours, varying according to the region. Nevertheless, Thai food retains its own distinctive character.

Chinese restaurants are quite common throughout the country. Western and Japanese restaurants are also present in big hotels as well as in tourist areas. Other foreign restaurants such as Vietnamese and Indian can also be found in tourist areas.

รับอะไร?
อันนี้น่าทาน
ดื่มอะไร?

What would you like?
I recommend this.
What would you like to drink?

ที่นี่ไม่มี...
คุณจะรับ...ไหมครับ?

We don't have...
Would you like...?

Hungry? หิวไหม?

I'm hungry/I'm thirsty.	ผม(ดิฉัน)หิว/ หิวน้ำ	pŏm (dì chán) hĭw/hĭw nárm
Can you recommend a good restaurant?	ช่วยแนะนำภัตตาคารดีๆ ให้หน่อยได้ไหม?	chûay néh nam pát tar karn dee dee hâi nòy dâi măi
Are there any inexpensive restaurants around here?	แถวนี้มีภัตตาคาร ที่ไม่แพงไหม?	tăirw née mee pát tar karn têe mâi pairng măi

If you want to be sure of getting a table in a well-known restaurant, it may be better to book in advance.

I'd like to reserve a table for 4.	ขอจองโต๊ะสำหรับสี่คน	kŏr jorng (d)tóh săm ràp sèe kon
We'll come at 8.	เราจะไปถึงนั่นตอนสองทุ่ม	row ja (b)pai tĕuhng nân (d)torn sŏrng tûm
Could we have a table...?	ขอโต๊ะ...ได้ไหม?	kŏr (d)tóh...dâi măi
in the corner	ที่มุมห้อง	têe mum hôrng
by the window	ติดหน้าต่าง	(d)tìt nâr (d)tàrng
outside	ด้านนอก	dârn nôrk
on the terrace	ที่ระเบียง	têe rá beang
in a non-smoking area	ในบริเวณห้ามสูบบุหรี่	nai boh rì weyn hârm sòop bu rèe

Asking and ordering ซักถามและสั่ง

Waiter/Waitress!	บ๋อย/คุณ	bŏy/kun
I'd like something to eat/drink.	ผม(ดิฉัน)อยากได้ อะไรมาทาน/ ดื่ม	pŏm (dì chán) yàrk dâi arai mar tarn/ dèurm

May I have the menu, please?	ขอดูรายการอาหารหน่อย ได้ไหม?	kŏr doo rai garn ar hărn nòy dâi măi
Do you have a set menu*/local dishes?	มีอาหารชุด/ พื้นบ้านไหม?	mee ar hărn chút/péurn bârn măi
What do you recommend?	มีอะไรน่าทานบ้าง?	mee arai nár tarn bârng
I like hot and spicy food.	ผม(ดิฉัน)ชอบอาหารรสจัด	pŏm (di chán) chôrp ar hărn rót jàt
Nothing too spicy, please.	ไม่เอารสจัดนะครับ(คะ)	mâi ow rót jàt ná kráp (kâ)
Do you have anything ready quickly?	มีอะไรที่เสร็จเร็วๆบ้าง?	mee arai têe sèht rehw rehw bârng
I'm in a hurry.	ผม(ดิฉัน)ต้องรีบไป	pŏm (di chán) (d)tông rêep (b)pai
I'd like...	ผม(ดิฉัน)อยากได้...	pŏm (di chán) yàrk dâi

Could we have a/an..., please?	ขอ...ได้ไหม?	kŏr...dâi măi
ashtray	ที่เขี่ยบุหรี่	têe kèar bu rèe
chopsticks	ตะเกียบ	(d)ta gèap
cup	ถ้วยกินน้ำ	tûay gin nárm
fork	ส้อม	sôrm
glass	แก้ว	gâiw
knife	มีด	mêet
napkin (serviette)	กระดาษเช็ดปาก	gra dàrt chét (b)pàak
plate	จาน	jarn
spoon	ช้อน	chórn
toothpicks	ไม้จิ้มฟัน	mái jîm făn
May I have some...?	ขอ...หน่อยได้ไหม?	kŏr...nòy dâi măi

bread	ขนมปัง	ka nŏm (b)pang
butter	เนย	noey
lemon	มะนาว	ma now
oil	น้ำมัน(มะกอก)	nám man (ma gòrk)
pepper	พริกไทย	prík tai
salt	เกลือ	gleua
seasoning	เครื่องปรุง	krêuang (b)prung
sugar	น้ำตาล	nárm (d)tarn
vinegar	น้ำส้มสายชู	nárm sôm săi choo

---

* A set menu is a number of pre-chosen courses, usually cheaper than à la carte.

Special diet *อาหารพิเศษ*

Some useful expressions for those with special requirements:

I'm on a diet.	ผม(ดิฉัน)กำลังลด ความอวน	pŏm (di chán) gam lang lód kwarm ûan
I'm vegetarian.	ผม(ดิฉัน)เป็นมังสวิรัติ	pŏm (di chán) (b)pehn mang sawi rát
I don't drink alcohol.	ผม(ดิฉัน)ไม่ดื่มอัลกอฮอยล์	pŏm (di chán) mâi dèurm al gor horl
I don't eat meat.	ผม(ดิฉัน)ไม่ทานเนื้อ	pŏm (di chán) mâi tarn néua
I mustn't eat food containing ...	ผม(ดิฉัน)จะ ตองไมทานอาหารทีมี...	pŏm (di chán) ja (d)tông mâi tarn ar hårn têe mee
flour/fat	แปง/ไขมัน	(b)pâirng/kǎi man
salt/sugar	เกลือ/น้ำตาล	kleua/nárm (d)tarn
Do you have ... for diabetics?	ทีนีมี...สำหรับ คนที่เป็นเบาหวานไหม?	têe nêe mee...sǎm ràp kon (b)pehn bow wǎrn mǎi
cakes	ขนมเคก	ka nŏm kéyk
fruit juice	น้ำผลไม	nárm pŏn la mái
a special menu	รายการอาหารพิเศษ	raì garn ar hårn pi sèyt
Do you have any vegetarian dishes?	ทีนีมีอาหารมังสวิรัติ บางไหม?	têe nêe mee ar hårn mang sawi rát bârng mǎi
Could I have cheese/ fruit instead of dessert?	ขอเนยแข็ง/ผลไม แทงของหวานไดไหม?	kŏr noey kǎihng/pŏn la mái tairn kŏrng wǎrn dâi mǎi
Can I have an artificial sweetener?	ขอน้ำตาลเทียม หนอยไดไหม?	kŏr nárm (d)tarn team nòy dâi mǎi

And ...

I'd like some more.	ขอสั่งเพิ่ม	kŏr sàng pêrm
Can I have more ..., please?	ขอ...เพิ่มไดไหม?	kŏr...pêrm dâi mǎi
Just a small portion.	ขอที่เล็กๆก็พอ	kŏr têe léhk léhk gôh por
Nothing more, thanks.	ไมรับอะไรแลว ขอบคุณ	mâi ráp arai láiw kòrp kun
Where are the toilets?	หองน้ำไปทางไหน?	hôrng nárm (b)pai tarng nǎi

What's on the menu? *รายการอาหารมีอะไรบ้าง?*

Menus are not usually displayed outside restaurants. Most restaurants in Bangkok and other large cities and tourist areas have menus in English. Look out for local specialities of the region: tiny spare-ribs with coriander root and peppercorns in the South; pork and ginger curry with sticky rice and chunky chilli dip with raw vegetables in the North; freshwater fish cooked with lemongrass in banana leaves in the North-East; and crab and prawns cooked with garlic in a clay pot on the Gulf Coast.

Under the headings below, you'll find alphabetical lists of dishes that might be offered on a Thai menu with their English equivalent. You can simply show the book to the waiter. If you want some fruit, for instance, let *him* point to what's available on the appropriate list. Use pages 36 and 37 for ordering in general.

Reading the menu   *ดูรายการอาหาร*

อาหารเรียกน้ำย่อย	ar hărn rêark nárm yôy	appetizers
เบียร์	bear	beer
เครื่องดื่ม	krêuang dèurm	beverages
เบอร์เกอร์	ber ger	burgers
ไก่	gài	chicken
ของหวาน	kŏrng wărn	desserts
อาหารประเภทไข่	ar hărn (b)pra pèyt kài	egg dishes
อาหารจานหลัก	ar hărn jarn làk	entrées
ปลา	(b)plar	fish
ผลไม้	pŏn la mài	fruit
ไอศครีม	ai sa kreem	ice cream
ก๋วยเตี๋ยว	gwáy těaw	noodles
เป็ดไก่	(b)pèt gài	poultry
ข้าว	kôw	salads
สลัด/ยำ	sa làt/yam	rice
อาหารทะเล	ar hărn ta ley	seafood
อาหารว่าง	ar hărn ra wârng	snacks
ซุป	súp	soups
ผัก	pàk	vegetables
เหล้าไวน์	lôw wai	wine

Breakfast   *อาหารเช้า*

Breakfast—*ar hărn chów* or *kôw chów*—literally means morning food, or morning rice. For Thais this is usually a bowl of rice soup, either flavoured with ground pork, chicken or prawns, or served plain with separate condiments such as salted fish, salted egg and pickled vegetables.

Most hotels and many restaurants in tourist areas serve Western style breakfasts of toast, butter and marmalade with orange juice and coffee. Breakfast cereals are much more difficult to come by. Ordering boiled eggs can also be a shock since the nearest Thai equivalent (*kài lûak*) really means scalded eggs. Two eggs are momentarily scalded with boiling water, then cracked into a glass and topped with pepper and soy sauce. Fried eggs are a safer bet!

I'd like breakfast, please.	ผม(ดิฉัน) อยากได้อาหารเช้า	pŏm (di chán) yàrk dâi ar hărn chów

I'll have a/an/ some...	ขอ...	kŏr
bacon and eggs	เบคอนกับไข่	bey korn gàp kài
boiled egg	ไข่ต้ม	kài (d)tôm
soft/hard	ไม่สุกมาก/เอาสุกๆ	mâi sùk mârk/ow sùk sùk
cereal	ซีเรียล	see re arl
eggs	ไข่	kài
fried eggs	ไข่ดาว	kài dow
scrambled eggs	ไข่คน	kài kon
scalded eggs	ไข่ลวก	kài lûak
fruit juice	น้ำผลไม้	nárm pŏn la mái
orange	น้ำส้ม	nárm sôm
ham and eggs	แฮมกับไข่ดาว	hairm gàp kài dow
jam	แยม	yairm
marmalade	แยมเปลือกส้ม	yairm (b)plèuak sôm
rice soup	โจ๊ก	jóek
with pork	โจ๊กหมู	jóek mŏo
with chicken	โจ๊กไก่	jóek gài
with prawns	โจ๊กกุ้ง	jóek gûng
with egg	โจ๊กใส่ไข่	jóek sài kài
toast	ขนมปังปิ้ง	ka nŏm (b)pang (b)pîng
yoghurt	โยเกิร์ต	yoe gèrt

May I have some...?	ขอ...หน่อยได้ไหม?	kŏr... nòy dâi măi
bread	ขนมปัง	ka nŏm (b)pang
butter	เนย	noey
(hot) chocolate	ช็อคโกแล็ต(ร้อน)	chók goe láiht (rórn)
coffee	กาแฟ	gar fair
decaffeinated	ชนิดไม่มีคาเฟอีน	cha nít mâi mee kar fey een
black/with milk	ดำ/ใส่นม	dam/sài nom
honey	น้ำผึ้ง	nárm pêuhng
milk	นม	nom
cold/hot	เย็น/ร้อน	yen/rórn
pepper	พริกไทย	prík tai
rolls	ขนมปังก้อน	ka nŏm (b)pang gôrn
salt	เกลือ	gleua
tea	ชา	char
with milk	ใส่นม	sài nom
with lemon	มะนาว	ma now
(hot) water	น้ำ(ร้อน)	nárm (rórn)

Starters (Appetizers) *อาหารเรียกน้ำย่อย*

Thai people don't usually have starters at meal time since every dish is served at the same time. However, it has become quite common, especially in the smart restaurants, to have starters. Thai pre-dinner snacks can include such tasty dishes as spicy sausage, nibbled with tiny cubes of fresh ginger, and grated raw papaya in a spicy dressing of fish sauce with fresh green chillies.

I'd like an appetizer.	ผม(ดิฉัน)อยากได้ อาหารเรียกน้ำย่อย	pŏm (di chán) yàrk dâi ar hărn rêark nárm yôy
What would you recommend?	มีอะไรน่าทานบ้าง?	mee arai nâr tarn bârng
ปีกไก่ยัดไส้	(b)pèek gài yát sâi	stuffed chicken wings
เกี๊ยวกรอบ	géaw gròrp	deep-fried, crispy wan ton
แหนมสด	năirm sòt	fresh sausage
ไส้กรอกอีสาน	sâi gròrk ee sărn	spicy North-Eastern sausage
ข้าวเกรียบกุ้ง	kôw grèarp gûng	rice cakes with prawn dip
ปลาหมึกย่าง	(b)pla mèuhk yârng	grilled squid

ปอเปี๊ยะ ((b)por (b)pía)	Thai spring rolls. Often served with a sweet sauce, these are more delicate and compact than Chinese spring rolls and are mildly flavoured.
กระทงทอง (gra tong torng)	Deep-fried batter cups filled with minced pork and spices.
ถุงเงินยวง (tŭng ngern yuang)	Delicate little cups of batter, filled with lightly curry-spiced pork.
สะเต๊ะหมู/เนื้อ (sa téh mŏo/néua)	Pork or beef satay. Originally introduced to Thailand through the southern region from Malaysia, satay is a delicious blend of spicy barbecued meat and hot peanut sauce.
ทอดมันปลา (tôrt man (b)plar)	Deep-fried, spicy fishcakes made from fresh fish fillets, flavoured with a spicy combination of chillies, coriander, galangal and lime.

ขนมปังหน้าหมู/กุ้ง

(ka nǒm (b)pang nâr móo/gûng)

Fried bread topped with minced pork or prawn; accompanied by a cucumber pickle dip, made with fresh chillies, these light but spicy toasts make a delicious starter.

Soups and curries ซุปและแกง

A typical selection of savoury dishes usually includes a soup and/or a curry. Thais always have their soup and curry at the same time as other savoury dishes, as soup was traditionally served as a beverage with the meal.

ต้มยำเห็ด	(d)tôm yam hèht	clear, hot and sour soup with mushroom
แกงจืดลูกชิ้นปลา	gairng jèurt lôok chín (b)plar	clear soup with fish balls
แกงจืดเกี้ยมฉ่าย	gairng jèurt gêarm chài	clear soup with pickled vegetables
แกงจืดสาหร่ายทะเล	gairng jèurt sǎr rài ta ley	clear soup with seaweed
แกงจืดรวมมิตร	gairng jèurt ruam mít	clear soup with a mixture of ingredients
ต้มจับฉ่าย	(d)tôm jàp chài	clear soup with pork ribs and mixed vegetables
แกงเลียง	gairng leang	clear soup with fresh vegetables, prawns and black pepper
ต้มโคล้ง	(d)tôm klóeng	hot and sour curry with dried fish and spices
ต้มเค็ม	(d)tôm kehm	salty soup

ต้มยำกุ้ง/ไก่

((d)tôm yam gûng/gài)

Clear, hot and sour soup with prawn or chicken. This soup, from the central region of Thailand, forms the perfect centrepiece of a typical Thai meal. It should be eaten with lots of rice, as it is flavoured with roasted chilli paste and lemongrass and is extremely hot!

ต้มข่าไก่
((d)tôm kàr gài)

Chicken and coconut milk soup flavoured with galanga. One of the most famous Thai dishes, this soup is rich with coconut milk, but sharp with the flavours of lemongrass, wild lime leaves and galanga, which is a citrus-scented member of the ginger family.

แกงจืดวุ้นเส้น
(gairng jèurt wún sêhn)

Clear soup with Chinese glass noodles, minced pork and vegetables. The delicate, silvery noodles are made from mung beans, and add a subtle texture to this mildly flavoured soup.

แกงจืดเต้าหู้
(gairng jèurt (d)tôw hôo)

Clear soup with tofu. Its name means "mildly flavoured", flavoured simply with fish sauce and spinach. This soup is traditionally served to soothe the effects of other dishes.

แกงส้มผักกระเฉด
(gairng sôm pàk gra chèyt)

Hot and sour curry with fish and pungent green vegetables. Unlike other Thai curries, made with sweet coconut milk, this one from the south of Thailand is based on the sharp, sour flavours of tamarind and lime.

Egg Dishes อาหารประเภทไข่

ไข่ดาว	kài dow	fried egg
ไข่เจียว	kài jeaw	deep-fried omelette
ไข่ลวก	kào lûak	soft boiled eggs
ยำไข่เค็ม	yam kài kèhm	salty egg salad

ไข่เจียวยัดไส้
(kài jeaw yát sâi)

Although called an omelette, this dish is more like a filled crêpe, with a sweetly flavoured stuffing of peppers, tomato and pork.

ไข่ลูกเขย
(kài lôok kŏei)

"Son-in-law" eggs. A popular Thai wedding dish, served as an accompaniment. Traditionally made from hard-boiled duck eggs, deep-fried with a coating of ground chillies, and eaten dripping with tamarind sauce.

Fish and seafood ปลาและอาหารทะเล

There are a large number of freshwater fish and seafood dishes in Thai cuisine, although the highland areas of the North and North-East might have a smaller selection compared to Bangkok and the coastal provinces of the South and the East.

I'd like some fish.	ผม(ดิฉัน)อยากทานปลา	pŏm (di chán) yàrk tarn (b)plar
What kind of seafood do you have?	มีอาหารทะเลอะไรบ้าง?	mee ar hărn ta ley arai bárng
ปลาทู	(b)plar too	mackerel
ปลาจาระเม็ด	(b)plar jar ra méht	pomfret
ปลากระพง	(b)plar gra pong	sea bass
ปลาหมึก	(b)plar mèuhk	squid
ปลาไหล	(b)plar lǎi	eel
ปลาช่อน	(b)plar chôn	serpent-headed fish
ปลาดุก	(b)plar dùk	catfish
ปลาสำลี	(b)plar săm lee	*samlee* fish
ปลากราย	(b)plar grai	*grai* fish
ปลาสลิด	(b)plar sa lìt	gourамy
กุ้ง	gûng	prawn
ล็อบสเต้อร์	lóp sa (d)têr	lobster
ปูทะเล	(b)poo ta ley	crab
หอยลาย	hǒy lai	scallops
หอยแมลงภู่	hǒy mairng pòo	mussels
หอยนางรม	hǒy nang rom	oyster

You may want to try one of these dishes:

ปลาสลิดทอดกรอบ	(b)plar sa lìt tôrt gròrp	crispy, deep-fried gouramy
ยำปลาสลิด	yam (b)plar sa lìt	spicy gouramy salad
ยำปลาดุกฟู	yam (b)plar dùk foo	spicy catfish salad
ผัดเผ็ดปลาดุก	pàt pèht (b)plar dùk	spicy stir-fried catfish
ปลาดุกย่าง	(b)plar dùk yârng	grilled catfish
ปลาเปรี้ยวหวาน	(b)plar (b)prîeaw wǎrn	sweet and sour fish
ปลาช่อนแปะซะ	(b)plar chôn (b)pàih sá	serpent-headed fish steamed with herbs
แกงส้มปลาช่อน	gairng sôm (b)plar chôrn	hot and sour fish curry with mixed vegetables
ห่อหมกปลา	hòr mòk (b)plar	steamed fish curry

ห่อหมกทะเล	hòr mòk ta ley	steamed seafood curry
ทอดมันปลา	tôrt man (b)plar	deep-fried spicy fishcakes
ปลาทูทอด	(b)plar too tôrt	deep-fried sardines
ปลาจาระเม็ดนึ่งเกี้ยมบ๊วย	(b)plar jar ra méht nêuhng gêarm búay	steamed pomfret with sour plums
ปลาหมึกย่าง	(b)plar mèuhk yârng	grilled squid
กุ้งเผา	gûng pŏw	roasted prawns
หอยลายผัดผงกะหรี่	hŏy lai pàt pŏng ga rèe	scallops fried with curry powder
หอยลายผัดน้ำพริกเผา	hŏy lai pàt nám prík pŏw	scallops fried with roasted chilli paste

ปลาสำลีเผา
(**(b)plar săm lee pŏw**)
Roasted *samlee* fish. A simple but delicious country dish, traditionally cooked in banana leaves on an open charcoal oven, flavoured with coriander and garlic.

กุ้งอบหม้อดิน
(**gûng òp môr din**)
Roasted prawns in a clay pot with soy sauce and pepper. This dish is Chinese in origin, combining soy and oyster sauces, sesame oil and ginger, but has been given a Thai flavour with the classic mix of coriander, peppercorns, garlic and fish sauce.

ปูผัดผงกะหรี่
(**(b)poo pàt pŏng ga rèe**)
Crab fried with curry powder. Despite its name, this dish is not particularly hot, but rather gently spiced with curry and without the usual heat of chillies.

ปูอบหม้อดิน
(**(b)poo òp môr din**)
Crab roasted in a clay pot with soy sauce and pepper.

ปลาราดพริก
(**(b)plar rârt prík**)
Fish topped with chillies. Called "three-flavoured fish", this dish is typical of Thai cuisine, combining the three elements of sweet, sour and hot.

baked	อบ	òp
boiled	ต้ม	(d)tôm
curried	แกง	gairng
fried	ผัด	pàt
deep-fried	ทอด	tôrt
grilled	ปิ้ง/ ย่าง	(b)pîng/ yârng
scalded	ลวก	lûak
smoked	รมควัน	rom kwan
steamed	นึ่ง	nêuhng

Meat เนื้อ

Pork and beef are common in Thai cuisines, while lamb is relatively rare. Meats are usually sliced or cut into small, lean pieces for ease of consumption and speed of cooking.

I'd like some...	ผม(ดิฉัน)อยากได้...	pŏm (di chán) yàrk dâi
beef	เนื้อวัว	néua wua
lamb	เนื้อลูกแกะ	néua lôok gàih
pork	เนื้อหมู	néua mŏo
veal	เนื้อลูกวัวอ่อน	néua lôok wua òrn

เบคอน	bey korn	bacon
เครื่องใน/ไส้	krêuang nai/sâi	chitterlings
เนื้อสัน	néua săn	fillet
หมูแฮมรมควัน	mŏo hairm rom kwan	(smoked) ham
ไต	(d)tai	kidneys
ขา(ลูกแกะ)	kăr (lôok) gàih	leg (of lamb)
ลูกชิ้นเนื้อ	lôok chín néua	meatballs
เนื้อแกะ	néua gàih	mutton
หางวัว	hărng wua	oxtail
หัวหมู/ ขาหมู	hŭa mŏo/kăr mŏo	pig's head/trotters
ไส้กรอก	sâi gròrk	sausage
ขาช่วงล่าง	kăr chûang lârng	shank
เนื้อสันนอก	néua săn nôrk	sirloin
หมูหัน	mŏo hăn	suckling pig
ตับอ่อน	(d)tàp òrn	sweetbreads
เนื้อสันใน	néua săn nai	tenderloin
ลิ้น	lín	tongue

baked	อบ	òp
barbecued	ปิ้ง/ย่าง	(b)pîng/yârng
boiled	ต้ม	(d)tôm
fried	ผัด/ทอด	pàt/tôrt
grilled	ปิ้ง/ย่าง	(b)pîng/yârng
roast	อบ	òp
sautéed	ผัด	pàt
stewed	ตุ๋น	(d)tŭn
very rare	ไม่เอาสุก	mâi ow sùk
underdone (rare)	เอาไม่ค่อยสุก	ow mâi kôy sùk
medium	สุกปานกลาง	sùk (b)parn glarng
well-done	เอาสุกๆ	ow sùk sùk

Some meat specialities อาหารจานพิเศษประเภทเนื้อ

เนื้อผัดพริก	néua pàt prík	beef fried with chillies
เนื้อผัดน้ำมันหอย	néua pàt nám man hŏy	beef fried with oyster sauce
เนื้ออบ	néua òp	roast beef
เนื้อตุ๋น	néua (d)tŭn	stewed beef
พะแนงเนื้อ/ หมู	pa nairng néua /mŏo	mild beef or pork curry
เนื้อทอด	néua tôrt	deep-fried beef
หมูย่าง	mŏo yârng	grilled pork
หมูทอดกระเทียม	mŏo tôrt gra team	pork fried with garlic
ผัดคะน้าหมูกรอบ	pàt ka ná mŏo gròrp	spinach fried with crispy pork
ขาหมูพะโล้	kăr mŏo pá lóe	leg of pork in cinnamon and star anise sauce
หมูกรอบ	mŏo gròrp	crispy roast pork
หมูแดง	mŏo dairng	red roast pork
หมูสะเต๊ะ	mŏo sa (d)téh	pork satay

เนื้อผัดกะเพรา
(néua pàt ga prow)
Beef fried with basil leaves. Sweet basil is deep-fried with strips of lean beef until crisp and glossy, giving this dish a lovely texture.

แกงมัสมั่นเนื้อ
(gairng ma sa mân néua)
Indian-style curry with beef or pork. Traditionally a special-occasion curry, this dish gets its name from "Muslim", and its Indian origins can be tasted in the sweet, rich blend of cinnamon, cloves, cardamom and nutmeg over a background of hot red chillies.

แกงเขียวหวานเนื้อ/หมู
(gairng kĕaw wărn néua/mŏo)
Fragrant green curry with beef or pork. An aromatic mixture of tastes: with hot green chillies, lemongrass and lime, sweetened with coconut milk, this curry is typically Thai.

ยำเนื้อย่าง
(yam néua yârng)
Spicy grilled beef salad. This dish is from the North-Eastern region of Thailand, where roasted rice powder adds texture and fragrance to a hearty salad tossed in chilli and lime dressing.

หมูผัดขิง
(mŏo pàt kĭng)
Pork fried with ginger. A dish frequently found in market and roadside foodstalls, where customers are tempted with strips of fragrant ginger, tender black mushrooms, and slabs of fresh pork.

Poultry เป็ดไก่

Chicken features heavily in Thai cuisine. Duck is also quite common. As with other meats, they are usually sliced or cut into small pieces, and fried swiftly to be crisp or tender.

ไก่ตอน	gài (d)torn	capon
ไก่	gài	chicken
หน้าอก/ขา/ปีก	nâr òk/kǎr/(b)pèek	breast/leg/wing
ไก่ย่าง	gài yârng	barbecued chicken
เป็ด	(b)pèht	duck
ลูกเป็ด	lôok (b)pèht	duckling
ห่าน	hàrn	goose
ไก่ป่า	gài (b)pàr	grouse
ไก่ต็อก	gài (d)tók	guinea fowl
นกกระทา	nók gra tar	partridge
นกพิราบ	nók pi rârp	pigeon
นกเป็ดน้ำ	nók (b)pèht nárm	teal
ไก่งวง	gài nguang	turkey
หมูป่า	mǒo (b)pàr	wild boar

Specialities อาหารจานพิเศษประเภท

ไก่ย่าง	gài yârng	grilled chicken
ไก่ทอด	gài tôrt	deep-fried chicken
ผัดกะเพราไก่	pàt ga prow gài	chicken fried with basil leaves
ไก่ผัดเม็ดมะม่วงหิมพานต์	gài pàt méht ma mûang hǐm ma parn	chicken fried with cashew nuts
ไก่ผัดขิง	gài pàt kǐng	chicken fried with ginger
ลาบไก่	lârp gài	spicy salad with minced chicken
พะแนงไก่	pa nairng gài	mild chicken curry
ตมยำไก่	(d)tôm yam gài	hot and sour chicken soup
ต้มข่าไก่	(d)tôm kàr gài	chicken in coconut milk flavoured with galanga
เป็ดย่าง	(b)pèht yârng	grilled duck
เป็ดตุ๋น	(b)pèht (d)tǔn	stewed duck
ลาบเป็ด	lârp (b)pèht	spicy salad with minced duck

แกงเขียวหวานไก่ (gairng kĕaw wărn gài)	Fragrant green curry with chicken. In Thai markets, this green curry, which is based on pungent, hot *kii noo* chillies, will often be served with tiny nests of white rice noodles.
แกงเผ็ดไก่ (gairng pèht gài)	Spicy red chicken curry. Flavoured with red chillies and Thai spices, this dish is topped with tiny, pea-sized green aubergines.
ไก่ห่อใบเตย (gài hòr bai (d)toey)	Chicken cooked in pandan leaves. Fresh pan-dan leaves are wrapped around tender pieces of chicken, and are then steamed and fried, imparting a delicate fragrance to the meat.
แกงเผ็ดเป็ดย่าง (gairng pèht (b)pèht yârng)	Hot red curry with grilled duck, combining Chinese and Thai flavours. Order lots of rice with this dish, as it takes its name from hot red chillies!

Rice and noodles *ข้าวและก๋วยเตี๋ยว*

Thais eat rice at all times of the day, though for breakfast and lunch they may opt for noodles. The boiled or steamed rice served in most ordinary restaurants and eating establishments is called *kow plow* or *kôw sŭay*. More exclusive restaurants may serve jasmine-scented rice (*kôw hŏrm ma lí*) which has a toasty and somewhat nutty flavour.

Fried rice is usually eaten as a complete meal rather than as an accompaniment to savoury dishes. Traditionally using left-over rice from the previous evening, it is fried up with pineapple, prawns and chillies, or spiced slivers of chicken.

In the North-East of Thailand, glutinous or sticky rice is steamed and served in baskets. Sticky rice (*kôw nĕaw*) is eaten with the fingers, rolled into balls and dipped into the spicy sauces of accompanying savoury dishes.

Noodles come in several different breadths and varieties, based either on rice or soya flour. While the type of noodle used for stir-fried dishes is traditionally set, you will be asked to make a choice for soup.

The most famous noodle dish of all is *pat tai*, which has some claim to be the national dish. Thais will adjust the flavour of their own *pat tai*, in a serious ritual, using an array of seasonings (*kruang prung*), including fish paste, crushed chillies, and chilli vinegar.

ก๋วยเตี๋ยวเส้นหมี่	gúay těaw sêhn mèe	fine thread noodles
ก๋วยเตี๋ยวเส้นเล็ก	gúay těaw sêhn léhk	medium thread noodles
ก๋วยเตี๋ยวเส้นใหญ่	gúay těaw sêhn yài	large thread noodles
ก๋วยเตี๋ยวเซียงไฮ้	gúay těaw sěang hái	short, clear noodles
วุ้นเส้น	wún sêhn	Chinese glass noodles
เส้นกวยจั๊บ	sêhn gúay jáp	short, clear noodles
บะหมี่	ba mèe	egg noodles
เส้นขนมจีน	sêhn ka nŏm jeen	fermented rice noodles

Why not sample some of these popular rice-based dishes?

ข้าวผัดกุ้ง/ปู/หมู	kôw pàt gûng/(b)poo/mŏo	fried rice with prawn/crab/pork
ข้าวผัดอเมริกัน	kôw pàt a mey ri gan	American fried rice
ข้าวคลุกกะปิ	kôw klúk ga (b)pì	fried rice mixed with fermented shrimp paste
ข้าวหมูแดง	kôw mŏo dairng	boiled rice with roast pork
ข้าวหน้าเป็ด	kôw nâr (b)pèht	boiled rice with roast duck
ข้าวมันไก่	kôw man gài	boiled rice with steamed chicken
ข้าวขาหมู	kôw kăr mŏo	boiled rice with stewed leg of pork
ข้าวแกง	kôw gairng	boiled rice topped with curry
แกงมัสมั่น	gairng ma sa mân	Indian style curry
แกงพะแนง	gairng pá nairng	mild curry
ข้าวแกงเขียวหวาน	kôw gairng kĕaw wărn	boiled rice with fragrant green curry
แกงเผ็ด	gairng pèht	hot red curry
ข้าวผัดพริกเนื้อ/หมู/ไก่	kôw pàt prík néua/mŏo/gài	spicy fried rice with beef/pork/chicken
ข้าวผัดพริกกระเพรา เนื้อ/หมู/ไก่	kôw pàt prík gra prow néua/mŏo/gài	fried rice with basil leaves and beef/pork/chicken

And here are some noodle-based dishes to try.

ก๋วยเตี๋ยวราดหน้า	gúay těaw rârt nâr	fried noodles in thickened sauce
ก๋วยเตี๋ยวผัดซีอิ๊ว	gúay těaw pàt see íw	noodles fried with soy sauce
ก๋วยเตี๋ยวน้ำ/แห้ง	gúay těaw nárm/hâirng	rice noodle soup/dry boiled rice noodles
บะหมี่น้ำ/แห้ง	ba mèe nárn/hâirng	egg noodle soup/dry boiled egg noodles
ก๋วยเตี๋ยวเรือ	gúay těaw reua	beef noodle soup
กวยเตี๋ยวเนื้อ/หมู/เป็ด/ไก่	gúay těaw néua/mǒo/(b)pèht/gài	rice noodle soup with beef/pork/duck/chicken
โกยซีหมี่	goey see mèe	fried noodles with chicken
ขนมจีนน้ำยา/น้ำพริก	ka nǒm jeen nám yar/nám pŕik	fermented rice noodles with sauce/curry

| ก๋วยเตี๋ยวผัดไทย (gúay těaw pàt tai) | Noodles fried with dried prawns and peanuts. A popular, classic Thai dish, found in all regions. Slender rice noodles are fried with a combination of sweet, sour and salty ingredients to give a piquant Thai flavour. |
| ข้าวซอย (kôw soy) | Spicy noodle soup with chicken or beef. *Kow soy* is a Thai/Burmese dish, common in open-air restaurants, combining a curry and coconut soup with crispy fried noodles. |

Sauces ซ้อส/น้ำจิ้ม

Most Thai sauces are spicy and a small quantity is sufficient. The most common sauce is chilli fish and shrimp sauce (น้ำปลาพริก —*nám (b)plar pŕik*), a real taste of Thailand around which a whole meal can be based, acting as a dip for raw vegetables and deep-fried fish. There are a number of spicy sauces, accompanied by raw vegetables, which become dishes in their own right. These include น้ำพริกอ่อง —*nám pŕik ong*, น้ำพริกหนุ่ม —*nám pŕik nùm* and น้ำพริกกะปิ —*nám pŕik ga pì*.

Vegetables and salads ผักและสลัด

It is not easy to find vegetarian food in Thailand, although large towns and cities, particularly those with substantial tourist populations, will have some vegetarian restaurants. Most ordinary restaurants will be prepared to cook vegetable and egg dishes without meat if asked.

หน่อไม้ฝรั่ง	nòr mái fa ràng	asparagus (tips)
มะเขือยาว	ma kĕua yow	aubergine (eggplant)
ถั่ว	tùa	beans
ถั่วผักยาว	tùa fàk yow	long beans
มะระ	má rá	bitter gourd
บร็อคโครี่	bròk koe rêe	broccoli
กระหล่ำ	gra làm	cabbage
แคร็อต	kair rôt	carrots
กระหล่ำดอยก	gra làm dòrk	cauliflower
คื่นชายฝรั่ง	kêuhn châi fa ràng	celery
พริก	prìk	chilli
ผักกาดขาว	pàk gàrt kŏw	Chinese leave
ผักชี	pàk chee	coriander
ข้าวโพด	kôw pôet	corn
แตงกวา	(d)tairng gwar	cucumber
ถั่วขก	tùa kàirk	lentils
ผักสลัด	pàk sa làt	lettuce
ผักรวมมิตร	pàk ruam mít	mixed vegetables
เห็ด	hèht	mushrooms
กระเจี๊ยบมอญ	gra jíap morn	okra
หอมหัวใหญ่	hŏrm hŭa yài	onions
พริกหยวก	prìk yùak	(sweet) peppers
เขียว/แดง	kĕaw/dairng	green/red
มันฝรั่ง	man fa ràng	potatoes
ฟักทอง	fák torng	pumpkin
ผักขม	pàk kŏm	spinach
ข้าวโพด	kôw pôet	sweetcorn
มันหวาน	man wărn	sweet potatoes
มะเขือเทศ	ma kĕua téyt	tomatoes
แฟง	fairng	vegetable marrow

Vegetables may be served...

boiled	ต้ม	(d)tôm
stewed	ตุ๋น	(d)tŭn
stir-fried	ผัด	pàt
stuffed	ยัดไส้	yát sâi

Here are some common vegetable dishes.

ซุปเห็ด	súp hèht	mushroom soup
ซุปผัก	súp pàk	vegetable soup
ซุปข้าวโพด	súp kôw pôet	sweetcorn soup
จับฉ่าย	jàp chài	clear mixed vegetable soup
ต้มยำเห็ด	(d)tôm yam hèht	hot and sour mushroom soup
ต้มข่าเห็ด	(d)tôm kàr hèht	mushrooms cooked in coconut milk and galanga
แกงเขียวหวานเจ	gairng kěaw wǎrn jey	fragrant green vegetable curry
แกงเผ็ดเจ	gairng pèht jey	hot red vegetable curry
แกงเลียงเจ	gairng leang jey	clear, spicy vegetable soup with pepper
แกงจืดรวมมิตรเจ	gairng jèurt ruam mít jey	clear mixed vegetable soup
ผัดเปรี้ยวหวานเจ	pàt (b)prêaw wǎrn jey	sweet and sour fried vegetables
ผัดผักรวมมิตรเจ	pàt pàk ruam mít jey	mixed fried vegetables
ผัดถั่วลันเตา ข้าวโพดอ่อนเจ	pàt tùa lan (d)tow kôw pôet òrn jey	mangetout peas fried with baby sweetcorn
ผัดซีอิ๊วเจ	pàt see íw jey	noodles stir fried with soy sauce
สลัดแขก	sa làt kàirk	fresh salad with peanut sauce
ลาบเห็ด	lârp hèht	spicy salad of minced mushrooms
ยำวุ้นเส้นเจ	yam wún sêhn jey	spicy Chinese glass noodle salad
ผักชุบแป้งทอด	pàk chúp (b)pâirng tôrt	deep-fried, battered vegetables
ปอเปี๊ยะเจ	(b)por (b)pía jey	vegetarian spring rolls
ไข่เจียว	kài jeaw	omelette
เต้าหู้ทอด	(d)tôw hôo tôrt	deep-fried bean curd

| ผัดผักบุ้ง (pàt pàk bûng) | Stir-fried water spinach. A delicious deep green vegetable with hollow stems and arrow-head shaped leaves, fried with garlic and peppercorns. |

| ผัดกะเพราเห็ดกับ ข้าวโพด (pàt ga prow hèht gàp kôw pôet) | Mushrooms fried with basil leaves and baby sweetcorn. |

ผัดไทยเจ Fried noodles with peanuts. This is perhaps
(pàt tai jey) the most commonly found vegetarian dish,
which can include chunks of crispy bean curd
and pickled white radish.

ยำถั่วพูเจ Spicy green bean salad with coconut sauce.
(yam tùa poo jey) The strongly flavoured sauce, with a rich,
creamy coconut base, is complemented per-
fectly by the spicy beans.

Herbs and spices สมุนไพรและเครื่องเทศ

โป๊ยกั๊ก	(b)póey gák	aniseed
กระชาย	gra chai	aromatic ginger
โหระพา	hŏe ra par	basil
ใบกระวาน	bai gra warn	bay leaf
ยี่หร่า	yêe ràr	caraway
พริก	prík	chillies
อบเชย	òp choey	cinnamon
กานพลู	garn ploo	clove
พริกไทยอ่อน	prík tai òrn	fresh peppercorns
ข่า	kàr	galanga
กระเทียม	gra team	garlic
ขิง	kĭng	ginger
ตะไคร้	(d)ta krái	lemongrass
มะนาว	ma now	lime
ใบมะกรูด	bai ma gròot	lime leaf
สะระแหน่	sa ra nàir	mint
มัสตาร์ด	ma sa (d)tàrt	mustard
ลูกจันทร์	lôok jan	nutmeg
พริกชี้ฟ้า	prík chée fár	paprika
ผักชีฝรั่ง	pàk chee fa ràng	parsley
พริกไทย	prík tai	pepper
หญ้าฝรั่น	yâr fa ràn	saffron
เกลือ	gleua	salt
งา	ngar	sesame
หอมเล็ก/หอมแดง	hŏrm léhk/ hŏrm dairng	shallot
ต้นหอม	(d)tôn hŏrm	spring onions
ใบกระเพรา	bai gra prow	sweet basil
ส้มซ่า	sôm sâr	sweet lime
มะขาม	ma kărm	tamarind
ขมิ้นผง	ka mîn pŏng	turmeric powder
วานิลา	war ni lar	vanilla

Fruit and nuts ผลไม้และลูกนัท

Fresh fruit, often exquisitely carved, is the favoured end-of-meal sweet in Thailand. Watch out for durian—this fruit smells like a sewer on a hot day, but if you can fight back the nausea, you will be rewarded with its delicious custardy sweet flesh.

Do you have any fresh fruit?	มีผลไม้สดไหม?	mee pŏn la mái sòt măi
I'd like a (fresh) fruit cocktail.	ผม(ดิฉัน)อยากได้ค็อกเทล ผลไม้(สด)	pŏm (di chán) yàrk dâi kôk teyn pŏn la mái (sòt)

อัลมอนด์	a la morn	almonds
แอปเปิ้ล	áihp (b)pêrn	apple
กล้วยหอม	glûay hŏrm	banana
เม็ดมะมวงหิมพานต์	méht ma mûang him má parn	cashew nuts
เชอรี่	cher rêe	cherries
เกาลัด	gow lát	chestnuts
มะพร้าว	ma prów	coconut
อินทผาลัม	in tá păr lam	dates
ผลไม้แห้ง	pŏn la mái hâirng	dried fruit
มะเดื่อ	ma dèua	figs
องุ่น	a ngùn	grapes
ฝรั่ง	faràng	guava
มะนาวเหลือง	ma now lĕuang	lemon
มะนาว	ma now	lime
ลิ้นจี่	lín jèe	lychee
มะม่วง	ma mûang	mango
แตงไทย	(d)tairng tai	melon
ส้ม	sôm	orange
ถั่วลิสง	tùa li sŏng	peanuts
ลูกแพร	lôok pair	pear
สับปะรด	sàp (b)pa rót	pineapple
ลูกพลัม	lôok plam	plums
ลูกพรุน	lôok prun	prunes
ลูกเกด	lôok gèyt	raisins
สตรอเบอร์รี่	sa (d)tror ber rêe	strawberries
ส้มจีน	sôm jeen	tangerine
แตงโม	(d)tairng moe	water melon

These are some of the more exotic fruit you may encounter at market stalls:

น้อยหน่า (nóy nàr)		custard apple: the green skin is easily peeled when ripe to reveal a sweet white flesh.

ทุเรียน (tú rearn)	durian: this huge, spiky green fruit with a soft, yellow flesh is only for the strong of stomach!
ขนุน (ka nŭn)	jackfruit: a large green fruit with a leathery, sweetish flavour.
ลองกอง (lorng gorng)	longan; a small round fruit with a brittle skin, and white flesh around a black stone.
มังคุด (mang kút)	mangosteen: considered the Queen of fruit. A hard, dark purple shell encloses delicious segmented, creamy-white flesh.
มะละกอ (ma lá gor)	papaya: a long, yellowy green fruit with a soft orange flesh.
ส้มโอ (sôm or)	pomelo: a tropical cousin of the grapefruit, served in sections.
เงาะ (ngóh)	rambutan: a sort of hairy lychee, with sweet opalescent flesh.
มะขาม (ma kărm)	tamarind: with a sour, fruity taste, this fruit is often sold as pulp for use in cooking.

Desserts—Pastries ของหวาน

Traditional Thai sweetmeats tend to be eaten as snacks rather than as desserts at the end of a meal. The ideal Thai meal will include two desserts—one dry, a cake-like sweet such as *méht kanoon*, made with egg, mung beans and sugar, and one liquid, such as bananas in fragrant coconut milk. Many restaurants also serve ice cream, referred to either as *ai sa kreem* or simply *ai tim*. Traditional ice creams are made from coconut milk (*ai tim ga tí*), but manufacturers now produce a wide range of Thai and Western flavours.

I'd like a dessert, please.	ผม(ดิฉัน) อยากได้ของหวาน	pŏm (di chán) yàrk dâi kŏrng wărn
What do you recommend?	มีอะไรน่าทานบ้าง?	mee arai nâr tarn bârng
Something light, please.	เอาอะไรที่ไม่หนักท้อง	ow arai têe mâi nàk tórng
Just a small portion.	ขอที่เล็กๆก็พอ	kŏr têe léhk léhk gôh por
ขนมหม้อแกง	ka nŏm môr gairng	steamed coconut cream sweet

ทองหยิบ	torng yìp	sweet made from deep-fried egg yolk
เม็ดขนุน	méht ka nŭn	sweet made from taro
ฝอยทอง	fŏy torng	sweet made from deep-fried egg
วุ้นกะทิ	wún ga tí	threads of scented sweet rice noodle
ขนมชั้น	ka nŏm chán	layers of sweet jellied coconut milk
ลอดช่องน้ำกะทิ	lôrt chông nárm ga tí	tapioca noodles in sweet coconut milk
บวชเผือก	bùat pèuak	taro stewed in fragrant, sweetened coconut milk
บัวลอยไข่หวาน	bua loy kài wărn	sour paste balls in sweet egg syrup
ข้าวต้มมัด	kôw (d)tôm mát	steamed sticky rice with banana or taro
สาคูถั่วดำ	săr koo tùa dam	black beans in sweetened coconut milk
ถั่วแปบ	tùa (b)pàihp	candied mung bean paste rolled in sesame seeds
ซาหริ่ม	sâr rìm	jellied noodles in sweet coconut milk
ทับทิมกรอบ	táp tim gròrp	jellied water chestnuts in coconut milk
ผลไม้รวม	pŏn la mái ruam	mixed fresh fruit

สังขยา
(săng ka yăr)

Steamed egg and coconut milk custard, made with duck eggs, palm sugar and coconut, so rich it will normally be served spooned over a mound of sticky rice.

กล้วยบวชชี
(glûay bùat chee)

Bananas stewed in fragrant, sweetened coconut milk. Its charming name means "bananas ordained as nuns", as this dessert has a creamy whiteness and delicate flavour.

กล้วยเชื่อม
(glûay chêuam)

Caramelized bananas. There are many varieties of Thai banana; the type usually used in this dessert is short, stubby and very sweet, made even sweeter with a syrupy sauce.

ข้าวเหนียวเปียก
(kôw nĕaw (b)pèark)

Boiled sticky rice in sweetened coconut milk, usually accompanied by mangoes. The still-warm sticky rice is left to soak in sweetened and salted coconut milk.

Drinks เครื่องดื่ม

The Thais' staple drink is plain water. You should not drink tap water in Thailand; bottled, filtered water is readily available. Ice is not always very clean, especially shaved ice, and should be avoided if you wish to be very careful.

Soft, carbonated drinks are also popular, though if you can, try to find the superb Thai soft drinks such as iced lemongrass, or *glûay bâhn*, a smooth banana drink sold by street vendors.

Beer เบียร์

Thai beer has a distinctive taste and makes a good accompaniment to an evening meal. There are two local beers (lager) generally available at most restaurants. Singha Beer is stronger and has a sweeter taste compared to its rival Kloster Beer. A number of exported beers are also available in big hotels and western restaurants. Beer is sold by the bottle and there are no restrictions on licensing hours.

What would you like to drink?	จะดื่มอะไร?	ja dèurm arai
I'd like a beer, please.	ขอเบียร์หน่อย	kŏr bear nòy
Have a beer!	เบียร์ที่หนึ่ง	bear têe nèuhng
A bottle of lager, please.	ขอเบียร์ขวดหนึ่ง	kŏr bear kùat nèuhng
A bottle of Singha beer, please.	ขอเบียร์สิงห์ขวดหนึ่ง	kŏr bear sing kùat nèuhng
A bottle of Kloster beer, please.	ขอเบียร์คลอสเตอร์ ขวดหนึ่ง	kŏr bear klor sa (d)ter kùat nèuhng

Wine เหล้าไวน์/เหล้าผลไม้

In Thailand wine is much less common than whisky and beer, and in fact is not the ideal accompaniment to Thai cuisine, with its strong hot flavours. Imported wine is only available in the big hotels and western restaurants.

May I have the wine list?	ขอดูรายการเหล้าไวน์ หน่อยได้ไหม?	kŏr doo rai garn lôw wai nòy dâi măi
I'd like a . . . of red wine/white wine.	ขอเหล้าไวน์แดง/ ไวน์ขาว...	kŏr lôw wai dairng/ wai kŏw

a bottle	ขวดหนึ่ง	kùat nèuhng
half a bottle	ครึ่งขวด	krêuhng kùat
a carafe	คาราฟ	kar rârf
a glass	แก้ว	gâiw
How much is a bottle of champagne?	แชมเปญขวดละเท่าไหร่?	chairm (b)peyn kùat lá tôw rài
Bring me another bottle/glass of..., please.	ขอ...อีกขวด/แก้ว	kŏr...èek kùat/gâiw

red	แดง	dairng
white	ขาว	kŏw
rosé	โรเซ่	roe sêy
sweet	สวีท	sa wèet
dry	คราย	da rai
sparkling	สปาร์คลิ้ง	sa (b)park gîng
chilled	เย็นๆ	yehn yehn
at room temperature	ที่อุณหภูมิห้อง	têe una ha poom hôrng

Other alcoholic drinks เครื่องดื่มที่มีอัลกอฮอล์อื่นๆ

Thai whisky (เหล้าวิสกี้ —lôw wí sa gêe), is taken primarily as a drink in its own right, served with snacks and appetizers, and is usually much diluted.

| I'd like a/an ... | ผม(ดิฉัน)อยากได้... | pŏm (di chán) yàrk dâi |

cognac	คอนยัค	korn yák
gin	จิน	jin
liqueur	เหล้าชนิดหวาน	lôw cha nít wărn
rum	เหล้ารัม	lôw ram
vermouth	เวอมัธ	wer mát
vodka	ว็อดก้า	wôd gâr
whisky	วิสกี้	wí sa gêe
neat (straight)	เพียว	peaw
on the rocks	ออนเดอะร็อค	orn der rók
with a little water	ใส่น้ำนิดเนึ่ง	sài nám nít neuhng
Give me a large gin and tonic, please.	ขอเหล้าจินกับ, โทนิคแก้วใหญ่	kŏr lôw jin gàp toe ník gâiw yài
Just a dash of soda, please.	ขอโซคานิดเนึ่ง	kŏr soe dar nít neuhng

Nonalcoholic drinks *เครื่องดื่มที่ไม่มีอัลกอฮอล์*

apple juice	น้ำแอ๊ปเปิ้ล	nàrm áihp (b)pêrn
boiled water	น้ำต้ม	nárm (d)tôm
iced coffee	กาแฟเย็น	garfair yehn
fruit juice	น้ำผลไม้	nárm pǒn la mái
lemonade	น้ำมะนาว	lehm ma néyt
lime juice	เติมมะเนต	nárm ma now
milk	นม	nom
milkshake	มิลค์เชค	milk chék
mineral water	น้ำแร่	nárm râir
fizzy (carbonated)	ชนิดมีก๊าซ	cha nít mee gàrt
still	ชนิดไม่มีก๊าซ	cha nít mâi mee gàt
plain water	น้ำเปล่า	nárm (b)plòw
orange juice	น้ำส้ม	nárm sôm
tomato juice	น้ำมะเขือเทศ	nárm ma kĕua téyt
tonic water	โทนิค	toe ník

Hot beverages *เครื่องดื่มร้อน*

Thais do not tend to drink coffee or tea with their food, unless it is Chinese tea. Nevertheless, coffee has become increasingly popular in urban areas as a morning drink and both coffee and tea are readily available in most parts of the country. Far more common is iced coffee served with evaporated milk. Iced tea is also delicious and refreshing, commonly flavoured with star anise, cinnamon and vanilla.

I'd like a/an ...	ขอ...ที่หนึ่ง	kŏr... têe nèuhng
(hot) chocolate	ช็อคโกแล็ค(ร้อน)	chôrk goe lâiht (rórn)
camomile tea	น้ำเก๊กฮวย	nàrm géhk huay
coffee	กาแฟ	gar fair
with cream	ใส่ครีม	sài kreem
with milk	ใส่นม	sài nom
black/decaffeinated coffee	ดำ/ ชนิดไม่มีคาเฟอีน	dam/cha nít mâi mee kar fey een
espresso coffee	กาแฟเอสเพรสโซ่	gar fair eyt sa prèyt sôe
mokka	ม็อคคา	mók gâr
herb tea	ชาสมุนไพร	char sa mŭn prai
rosehip tea	น้ำกระเจี๊ยบ	nàrm gra jéarp
tea	ชา	char
Chinese tea	ชาจีน	char jeen
cup of tea	น้ำชาถ้วยหนึ่ง	nárm char tûay nèuhng
with milk/lemon	ใส่นม/ใส่มะนาว	sài nom/sài ma now

Complaints   ต่อว่า

There's a plate/glass missing.	ขอจาน/ แก้วอีกที่หนึ่ง	kŏr jarn/gâiw èek têe nèuhng
I don't have a knife/ fork/spoon.	ขอมีด/ ส้อม/ ช้อนอันหนึ่ง	kŏr mêet/ sôrm/ chórn an nèuhng
That's not what I ordered.	อันนี้ผม(ดิฉัน)ไม่ได้สั่ง	an née pŏm (di chán) mâi dâi sàng
I asked for...	ผมสั่ง...	pŏm sàng
There must be some mistake.	คงมีอะไรผิดพลาด	kong mee arai pìt plârt
May I change this?	ขอเปลี่ยนอันนี้ได้ไหม?	kŏr (b)plèarn an née dâi mái
I asked for a small portion (for the child).	ผม(ดิฉัน)ขอที่เล็กๆ (สำหรับเด็ก)	pŏm (di chán) kŏr têe léhk léhk (săm ràp dèhk)
The meat is...	เนื้อนี้...	néua nêe
overdone	สุกเกินไป	sùk gern (b)pai
underdone	สุกไม่พอ	sùk mâi por
too rare	ดิบเกินไป	dìp gern (b)pai
too tough	เหนียวเกินไป	něaw gern (b)pai
This is too...	อันนี้...เกินไป	an nêe... gern (b)pai
bitter/salty/sweet	ขม/ เค็ม/ หวาน	kŏm/kehm/wǎrn
I don't like this.	ผม(ดิฉัน)ไม่ชอบอันนี้เลย	pŏm (di chán) mâi chôrp an née loey
The food is cold.	อาหารเย็นชืดแล้ว	ar hǎrn yehn chêut láiw
This isn't fresh.	อันนี้ไม่สดเลย	an nêe mâi sòt loey
What's taking you so long?	ทำไมนานจังเลย?	tam mai narn jang loey
Have you forgotten our drinks?	เราสั่งเครื่องดื่มไป นานแล้วนะ	row sàng krêuang dèurm (b)pai narn láiw ná
The wine doesn't taste right.	เหล้าไวน์รสชาติไม่เข้าที่	lôw wai rót chârt mâi kôw têe
This isn't clean.	มันไม่สะอาด	man mâi sa àrt
Would you ask the head waiter to come over?	ช่วยเรียกหัวหน้าบ๋อย มานี่หน่อยได้ไหม?	chûay rêak hǔa nâr bŏy mar nêe nòy dâi mái

The bill (check) เช็คบิล

In cheaper establishments your bill will be calculated by counting the plates you have on the table in front of you at the end of the meal and will be given to you verbally. In the more expensive restaurants, however, you will be given a slip of paper. It is appropriate to tip 10–20 baht.

I'd like to pay.	เก็บเงินด้วย	gèhp ngern dûay
We'd like to pay separately.	คิดเงินแยกกันนะ	kít ngern yâirk gan ná
I think there's a mistake in this bill.	ผม(ดิฉัน)คิดว่าบิล ใบนี้มีอะไรผิดอยู่อย่าง	pŏm (di chán) kít wâr bin bai née mee arai pìt yòo yàrng
What's this amount for?	อันนี้ค่าอะไรบ้าง?	an nèe kâr arai bârng
Is service included?	รวมค่าบริการแล้ว หรือยัง?	ruam kâr boe ri garn láiw rĕur yang
Is the cover charge included?	รวมค่าบริการต่อหัว ต่อคนแล้วหรือยัง?	ruam kâr boe ri garn (d)tòr hŭa (d)tòr kon láiw rĕur yang
Is everything included?	รวมทุกอย่างแล้วใช่ไหม?	ruam túk yàrng láiw châi măi
Do you accept traveller's cheques?	จ่ายเป็นเช็คเดินทาง ได้ไหม?	jài (b)pehn chéhk dern tarng dâi măi
Can I pay with this credit card?	จ่ายด้วยบัตร เครดิตได้ไหม?	jài dûay bàt kroy dít dâi măi
Please round it up to...	รวมทั้งหมดแล้วเก็บที่...	ruam táng mòt láiw gèhp têe
Keep the change.	เก็บเงินทอนเอาไว้	gèhp ngern torn ow wái
That was delicious.	อร่อยมาก	a ròy mârk
We enjoyed it, thank you.	อร่อยมาก ขอบคุณ	a ròy mârk kòrp kun

รวมค่าบริการแล้ว
SERVICE INCLUDED

TIPPING, see inside back-cover

Snacks—Picnic อาหารว่าง ปิ๊กนิค

Give me two of these and one of those.	ขออันนี้สองอันและอันนั้นอันหนึ่ง	kŏr an née sŏrng an láih an née an nèuhng
to the left/right	ด้านซ้าย/ ด้านขวา	dârn sái/ dârn kŵar
above/below	ข้างบน/ ข้างล่าง	kârng bon/kârn lârng
It's to take away.	ใส่ห่อไปกินที่บ้าน	sài hòr (b)pai gin têe bârn
I'd like a piece of cake.	ขอขนมเค้กชิ้นหนึ่ง	kŏr ka nŏm kéhk chín nèuhng
omelette	ไข่เจียว	kài jeaw
open sandwich	แซนด์วิชไม่ต้องห่อ	sairn wít mâi (d)tôrng hòr
with ham	ใส่แฮม	sài hairm
with cheese	ใส่ชีส(เนยแข็ง)	sài chêet (noey kǎihng)
sandwich	แซนด์วิช	sairn wít
I'd like a/an/ some...	ผม(ดิฉัน)อยากได้...	pŏm (di chán) yàrk dâi

apples	แอ๊ปเปิ้ล	áihp (b)pêrn
bananas	กล้วยหอม	glûay hŏrm
biscuits (Br.)	ขนมปังกรอบ	ka nŏm (b)pang gròrp
beer	เบียร์	bia
bread	ขนมปัง	ka nŏm (b)pang
butter	เนย	noey
cheese	เนยแข็ง	noey kǎihng
chips (Br.)	มันทอด	man tôrt
coffee	กาแฟ	gar fair
cookies	คุกกี้	kúk gêe
eggs	ไข่	kài
grapes	องุ่น	a ngùn
ice cream	ไอศครีม	ai sɛ kreem
milk	นม	nom
mustard	มัสตาร์ด	mát sa tàrt
oranges	ส้ม	sôm
pepper	พริกไทย	prík tai
roll	ขนมปังก้อน	ka nŏm (b)pang gôn
salt	เกลือ	gleua
sausage	ไส้กรอก	sâi gròrk
sugar	น้ำตาล	nárm (d)tarn
tea bags	ชาชนิดถุง	char cha nít tǔng
yoghurt	โยเกิร์ต	yoe gèrt

Travelling around

Plane เครื่องบิน

Most internal flights are operated by Thai Airways International (การบินไทย —*garn bin tai*) which flies to the major cities of each region of the country. Tickets can be purchased through travel agents or at the domestic terminal of Don Muang (*dorn meuang*) airport. The smaller airline company, Bangkok Airways, flies between Bangkok and Hua Hin and Koh Samui.

Is there a flight to Chiang Mai?	มีเที่ยวบินไปเชียงรายไหม?	mee têaw bin (b)pai cheang mài măi
Is it a direct flight?	เป็นเที่ยวบินตรง หรือเปล่า?	(b)pehn têaw bin (d)trong rĕua (b)plòw
When's the next flight to Chiang Mai?	เที่ยวบินไปเชียงใหม่เที่ยว ต่อไปออกกี่โมง?	têaw bin (b)pai chearng mài têaw (d)tòr (b)pai òrk gèe moeng
Is there a connection to Lampang?	มีเครื่องบินต่อไปที่ ลำปางหรือเปล่า?	mee krêuang bin (d)tòr (b)pai têe lam parng rĕua (b)plòw
I'd like to book a ticket to Phuket.	ผม(ดิฉัน)ต้องการ จองตั๋วไปภูเก็ต	pŏm (di chán) tôrng garn jorng tŭa (b)pai poo gèht
single (one-way)	เที่ยวเดียว	têaw deaw
return (round trip)	ไปกลับ	(b)pai glàp
business class	ชั้นสำหรับนักธุรกิจ	chán săm ràp nák tu rá gìt
aisle seat	ที่นั่งติดทางเดิน	têe nâng (d)tìt tarng dern
window seat	ที่นั่งติดหน้าต่าง	têe nâng (d)tìt nâr tàrng
What time do we take off?	เครื่องบินจะออกกี่โมง?	krêuang bin ja òrk gèe moeng
What time should I check in?	จะต้องเช็คอินตอนกี่โมง?	ja tôrng chehk in (d)torn gèe moeng
Is there a bus to the airport?	มีรถประจำทาง ไปสนามบินไหม?	mee rót pra jam tarng (b)pai sa nărm bin măi
What's the flight number?	เที่ยวบินที่เท่าไหร่?	têaw bin têe tôw rài
What time do we arrive?	เราจะไปถึงที่นั่นตอนกี่โมง?	row ja (b)pai tĕuhng nân (d)torn gèe moeng

I'd like to ... my reservation.	ผม(ดิฉัน)อยากจะ... การจองตัว	pŏm(di chán) yàrk ja... garn jorng tŭa
cancel	ยกเลิก	yók lêrk
change	เปลี่ยนแปลง	plèarn plairng
confirm	ยืนยัน	yeurn yan

ขาเข้า ARRIVAL	ขาออก DEPARTURE

Train รถไฟ

Several trains run each day between Bangkok's main line Hualampong (*hŭa lam poeng*) railway station and the North, South and North-East regions of the country. Most of the trains depart between late afternoon and early evening in order to arrive at their final destination early the following morning. In addition to this some trains to the south operate from the much smaller station of Bangkok Noi. This is also the station used for trains to Kanchanaburi. Trains to Eastern Thailand run from Makkasan (*mák ga săn*) station.

Thai trains are classified either as:

รถธรรมดา (rót tam ma dar)	Ordinary train; a painfully slow service stopping at local stations. Provides third class facilities only.
รถเร็ว (rót rehw)	Rapid train; but only relatively faster than the "ordinary" train. Tends to offer only second and third class seats.
รถด่วน (rót dùan)	Long distance express with first and second class facilities, stopping at major stations only.

Whilst third class train travel is exceptionally cheap it is not advised for long journeys because of the very hard seats. Second class offer reclining seats with a fan or sleepers with either fan or air-conditioning.

Second and first class tickets should be booked in advance either through a travel agent or direct from the station itself. Third class tickets can be bought immediately prior to departure.

Visit Thailand Rail Passes (เรวพาส —*rew pars*) can be bought by overseas visitors to Thailand. Blue Passes are valid for second or third class travel for 20 days excluding supplementary charges. Red Passes do include supplementary charges.

ตู้นอน ((d)tôo norn)	Second class sleepers are good value and comfortable. The seats convert into a lower and an upper bunk, and the top one is slightly cheaper than the lower. First class accommodation is in private cabins have air conditioning and an optional fan and seats which convert into sleeping berths.
รถดีเซลราง (rót dee sehn rarng)	Air conditioned diesel "sprinters" operate on some lines, providing a faster and efficient service. The price of the ticket also includes a meal and refreshments.

Train travel is cheap in Thailand, but small supplements are charged for express and rapid trains. Children are charged under a a range of reduced prices calculated by age and height. There are measuring boards at all railway stations and on the trains themselves.

To the railway station ไปสถานีรถไฟ

Where's the railway station?	สถานีรถไฟอยู่ที่ไหน?	sa tăr nee rót fai yòo têe năi
Taxi!	แท็กซี่	táihk sêe
Take me to the...	ไปส่งผม(ดิฉัน)ที่...หน่อย	(b)pai sòng pŏm (dì chán) têe...nòy
main railway station	สถานีรถไฟ	sa tăr nee rót fai
What's the fare?	เท่าไหร?	tôw rài

ทางเข้า	ENTRANCE
ทางออก	EXIT
ชานชลา	TO THE PLATFORMS
ประชาสัมพันธ์	INFORMATION

Where's the ...? ...*อยู่ที่ไหน?*

Where is/are (the)...?	...อยู่ที่ไหน?	... yòo têe nǎi
bar	บาร์	bar
booking office	ที่จองตั๋ว	têe jorng tǔa
currency exchange office	ที่แลกเงิน	têe lâirk ngern
left-luggage office (baggage check)	ที่ฝากกระเป๋าและสัมภาระ	têe fàrk gra pǒw láih sǎm par rá
lost property (lost and found) office	แผนกของหาย	pa nàirk kǒrng hǎi
luggage lockers	ตู้เก็บสัมภาระ	(d)tôo gèhp sǎm par rá
newsstand	แผงขายหนังสือพิมพ์	pǎirng kǎi náng sěur pim
platform 7	ชานชลาที่ ๗	charn cha lar têe jèht
reservations office	แผนกสำรองที่นั่งล่วงหน้า	pa nàirk sǎm rorng têe nâng lûang nâr
restaurant	ร้านอาหาร	rárn ar hǎrn
ticket office	แผนกจำหน่ายตั๋ว	pa nàirk jam nài tǔa
waiting room	ห้องพักผู้โดยสาร	hórng pák pôo doey sǎrn
Where are the toilets?	ห้องน้ำอยู่ที่ไหน?	hórng nárm yòo têe nǎi

Inquiries สอบถาม

When is the ... train to Nongkhai?	รถไฟไปหนองคายคัน ...ออกเมื่อไหร่?	rót fai (b)pai nǒrng kai kan ... òrk mêua rài
first/last/next	แรก/สุดท้าย/ต่อไป	râirk/sùt tái/(d)tòr (b)pai
What time does the train to Kanchanaburi leave?	รถไฟไปกาญจนบุรี ออกกี่โมง?	rót fai (b)pai garn ja na bu ree òrk gèe moeng
What's the fare to Ayutthaya?	ค่ารถไฟไปอยุธยาเท่าไหร่?	kâr rót fai (b)pai a yú ta yar tôw rài
Is it a through train?	ไม่ต้องเปลี่ยน รถไฟใช่ไหม?	mâi tôrng plèarn rót fai cháy mǎi
Do I have to change trains?	ผม(ดิฉัน)จะต้องเปลี่ยน รถหรือเปล่า?	pǒm (di chán) ja tôrng plèarn rót rěua (b)plòw
Is the train running on time?	รถไฟวิ่งตรงเวลาไหม?	rót fai wîng (d)trong wey lar mǎi

TAXI, see page 21

What time does the train arrive in Phitsanulok?	รถไฟจะไปถึงพิษณุโลกตอนกี่โมง?	rót fai ja (b)pai těuhng pít san nú lôek (d)torn gêe moeng
Is there a dining car/ sleeping car on the train?	มีรถเสบียง/รถนอนในขบวนนี้หรือเปล่า?	mee rót sabeang/rót norn nai kabuan née rěua (b)plòw
Does the train stop in Khon Kaen?	รถไฟหยุดที่ขอนแก่นหรือเปล่า?	rót fai yùt têe kǒrn kàihn rěua (b)plòw
Which platform does the train to Nongkhai leave from?	รถไฟไปหนองคายออกจากชานชลาไหน?	rót fai (b)pai nǒrng kai òrk jark charn cha lar nǎi
Which platform does the train from Chiang Mai arrive at?	รถไฟจากเชียงใหม่จะเขาจอดชานชลาไหน?	rót fai jark cheang mài ja kòw jort charn cha lar nǎi
I'd like a time-table.	ขอตารางเดินรถหน่อย	kǒr (d)tar rarng dern rót nòy

---

คุณจะต้องเปลี่ยนรถที่...	You have to change at...
ชานชลาที่ ๗...	Platform 7 is...
อยู่ที่โน่น	over there
อยู่ด้านซ้ายมือ/อยู่ด้านขวามือ	on the left/on the right
มีรถไฟไป...ตอน...	There's a train to... at...
รถไฟคุณจะออกจากชานชลาที่ ๘	Your train will leave from platform 8.
รถไฟจะช้า...นาที	There will be a delay of... minutes.
ชั้นหนึ่งอยู่หัวขบวน/ตรงกลาง/ท้ายขบวน	First class at the front/in the middle/at the rear.

Tickets ตั๋ว

I'd like a ticket to Lop Buri.	ขอตั๋วไปลพบุรีใบหนึ่ง	kǒr (d)tǔa (b)pai lóp buree bai nèuhng
single (one-way)	เที่ยวเดียว	têaw deaw
return (round trip)	ไปกลับ	(b)pai glap
first/second class	ชั้นหนึ่ง/ชั้นสอง	chán nèuhng/chán sǒrng
half price	ครึ่งราคา	krêuhng rar kar

Reservation สำรองที่นั่ง

I'd like to reserve a...	ผม(ดิฉัน) ต้องการสำรอง...	pŏm (di chán) (d)tông garn săm rorng
seat (by the window)	ที่นั่ง(ติดหน้าต่าง)	têe nâng ((d)tìt nâr (d)tàrng)
berth	เตียงนอน	teang norn
upper	ชั้นบน	chán bon
lower	ชั้นล่าง	chán lârng
berth in the sleeping car	เตียงนอนในตู้นอน	teang norn nai tôo norn

All aboard บนรถไฟ

Is this the right platform for the train to Hat Yai?	ชานชลานี้ไปหาดใหญ่ ใช่ไหม?	charn cha lar née (b)pai hàrt yài châi măi
Is this the right train to Phetchaburi?	รถไฟขบวนนี้ไปเพชรบุรี ใช่ไหม?	rót fai kabuan née (b)pai péht buree châi măi
Excuse me. Could I get past?	ขอโทษ ขอผ่านไปหน่อย?	kŏr tôet kŏr pàrn (b)pai nòy
Is this seat taken?	ตรงนี้มีคนนั่งไหม?	(d)trong née mee kon nâng măi

สูบบุหรี่ได้	ห้ามสูบบุหรี่
SMOKER	**NONSMOKER**

I think that's my seat.	นั่นเป็นที่นั่งของผม(ดิฉัน)	nân (b)pehn têe nâng kŏrng pŏm(di chán)
Would you let me know before we get to Surin?	ช่วยบอกก่อนที่จะถึง สุรินทร์หน่อยได้ไหม?	chûay bòrk gòrn têe ja tĕuhng su rin nòy dâi măi
What station is this?	สถานีอะไรนี่?	sa tăr nee arai née
How long does the train stop here?	รถไฟจะ จอดที่นี่นานแค่ไหน?	rót fai ja jòrt têe née narn kàir năi
When do we arrive in Lampang?	เราจะถึงลำปาง ตอนกี่โมง?	row ja tĕuhng lam (b)parng (d)torn gèe moeng

Sleeping การนอน

Are there any free compartments in the sleeping car?	มีที่ว่างในรถนอน หรือเปล่า?	mee têe wârng nai rót norn rĕua (b)plòw

Where's the sleeping car?	รถนอนอยู่ที่ไหน?	rót norn yòo têe năi
Where's my berth?	เตียงนอนผม (ดิฉัน)อยู่ที่ไหน?	teang norn pŏm (di chán) yòo têe năi
I'd like a lower berth.	ผม(ดิฉัน)อยากได้ เตียงนอนชั้นล่าง	pŏm (di chán) yàrk dâi teang norn chán lârng
Would you wake me at 7 o'clock?	ช่วยปลุกคุณ เจ็ดโมงได้ไหม?	chûay (b)plùk (d)torn jèht moeng dâi măi

Eating *การกิน*

Long distance trains have a buffet car where you can go and sit to have a meal. Alternatively you can order from your seat and have your meal brought to you. Buffet staff will also pass through the train with plates of ready-prepared food such as fried rice (ข้าวผัด —*kôw pàt*).

On local trains running shorter distances vendors board the trains at each stop and pass through the carriage with bags of steamed sticky rice, cured beef, grilled chicken, fried rice and other snacks.

| Where's the dining-car? | รถเสบียงอยู่ที่ไหน? | rót sa bearng yòo têe năi |

Baggage—Porters *กระเป๋า คนยกกระเป๋า*

Porter!	คนยกกระเป๋า	kon yók gra (b)pŏw
Can you help me with my luggage?	ช่วยจัดการกับกระเป๋า ผม(ดิฉัน)หน่อยได้ไหม?	chûay jat garn gàp gra (b)pŏw pŏm (di chán) nòi dâi măi
Where are the luggage trolleys (carts)?	รถเข็นอยู่ที่ไหน?	rót kěhn yòo têe năi
Where are the luggage lockers?	ตู้เก็บของอยู่ที่ไหน?	(d)tôo gèhp kŏrng yòo têe năi
Where's the left-luggage office (baggage check)?	ที่ฝากกระเป๋าและ สัมภาระอยู่ที่ไหน?	têe fàrk gra (b)pŏw laih săm par rá yòo têe năi
I'd like to leave my luggage, please.	ผม(ดิฉัน)อยากฝาก กระเป๋าหน่อย	pŏm (di chán) yàrk fàrk gra (b)pŏw nòi

---

การลงทะเบียน กระเป๋า
REGISTERING (CHECKING) BAGGAGE

PORTERS, see also page 18

Coach (long-distance bus) รถทัวร์

Coaches are a popular method of long-distance travel for Thais and are much faster than the trains. The three major coach stations in Bangkok operate services to all regions of the country with air-conditioned tour buses. The tour buses classed as VIP (วีไอพี —*wee ai pee*) have fully reclining seats. A hostess is available to serve refreshments and long-distance journeys include a stop off at a restaurant en route.

In addition to coach and tour bus service, ordinary buses (รถบขส —*rót bor kŏr sŏr*) also travel to all provinces in the country. They are usually bright orange in colour, are not air-conditioned and are tightly packed with seating designed for small-framed Thais so they can be rather cramped. They are very cheap but not recommended for long-distance travel.

When's the next coach to ...?	รถคันหน้าที่จะ ไป...ออกกี่โมง?	rót kan nâr têe ja (b)pai...òrk gèe moeng
Does this coach stop at ...?	รถคันนี้จะ จอดที่...หรือเปล่า?	rót kan née ja jòrt têe...rěua (b)plòw
How long does the journey (trip) take?	ใช้เวลาเดินทางเท่าไหร่?	chái wey lar dern tarng tôw rài

Bus รถเมล์/รถประจำทาง

Bangkok has the largest bus service of any Thai city and buses run very frequently. In recent years longer red and cream buses have begun to replace the older blue and cream ones, and are safer in that they have doors which close while the bus is moving. The fare varies accordingly, and is collected by a conductor or conductress with a long, steel tube-shaped receptacle in which tickets and change are kept.

In the provinces bus services are usually converted lorries or pick-up trucks called *sŏng tăiw*, which literally means "two rows" referring to the two benches on either side of the vehicle. The *sŏng tăiw* may or may not have route numbers on the sides.

Which bus goes to the town centre?	รถเมล์สายไหน ไปในเมืองบาง?	rót mey săi năi (b)pai nai meuang bârng

Where can I get a bus to the Grand Palace?	ไปวัดพระแก้วไปรถเมล์ สายไหนได้บ้าง?	(b)pai wát pfa gâiw (b)pai rót mey săi năi dâi bârng
Which bus do I take to Siam Square?	ไปสยามสแควร์ไป รถเมลสายไหนได้บ้าง?	(b)pai sa yǎrm sa kwair (b)pai rót mey săi năi dâi bârng
Where's the bus stop?	ป้ายรถเมล์อยู่ที่ไหน?	(b)pâi rót mey yòo têe năi
When is the ... bus to Rangsit?	รถเมล์ไปรังสิต ...ออกกี่โมง?	rót mey (b)pai rang sìt...òrk gèe moeng
first/last/next	คันแรก/ คันสุดท้าย/	kan râirk/kan sùt tái/kan (d)tòr (b)pai
How much is the fare to ...?	คันต่อไป คารถไป...เท่าไหร่?	kâr rót (b)pai...tôw rài
Do I have to change buses?	ผม(ดิฉัน)จะต้องต่อ รถเมล์หรือเปล่า?	pŏm (di chán) ja (d)tôrng (d)tòr rót mey rĕua (b)plòw
How many bus stops are there to ...?	ไป...ประมาณกี่ป้าย?	(b)pai...(b)pra marn gèe (b)pâi
Will you tell me when to get off?	ช่วยบอกให้ผม(ดิฉัน) ลงด้วย?	chûay bòrk hâi pŏm (di chán) long dûay
I want to get off at Banglamphu.	ผม(ดิฉัน)จะลงที่บางลำภู	pŏm (di chán) ja long têe barng lam poo

ป้ายรถเมล์
BUS STOP

Boat service *บริการทางเรือ*

Once known as the Venice of the East, the majority of Bangkok's canals have now been filled in. But long-tail boats do still travel along the remaining canal of the city and speedboats operate along the main Chao Praya (*jôw pfa yar*) River. The Express boat (เรือด่วน —*reua dùan*) can be picked up from the pier at the Oriental Hotel and passes the Grand Palace on its way up river to the market at Nontaburi (*non tá bu ree*), just north of Bangkok. Like a bus, tickets are purchased on board. River trips are also available in the North of Thailand.

When does the next boat for... leave?	เรือไป...ลำต่อไป ออกกี่โมง?	reua (b)pai...lam (d)tòr (b)pai òrk gèe moeng
Where's the embarkation point?	ลงเรือได้ที่ไหน?	long reua dâi têe nǎi
How long does the crossing take?	ใช้เวลาข้ามไปนานไหม?	chái wey lar kârm (b)pai narn mǎi
Which port(s) do we stop at?	เราจะจอดที่ท่าไหนบ้าง?	row ja jòrt têe târ nǎi bârng
I'd like to take a cruise/ tour of the harbour.	ผม(ดิฉัน)อยากจะลอง เรือเที่ยวแถวท่าจอดเรือ	pǒm (di chán) yàrk ja lông reua têaw tǎiw târ jòrt reua

boat	เรือ	reua
cabin	ห้องนอนในเรือ	hôrng norn nai reua
single/double	ห้องเดี่ยว/ ห้องคู่	hôrng dèaw/hôrng kôo
canal trip	ลองแม่น้ำ	lông mâir nárm
deck	ดาดฟ้าเรือ	dàrt fár reua
ferry	เรือข้ามฟาก	reua kârm fârk
hydrofoil	เรือไฮโดรฟอย	reua hǎi droe foi
life belt/boat	เข็มขัดนิรภัย/ เรือชูชีพ	kěhm kàt ni rá pay/reua choo chêep
port	ท่าเรือ	târ reua
reclining seat	ที่นั่งเอนหลัง	têe nâng eyn lǎng
river cruise	ลองแม่น้ำ	lông mâir nárm
ship	เรือกำปั่น/ เรือทะเล	reua gam (b)pàn/reua ta ley
steamer	เรือกลไฟ	reua gon fai

Bicycle hire *เช่ารถจักรยาน*

It is too dangerous to ride a bicycle amidst Bangkok's jostling traffic but bicycle hire is available from guest houses and shops catering for tourists in the provinces. Remember that the sun is extremely strong and cycling without the shade of a hat and sun block is an efficient way to get burned.

I'd like to hire a... bicycle.	ผม(ดิฉัน)อยากเช่า จักรยานสักคัน...	pǒm (di chán) yàrk chôw jàk ra yarn sàk kan
5-gear	(แบบ)ห้าเกียร์	(bàirp) hâr gear
mountain	(แบบ)เมาเทนไบค์	(bàirp) mow têyn bai

Other means of transport *การเดินทางวิธีอื่นๆ*

helicopter	เฮลิคอปเตอร์	hey li kôrp ter
motorbike/scooter	จักรยานยนต์/	jàk ra yarn yon/rót sa gôot
	รถสกุตเตอร์	ter

Or perhaps you prefer:

to hitchhike	โบกรถ	bòek rót
to walk	เดิน	dern

Car *รถยนต์*

Driving in Thailand is on the left. While most major highways are in a reasonable state of repair, road safety is not uppermost in the Thai mind; many Thais drive with the fatalistic philosophy of good and bad karma—that when the day of your death is due even a toothpick will kill you. As a result road accidents are the cause of a large number of fatalities each year. Insurance, like the wearing of seat belts, is currently not compulsory, though this may soon change.

The official speed limit is 60 kph in towns and 80kph on highways, but rules are liberally interpreted. Driving along the middle of the road or using the verge to overtake is common practice.

Fuel and oil are readily available in both regular and super, dispensed by the litre.

Where's the nearest filling station?	ปั้มน้ำมันใกล้ ที่สุดอยู่ไหน?	(b)pâm nám man glâi têe sùt yòo nǎi
Fill it up, please.	เติมเต็มถัง	(d)term (d)tehm tǎng
Give me... litres of petrol (gasoline).	เติมเบนซิน...ลิตร	(d)term behn sin...lít
super (premium)/ regular/unleaded/ diesel	ซุปเปอร์/ธรรมดา/ ไร้สารตะกั่ว/ดีเซล	sup per/tam ma dar/rái sǎrn (d)ta gùa/dee seyn
Please check the...	ช่วยดู...ให้ด้วย	chûay doo... hâi dûay
battery	แบตเตอรี่	bàirt ter rêe
brake fluid	น้ำมันเบรก	nám man brèyk
oil/water	น้ำมันเครื่อง/หม้อน้ำ	nám man krêuang/môr nárm

CAR HIRE, see page 20

Would you check the tyre pressure?	ช่วยดูลมยางรถ ให้ด้วยได้ไหม?	chûay doo lom yarng rót hâi dûay dâi măi
1.6 front, 1.8 rear.	ด้านหน้า๑.๖ หลัง๑.๘	dârn nâr nèuhng jùt hòk lăng nèuhng jùt (b)pàirt
Please check the spare tyre, too.	ช่วยดูยางสำรองให้ด้วย	chûay doo yarng săm rorng hâi dûay
Can you mend this puncture (fix this flat)?	ช่วยปะยางที่รั่ว ให้ด้วยได้ไหม?	chûay (b)pà yarng têe rûa hâi dûay dây măi
Would you change the... please?	ช่วยเปลี่ยน... ให้ด้วยได้ไหม?	chûay plèarn... hâi dûay dây măi
bulb	หลอดไฟ	lòrt fai
fan belt	สายพานพัดลม	săi parn pát lom
spark(ing) plugs	หัวเทียน	hŭa tearn
tyre	ยาง	yarng
wipers	ที่ปัดน้ำฝน	têe (b)pàt nárm fŏn
Would you clean the windscreen (windshield)?	ช่วยทำความสะอาด กระจกหน้ารถยนต์ ให้หน่อยได้ไหม?	chûay tam kwarm sa àrt gra jòk nâr rót yon hâi nòy dâi măi

Asking the way—Street directions ถามทาง ทิศทางตามถนน

Can you tell me the way to...?	ช่วยบอกทางไป...ให้ หน่อยได้ไหม?	chûay bòrk tarng (b)pai...hâi nòy dâi măi
In which direction is...?	...ไปทางไหน?	... (b)pai tarng năi
How do I get to...?	ผม(ดิฉัน)จะไปที่... ไปยังไง?	pŏm (di chán) ja (b)pai têe...(b)pai yang ngai
Are we on the right road for...?	เราอยู่บนถนนสายที่ถูก หรือเปล่าที่จะไป...?	row yòo bon ta nŏn săy têe tòok rĕua (b)plòw têe ja (b)pai
How far is the next village?	หมู่บ้านข้างหน้าอยู่อีกไกล ไหม?	mòo bârn kârng nâr yòo èek glai măi
How far is it to... from here?	จากนี้ไป...ไกลไหม?	jàrk née (b)pai...glai măi
Is there a motorway (expressway)?	มีทางด่วนหรือเปล่า?	mee tarng dùan rĕua (b)plòw

How long does it take by car/on foot?	ใช้เวลาเดินทาง เท่าไหร่ถ้าไปโดยรถยนต์/ ถ้าเดินไป?	châi wey lar dern tarng tôw rài târ (b)pai rót yon/ târ dern (b)pai
Is traffic allowed in the town centre?	ที่ใจกลางเมือง รถวิ่งได้ไหม?	têe jai glarng meuang rót wîng dâi măi
Can you tell me where . . . is?	ช่วยบอกผม(ดิฉัน) หน่อยว่า...อยู่ที่ไหน?	chûay bòrk pŏm (di chán) nòi wâr...yòo têe năi
How can I find this place/address?	ผม(ดิฉัน)จะหาสถานที่/ ที่อยู่นี้ได้ยังไง?	pŏm (di chán) ja hăr sa tărn têe/têe yòo nêe dâi yang ngai
Where's this?	นี่ที่ไหน?	née têe năi
Can you show me on the map where I am?	ช่วยชี้ในแผนที่ให้ดูหน่อย ว่าตอนนี้ผม(ดิฉัน) อยู่ที่ไหน?	chûay chée nai păirn têe hâi doo nòy wâr (d)torn nêe pŏm (di chán) yòo têe năi
Where are the nearest public toilets?	ห้องน้ำสาธารณะที่ใกล้ ที่สุดอยู่ที่ไหน?	hôrng nárm să tar ra ná têe glâi têe sùt yòo têe năi

คุณมาผิดถนนแล้ว	You're on the wrong road.
ตรงไป	Go straight ahead.
มันอยู่ที่นั่นด้านซ้ายมือ/ ขวามือ	It's down there on the left/ right.
ด้านตรงข้าม/ด้านหลัง	opposite/behind . . .
ติดกับ/เลย...ไป	next to/after . . .
ทิศเหนือ/ทิศใต้	north/south
ทิศตะวันออก/ทิศตะวันตก	east/west
ไปถึงสี่แยกแรก/ที่สอง	Go to the first/second crossroads (intersection).
เลี้ยวซ้ายที่แยกไฟแดง	Turn left at the traffic lights.
เลี้ยวขวาที่หัวมุมข้างหน้า	Turn right at the next corner.
ไปถนน...	Take the . . . road.
มันเป็นถนนวันเวย์	It's a one-way street.
คุณจะต้องกลับไปที่...	You have to go back to . . .
ไปตามป้ายบอกทางไปชลบุรี	Follow signs for Chon Buri.

Parking *การจอดรถ*

Is there a car park nearby?	มีที่จอดรถใกล้ ๆแถวนี้ไหม?	mee têe jòrt rót glâi glâi tǎiw née mǎi
May I park here?	ผม(ดิฉัน)จอดรถ ตรงนี้ได้ไหม?	pǒm (di chán) jòrt rót (d)trong née dâi mǎi
How long can I park here?	ผม(ดิฉัน) สามารถจอดรถที่นี่ได้ นานแค่ไหน?	pǒm (di chán) sǎr mârt jòrt têe nêe dâi narn kâir nǎi
What's the charge per hour?	ค่าจอดเท่าไหร่ต่อชั่วโมง?	kâr jòrt tôw rài (d)tòr chûa moeng

Breakdown—Road assistance *รถเสีย ความช่วยเหลือบนถนน*

You can either call the firm from which you hired the car or the Highway Police Patrol Centre (*gorng bang káp garn (d)tam rûat tarng lûang*).

Where's the nearest garage?	อู่รถที่ใกล้ที่สุดอยู่ที่ไหน?	òo rót têe glâi têe sùt yòo têe nǎi
My car has broken down.	รถผม(ดิฉัน)เสีย	rót pǒm (di chán) sěar
Where can I make a phone call?	ผม(ดิฉัน)จะไปโทรศัพท์ ได้ที่ไหน?	pǒm (di chán) ja (b)pai toe ra sàp dâi têe nǎi
I've had a break-down at...	รถผม(ดิฉัน)เสียที่...	rót pǒm (di chán) sěar têe
Can you send a mechanic?	คุณช่วยส่งช่าง มาดูได้ไหม?	kun chûay sòng chârng mar doo dâi mǎi
My car won't start.	รถผม(ดิฉัน)สตาร์ทไม่ติด	rót pǒm (di chán) sa tàrt mâi (d)tìt
The battery is dead.	แบตเตอรี่หมด	bàiht ter rèe mòt
I've run out of petrol (gasoline).	รถผม(ดิฉัน)น้ำมันหมด	rót pǒm (di chán) nárm man mòt
I have a flat tyre.	รถผม(ดิฉัน)ยางแบน	rót pǒm (di chán) yarng bairn
The engine is over-heating.	เครื่องยนต์ร้อนเกินไป	krêuang yon rórn gern (b)pai
There's something wrong with the...	มีอะไรผิดปกติที่...	mee arai pìt (b)pòk a tì têe
brakes	เบรก	brèyk
carburettor	คาร์บิวเรเตอร์	kar biw rey ter

exhaust pipe	ท่อไอเสีย	tôr ai sěar
wheel	ล้อรถ	lór rót
Can you send a break-down van (tow truck)?	คุณช่วยส่งรถลาก มาช่วยหน่อยได้ไหม?	kun chûay sòng rót lârk mar chûay nòy dâi mǎi
How long will you be?	อีกนานไหมถึงจะมาได้?	èek narn mǎi tǔeng ja mar dâi
Can you give me an estimate?	บอกคร่าวๆ ได้ไหมว่าเท่าไหร่?	bòrk krôw krôw dâi mǎi wâr tôw rài

Accident—Police อุบัติเหตุ ตำรวจ

Please call the police.	ช่วยเรียกตำรวจด้วย	chûay rêark tam rûat dûay
There's been an accident. It's about 2 km from ...	มีอุบัติเหตุ ห่างจาก...ประมาณ ๒กิโลเมตร	mee u ba tì hèyt hàrng jàrk...(b)pra marn sǒrng gi loe méht
Where's there a telephone?	แถวนี้มีโทรศัพท์ที่ไหน?	tǎiw née mee toe ra sàp tôe nǎi
Call a doctor/an ambulance quickly.	เรียกหมอ/รถพยาบาล มาเร็วเข้า	rêark mǒr/rót pa yar barn mar rehw kôw
Here's my driving licence.	นี่ใบขับขี่ของผม(ดิฉัน)	née bai kàp kèe kǒrng pǒm(di chán)
What's your name and address?	คุณชื่ออะไรและอยู่บ้าน เลขที่เท่าไหร่?	kun chêur arai láih yòo bârn lêyk têe tôw rài
What's your insurance company?	บริษัทประกันของคุณ ชื่ออะไร?	bo ri sàt (b)pra gan kǒrng kun chêur arai

Road signs ป้ายจราจร

Most road signs are international pictographs.

หยุด	STOP
ระวัง ถนนกำลังซ่อม	CAUTION ROADWORKS
อันตราย	DANGER
ห้ามผ่าน	NO PASSING
ห้ามเข้า	NO ENTRY
ทางออก	EXIT
ขับช้าๆ	DRIVE SLOWLY
เปลี่ยนเส้นทาง	DIVERSION (DETOUR)
ทางโค้ง	BEND
ห้ามรถเข้า	NO VEHICLES
ห้ามเลี้ยว	NO TURNING
ห้ามจอด	NO PARKING

Sightseeing

The Head Office of the Tourist Authority of Thailand (TAT) is on Ratchadamnern Nok (*rârt cha dam nern nòrk*) Avenue, Bangkok 10100, and has leaflets, maps and an advice centre. TAT also has smaller offices in other provincial capitals of Thailand, with maps of the town frequently displayed outside.

Where's the tourist office?	สำนักงาน ทองเที่ยวอยู่ที่ไหน?	săm nák ngarn tôrng têaw yòo têe năi
What are the main points of interest?	มีสถานที่ที่น่าสนใจหลักๆ อะไรบาง?	mee sa tărn têe nâr sŏn jai arai bârng
We're here for...	เราอยู่ที่นี่...	row yòo têe née
only a few hours	แค่ไม่กี่ชั่วโมง	kâir mâi gèe chûa moeng
a day	วันเดียว	wan deaw
a week	อาทิตย์หนึ่ง	ar tít nèuhng
Can you recommend a sightseeing tour/ an excursion?	คุณช่วยแนะนำทัวร์ นำเที่ยว/รายการนำเที่ยว ให้หน่อยได้ไหม?	kun chûay náih nam tua nam têaw/rai garn nam têaw hâi nòy dâi mái
Where do we leave from?	เราจะออกเดินทาง จากที่ไหน?	row ja òrk dern tarng jàrk têe năi
Will the bus pick us up at the hotel?	รถจะมารับเรา ที่โรงแรมหรือเปล่า?	rót ja mar ráp row têe roeng rairm rĕua (b)plòw
How much does the tour cost?	ค่าทัวร์เท่าไหร่?	kâr tua tôw rài
What time does the tour start?	รายการนำเที่ยวนี้จะ เริ่มตอนกี่โมง?	rai garn nam têaw née ja rêrm (d)torn gèe moeng
What time do we get back?	เราจะกลับมาถึง ที่นี่กี่โมง?	row ja glàp mar tĕuhng têe nêe gèe moeng
Do we have free time in ...?	เรามีเวลาว่าง ที่...หรือเปล่า?	row ja mee wey lar wârng têe...rĕua (b)plòw
Is there an English-speaking guide?	มีไก๊ด์(มัคคุเทศก์) พูดภาษาอังกฤษ หรือเปล่า?	mee gái (mák ku têyt) pôot par săr ang grìt rĕua (b)plòw

I'd like to hire a private guide for...	ผม(ดิฉัน)ต้องการ ไกด์ส่วนตัวสัก...	pŏm (di chán) (d)tôrng garn gái sùan (d)tua sàk
half a day	ครึ่งวัน	krêuhng wan
a day	วันหนึ่ง	wan nèuhng
Where is/Where are the...?	...อยู่ที่ไหน?	... yòo têe năi
Ancient City	เมืองโบราณ	meuang borarn
art gallery	หอศิลป์	hŏr sĭn
botanical gardens	สวนพฤกษชาติ	sŭan prúk sa chârt
building	อาคาร	ar karn
business district	ย่านธุรกิจ	yârn tu rá gìt
castle	ปราสาท	(b)prar sàrt
catacombs	อุโมงค์	u moeng
cathedral	วิหาร	wi hărn
cave	ถ้ำ	tâm
cemetery	ป่าช้า	(b)pàr chár
city centre	ใจกลางเมือง	jai glarng meuang
chapel	โรงสวด	roeng sùat
church	โบสถ์	bòet
concert hall	ที่แสดงดนตรี	têe sa dăirng don (d)tree
convent	คอนแวนท์	korn wairn
court house	ศาล	sărn
downtown area	ย่านในเมือง	yârn nai meuang
embankment	เขื่อน	kèuan
exhibition	นิทรรศการ	ní tát sa garn
factory	โรงงาน	roeng ngarn
fair	งานออกร้าน	ngarn òrk rárn
floating market	ตลาดน้ำ	(d)ta làrt nárm
fortress	ป้อมปราการ	pôrm prar garn
fountain	น้ำพุ	nárm pú
gardens	สวน	sŭan
harbour	ท่าจอดเรือ	tâ jòrt reua
lake	ทะเลสาบ	ta ley sàrp
library	หองสมุด	hôrng sa mùt
market	ตลาด	(d)ta làrt
memorial	อนุสรณ์สถาน	ar nú sŏrn sa tărn
monastery	วัด	wát
monument	อนุสาวรีย์	ar nú sŏw a ree
museum	พิพิธภัณฑ์	pi pít ta pan
old town	เมืองเก่า	meuang gòw
palace	วัง	wang
park	สวนสาธารณะ	sŭan săr tar ra ná
parliament building	ตึกรัฐสภา	(d)tèuhk rát ta sa par
planetarium	ท้องฟ้าจำลอง	tórng fár jam lorng
royal palace	พระราชวัง	pfra rârt cha wang
ruins	โบราณสถาน	boe rarn sa tărn

shopping area	ย่านช้อปปิ้ง	yârn chóp (b)pîng
square	จตุรัส	jà (d)tu rát
stadium	สนามกีฬา	sa nǎrm gee lar
statue	รูปปั้น	rôop (b)pân
stock exchange	ตลาดหุ้น	(d)ta làrt hûn
temple	วัด	wát
theatre	โรงละคร	roeng la korn
tomb	สุสาน	su sǎrn
town hall	ศาลาว่าการจังหวัด	sǎr lar wâr garn jang wàt
university	มหาวิทยาลัย	ma hǎr wít ta yar lay
zoo	สวนสัตว์	sǔan sàt

Admission ค่าผ่านประตู

Museums, galleries and tourist attractions are often half price or free on Sundays.

Is... open on Sundays?	...เปิดวันอาทิตย์ไหม?	... (b)pèrt wan ar tít mǎi
What are the opening hours?	เปิดเวลาเท่าไหร่?	(b)pèrt wey lar tôw rài
When does it close?	ปิดตอนไหน?	(b)pìt (d)torn nǎi
How much is the entrance fee?	ค่าผ่านประตูเท่าไหร่?	kâr pàrn (b)pra (d)tòo tôw rài
Is there any reduction for (the)...?	มีราคาพิเศษสำหรับ...ไหม?	mee rar kar pi sèyt sǎm ràp...mǎi
children	เด็ก	dèhk
disabled	คนพิการ	kon pi garn
groups	กลุ่ม	glùm
pensioners	ผู้ที่รับเงินบำนาญ	pôo têe ráp ngern bam narn
students	นักศึกษา	nák sèuhk sǎr
Do you have a guide-book (in English)?	คุณมีหนังสือนำเที่ยว (เป็นภาษาอังกฤษไหม?	kun mee náng sěur nam têaw ((b)pehn par sǎr ang grìt) mǎi
Can I buy a catalogue?	ขอซื้อแคตตาล็อกหน่อย?	kǒr séur kâirt (d)tar lôk nòy
Is it all right to take pictures?	ถ่ายรูปที่นี่ได้ไหม?	tài rôop têe née dâi mǎi

| ไม่เก็บค่าผ่านประตู
ห้ามเอากล้องถ่ายรูปเข้าไป | ADMISSION FREE
NO CAMERAS ALLOWED |

| Is there easy access for the disabled? | มีสิ่งอำนวยความสะดวก สำหรับคนพิการไหม? | mee sìng am nuay kwarm sa dùak săm ràp kon pi garn măi |
| Are there facilities/ activities for children? | มีสิ่งอำนวยความสะดวก/ กิจกรรมสำหรับเด็กไหม? | mee sìng am nuay kwarm sa dùak/gìt ja gam săm ràp dèhk măi |

Who—What—When? ใคร-อะไร-เมื่อไหร่?

What's that building?	อาคารหลังนั้นคืออะไร?	ar karn lăng nán keur arai
Who was the...?	ใครเป็น...?	krai (b)pehn
architect	สถาปนิก	sa thăr (b)pa ník
artist	ศิลปิน	sĭn la (b)pin
painter	จิตรกร	jìt ra gorn
sculptor	ประติมากร	(b)pra (d)tì mar gorn
Who built it?	ใครเป็นคนสร้าง?	krai (b)pehn kon sârng
Who painted that picture?	ใครเป็นคนวาดภาพนั้น?	krai (b)pehn kon wârt pârp nán
When did he live?	เขาเกิดสมัยไหน?	kow gèrt sa măy năi
When was it built?	อันนี้สร้างขึ้นมาเมื่อไหร่?	an nee sârng kêuhn mar mêua rài
We're interested in...	เราสนใจ...	row sŏn jai
antiques	โบราณวัตถุ	boe rarn wát tù
archaeology	โบราณคดี	boe rarn ka dee
art	ศิลปะ	sĭn la (b)pà
botany	พฤกษศาสตร์	prúk sa sârt
ceramics	เครื่องปั้นดินเผา/เซรามิค	krêuang (b)pân din pŏw/ sey rar mík
coins	เหรียญกษาปณ์	rĕarn ga sàrp
fine arts	วิจิตรศิลป์	wi jìt sĭn
geology	ธรณีวิทยา	to ran ee wít ta yar
handicrafts	งานฝีมือ	ngarn fĕe meur
history	ประวัติศาสตร์	(b)pra wát tì sàrt
medicine	เวชกรรม/การแพทย์	wêyt cha gam/garn pâirt
music	ดนตรี	don (d)tree
natural history	ธรรมชาติวิทยา	tam ma chârt wít ta yar
ornithology	ปักษีวิทยา	(b)pàk sĕe wít ta yar
painting	จิตรกรรม	jìt ra gam
religion	ศาสนา	sàrt sa năr
sculpture	ประติมากรรม	(b)pra (d)tì mar gam
zoology	สัตววิทยา	sàt wít ta yar

Where's the ... department?	แผนก...อยู่ที่ไหน?	pa nàirk...yòo têe năi
It's ...	มัน...	man
amazing	น่าทึ่ง	nâr têuhng
awful	แย่มาก	yâir mârk
beautiful	สวย	sŭay
gloomy	น่าเศร้า	nâr sôw
impressive	น่าประทับใจ	nâr (b)pra táp jai
interesting	น่าสนใจ	nâr sŏn jai
magnificent	งดงามมาก	ngót ngarm mârk
pretty	น่ารักดี	nâr rák dee
strange	แปลก	plàirk
superb	เยี่ยมมาก	yêarm mârk
terrifying	น่ากลัว	nâr glua
ugly	น่าเกลียด	nâr glèart

Churches—Religious services โบสถ์

Buddhist temples (*wát*) proliferate in Thailand and almost all villages have a local temple. In the towns and cities temples may be much larger and ornate. The buildings within the temple complex include a chapel for prayer (*bòet*), a chapel for Buddha images (*wi hǎrn*) and cells (*gu (d)ti*) where the monks live.

While temples make popular tourist attractions, it should be remembered that they are places of worship where a certain etiquette must be obeyed. It is not appropriate to enter a temple in shorts or very informal clothing and you will be asked to remove your shoes. Feet are considered a debased part of the body and it causes offence to point them at people, and especially at Buddha images and monks.

Is there a ... near here?	มี...แถวนี้ไหม?	mee...tǎiw née mǎi
temple	วัด	wát
Catholic church	โบสถ์คาทอลิค	bòet kàr tor lík
Protestant church	โบสถ์โปรแตสแตนท์	bòet proe tairt sa tairn
mosque	มัสยิด/สุเหร่า	mát sa yít/sù ròw
synagogue	สุเหร่ายิว	sú ròw yiw
What time is ...?	เวลา...กี่โมง?	wey lar...gèe moeng
mass/the service	คนทั่วไป/สวดมนต์	kon tûa (b)pai/sùat mon
I'd like to visit the temple.	ผม(ดิฉัน)อยากจะแวะ ไปโบสถ์	pǒm (di chán) yàrk ja wéh (b)pai bòet

| Should I take off my shoes? | ต้องถอดรองเท้าไหมครับ(คะ) | (d)tôrng tòrt rorng tów mái kráp (ká) |

In the countryside ในชนบท

How far is it to...?	ไป...ไกลไหม?	(b)pai...glai mǎi
Can we walk there?	เราสามารถเดินไปได้ไหม?	row sǎr mârt dern (b)pai dâi mǎi
What kind of... is that?	นั่น...ประเภทไหน?	nân...(b)pra pêyt nǎi
animal	สัตว์	sàt
bird	นก	nók
flower	ดอกไม้	dòrk mái
tree	ต้นไม้	(d)tôn mái

Landmarks จุดสังเกตเห็นได้ชัด

bridge	สะพาน	sa parn
cliff	หน้าผา	nâr pǎr
farm	นา/ไร่	nar/râi
field	ทุ่ง	tûng
footpath	ทางเท้า	tarng tów
forest	ป่า	(b)pàr
garden	สวน	sǔan
hill	เนินเขา	nern kǒw
house	บ้าน	bârn
lake	ทะเลสาบ	ta ley sàrp
meadow	ทุ่งหญ้า	tûng yâr
mountain	ภูเขา	poo kǒw
(mountain) pass	ช่องเขา	chôrng kǒw
path	ทางเดิน	tarng dern
peak	ยอดเขา	yôrt kǒw
pond	บ่อน้ำ	bòr nárm
river	แม่น้ำ	máir nárm
road	ถนน	ta nǒn
sea	ทะเล	ta ley
spring	บ่อน้ำแร่	bòr nárm râir
valley	หุบเขา	hùp kǒw
village	หมู่บ้าน	mòo bârn
wall	กำแพง	gam pairng
waterfall	น้ำตก	nárm (d)tòk
wood	ป่า	(b)pàr

ASKING THE WAY, see page 76

Relaxing

Cinema (movies)—Theatre โรงหนัง โรงละคร

The Thai word for film is *năng*, meaning leather, hide or skin, and is derived from traditional performances of shadow theatre in which leather cut-out puppets were shown against a lighted screen. Traditional shadow puppet performances are only to be found in Southern Thailand, having originated in Java.

There are several modern-day cinemas in Bangkok showing international films with Thai subtitles and other cinemas which show only Thai films. Cinema prices are cheap and advance bookings are not usually necessary. The national anthem is always played at the beginning of the programme as an accompaniment to pictures of the Thai Royal Family during which it is obligatory to stand. A film guide is given in the daily newspapers.

Traditional Thai masked drama, or *koen*, is performed at the National Theatre and performance details are given in the daily newspaper. *Koen* performances re-enact scenes from the Indian epic the Ramayana, known in Thai as the Ramakien.

Lí-gey or folk theatre is rather like pantomime and is often performed in dazzling costumes at night in side streets or night markets, particularly up country.

What's on at the cinema tonight?	คืนนี้มีหนังเรื่องอะไรฉาย?	keurn née mee năng rêuang arai chăi
What's playing at the... Theatre?	ที่โรงละคร...มีละคร เรื่องอะไรเล่น?	têe roeng la korn...mee la korn rêuang arai lêhn
What sort of play is it?	มันเป็นละครประ เภทไหน?	man (b)pehn la korn (b)pra pêyt năi
Who's it by?	เป็นละครของใคร?	(b)pehn la korn kŏrng krai
Can you recommend a...?	ช่วยแนะนำ... ให้หนอยได้ไหม?	chûay náih nam...hâi nòy dâi măi
good film	หนังดีๆ	năng dee dee
comedy	ละครตลก	la korn (d)ta lòk

masked drama	โขน	kŏen
musical	ละครเพลง	la korn pleyng
Where's that new film directed by... being shown?	หนังเรื่องใหม่ที่กำกับ โดย...ฉายที่ไหน?	năng rêuang mài têe gam gàp doey...chăi têe năi
Who's in it?	มีใครเล่นบ้าง?	mee krai lêhn bârng
Who's playing the lead?	ใครเล่นเป็นดารานำ?	krai lêhn (b)pehn dar rar nam
Who's the director?	ใครเป็นผู้กำกับ?	krai (b)pehn pôo gam gàp
At which theatre is that new play by... being performed?	ละครเรื่องใหม่ของ... เล่นที่ไหน?	la korn rêuang mài kŏrng...lêhn têe năi
Is there a shadow puppet show on somewhere?	มีการเล่นหนังตะลุง ที่ไหนบางไหม?	mee garn sadairng năng (d)talung têe năi bârng măi
What time does it begin?	เริ่มกี่โมง?	rêrm gèe moeng
Are there any seats for tonight?	มีที่นั่งสำหรับค่ำนี้ หรือเปล่า?	mee têe nâng săm ràp kâm née rĕua plòw
How much are the seats?	ตั๋วใบละเท่าไหร่?	(d)tŭa bai lá tôw rài
I'd like to reserve 2 seats for the show on Friday evening.	ผม(ดิฉัน)อยากจะจองที่นั่ง ๒ที่สำหรับการแสดง เย็นวันศุกร	pŏm (di chán) yàrk ja jorng têe nâng sŏrng têe săm ràp garn sa dairng yehn wan sùk
Can I have a ticket for the matinee on Tuesday?	ขอตั๋วใบหนึ่งสำหรับ รอบกลางวันวันอังคาร	kŏr tŭa bai nèuhng săm ràp rôrp glarng wan wan ang karn
I'd like a seat in the stalls (orchestra).	ผม(ดิฉัน)อยากได้ที่นั่ง ชั้นดีหน้าเวที	pŏm (di chán) yàrk dâi têe nâng chán dee nâr wey tee
Not too far back.	ไม่เอาที่ไกลเกินไป	mâi ow têe glai gern (b)pai
Somewhere in the middle.	เอาที่นั่งแถวกลางๆ	ow têe nâng tăiw glarng glarng
How much are the seats in the circle (mezzanine)?	ที่นั่งชั้นลอย?	têe nâng chán loy an lá tôw rài
May I have a programme, please?	ขอสูจิบัตรด้วย?	kŏr sŏo ji bàt dûay

DAYS OF THE WEEK, see page 151

| Where's the cloakroom? | ห้องรับฝากเสื้อและสิ่งของอยู่ที่ไหน? | hôrng ráp fàrk sêua láih sìng kŏrng yòo têe năi |

| ขอโทษ ขายหมดแล้ว มีที่นั่งเหลืออยู่ไม่กี่ที่ บนชั้นลอย | I'm sorry, we're sold out. There are only a few seats left in the circle (mezzanine). |
| ขอดูตั๋วหน่อย? ที่นั่งคุณอยู่นี่ | May I see your ticket? This is your seat. |

Opera—Ballet—Concert อุปรากร บัลเลต์ คอนเสิร์ต

Can you recommend a(n) ...?	ช่วยแนะนำ...ดีๆให้หนอยได้ไหม?	chûay náih nam...dee dee hâi nòy dâi măi
ballet	บัลเลต์	ban lêy
concert	คอนเสิร์ต	kŏrn sèrt
opera	อุปรากูร	ù (b)pa rar gorn
operetta	ละครรองขนาดสั้น	la korn rórng ka nàrt sân
Where's the concert hall?	ที่แสดงดนตรี	têe sa dairng don (d)tree
What's on at the opera tonight?	คืนนี้อุปรากรเล่นเรื่องอะไร?	keurn née ù (b)pa rar gorn lêhn rêuang arai
Who's singing/ dancing?	ใครร้อง/(เต้น)รำ?	krai rórng/((d)têhn) ram
Which orchestra is playing?	ออเคสตร้าวงไหนเล่น?	or key sa trăr wong năi lêhn
What are they playing?	พวกเขาเล่นเพลงอะไร?	pûak kŏw lêhn pleyng arai
Who's the conductor/ soloist?	ใครเป็นวาทยากร (คอนดักเตอร์)/ ใครเดี่ยว?	krai (b)pehn wârt ta yar gorn (kŏrn dàk ter)/ krai dèaw

Nightclubs—Discos ไนท์คลับ ดิสโก้

| Can you recommend a good nightclub? | ช่วยแนะนำไนท์คลับดีๆให้หนอยได้ไหม? | chûay náih nam nai klàp dee dee hâi nòy dâi măi |

Is there a floor show?	มีฟลอร์โชว์ไหม?	mee flor choe mǎi
What time does the show start?	การแสดงจะเริ่มตอนกี่โมง?	garn sa dairng ja rêrm (d)torn gèe moeng
Is evening dress required?	ต้องแต่งชุดราตรีสโมสรไหม?	(d)tông (d)tàihng chút rar (d)tree sa mǒe sǒrn mǎi
Where can we go dancing?	เราจะไปเต้นรำได้ที่ไหนบ้าง?	row ja (b)pai têhn ram dâi têe nǎi bârng
Is there a disco-theque in town?	ในเมืองมีดิสโก้เธคไหม?	nai meuang mee dìt sa gôe téhk mǎi
Would you like to dance?	คุณอยากไปเต้นรำไหม?	kun yàrk (b)pai têhn ram mǎi

Sports กีฬา

Popular sports include Thai boxing (*muay tai*) which differs from Western-style boxing in that it permits the use of the feet. It can be seen in Bangkok at the city's two major stadium at Lumpini and Ratchadamnern.

Some sports organized for tourist participation include golf, water-skiing, windsurfing, scuba diving, sailing, fishing, swimming and tennis. Large hotels often have their own fitness centres with weight training facilities and saunas.

Is there a football (soccer) match anywhere this Saturday?	มีฟุตบอลแข่งที่ไหนบ้างไหมเสาร์นี้?	mee fút born kàihng têe nǎi bârng mǎi sǒw née
Which teams are playing?	ทีมไหนกับทีมไหนแข่งกัน?	teem nǎi gàp teem nǎi kàihng gan
Can you get me a ticket?	คุณช่วยซื้อตั๋วให้ใบหนึ่งหน่อยได้ไหม?	kun chûay séur tǔa hâi bai nèuhng nòy dâi mǎi
I'd like to see a kick boxing match.	ผม(ดิฉัน)อยากดูมวยไทยสักนัด	pǒm (di chán) yàrk doo muay tai sàk nát
What's the admission charge?	ค่าผ่านประตูเท่าไหร่?	kâr pàrn (b)pra (d)tòo tôw rài
Where's the nearest golf course?	สนามกอล์ฟที่ใกล้ที่สุดอยู่ที่ไหน?	sa nǎrm gorf têe glâi têe sùt yòo têe nǎi

basketball	บาสเก็ตบอล	bàrt sa gèht born
boxing	ชกมวย	chók muay
car racing	แข่งรถ	kàihng rót
cycling	แข่งจักรยาน	kàihng jàk ra yarn
football (soccer)	ฟุตบอล	fút born
horse racing	แข่งม้า	kàihng már
(horse-back) riding	ขี่ม้า	kèe már
mountaineering	ปีนเขา	(b)peen kŏw
skiing	สกี	sa gee
swimming	ว่ายน้ำ	wâi nárm
tennis	เทนนิส	teyn nít
volleyball	วอลเลย์บอล	worn lêy born

Where are the tennis courts?	สนามเทนนิสอยู่ที่ไหน?	sa nǎrm teyn nít yòo têe nǎi
What's the charge per ...?	ต้องเสียค่าเล่น เท่าไหร่คอ...?	(d)tôrng sěar kâr lêhn tôw rài (d)tòr
day/round/hour	วัน/รอบ/ชั่วโมง	wan/rôrp/chûa moeng
Can I hire (rent) rackets?	ผมจะขอเช่า ไม้แร็กเกตได้ไหม?	pǒm ja kǒr chôw mái râihk gèht dâi mǎi
Where's the race course (track)?	ลู่วิ่งอยู่ที่ไหน?	lôo wîng yòo têe nǎi
Is there any good fishing around here?	แถวนี้มีที่ตกปลา ดีๆ ไหม?	tǎiw née mee têe (d)tòk (b)plar dee dee mǎi
Do I need a permit?	ผม(ดิฉัน)ต้องขอ อนุญาตหรือเปลา?	pǒm (di chán) (d)tôrng kǒr an nú yârt rěua (b)plòw
Where can I get one?	ผม(ดิฉัน)จะขอ อนุญาตได้ที่ไหน?	pǒm (di chán) ja kǒr an nú yârt dâi têe nǎi
Can one swim in the lake/river?	ทะเลสาบ/แม่น้ำนี้ ว่ายน้ำได้ไหม?	ta ley sàrp/mâir nárm née wâi nárm dâi mǎi
Is there a swimming pool here?	ที่นี่มีสระว่ายน้ำไหม?	têe nêe mee sà wâi nárm mǎi
Is it open-air or indoor?	อยู่กลางแจ้งหรืออยู่ในร่ม?	yòo glarng jâirng rěua yòo nai rôm
What's the temperature of the water?	น้ำอุณหภูมิเท่าไหร่?	nárm ùn a pǒom tôw rài

On the beach บนชายหาด

Thailand is well endowed with beautiful beaches, along the coast of the Gulf of Thailand, and with off-shore islands. The islands of Koh Samet (four hours by bus to the east of Bangkok) and Koh Samui, and Phuket in the far south, are popular tourist destinations.

Is there a sandy beach?	มีหาดทรายไหม?	mee hàrt sai mǎi
Is it safe to swim here?	ที่นี่ปลอดภัยพอที่จะว่ายน้ำได้ไหม?	têe nee (b)plòrt pai por têe ja wâi nárm dâi mǎi
Is there a lifeguard?	มียามคอยช่วยไหม?	mee yarm koy chûay mǎi
Is it safe for children?	ปลอดภัยสำหรับเด็กหรือเปล่า?	(b)plòrt pai sǎm ràp dèk rěua (b)plòw
The sea is very calm.	ทะเลสงบมาก	ta ley sa ngòp mârk
There are some big waves.	มีคลื่นขนาดใหญ่บ้าง	mee klêurn ka nàrt yài bârng
Are there any dangerous currents?	มีกระแสน้ำที่อันตรายบ้างไหม?	mee gra sǎir nárm têe an ta rai bârng mǎi
What time is high tide/low tide?	น้ำขึ้น/น้ำลงตอนกี่โมง?	nárm kêuhn/nárm long (d)torn gèe moeng
I want to hire (rent) a/an/ some...	ผม(ดิฉัน)อยากเช่า...	pǒm (dì chán) yàrk chôw
bathing hut (cabana)	ที่อาบน้ำ	têe àrp nárm
deck chair	เก้าอี้ผ้าใบ	gôw êe pâr bai
motorboat	เรือยนต์	reua yon
rowing-boat	เรือพาย	reua pai
sailing boat	เรือใบ	reua bai
skin-diving equipment	เครื่องมือดำน้ำ	krêuang meur dam nárm
sunshade (umbrella)	ร่มกันแดด	rôm gan dàirt
surfboard	กระดานโต้คลื่น	gra darn (d)tôe klêurn
water-skis	สกีน้ำ	sa gee nárm
windsurfer	วินด์เซิร์ฟ	win sêrf

ชายหาดส่วนตัว	PRIVATE BEACH
ห้ามว่ายน้ำ	NO SWIMMING

Making friends

Introductions   แนะนำตัว

On being introduced Thais will place both palms together beneath their chin, fingers pointing upwards. This guesture is known as ไหว้ —wâi. You will find most Thais very friendly and willing to strike up a conversation.

Smart, conservative dress is appreciated, particularly if you are invited to a Thai home. Do not touch anyone on the head, which is considered sacred, and avoid pointing your feet towards another's body.

The polite form of calling Thais by their name is the same whether speaking to a man or woman: the title *kun* followed by their first name.

May I introduce Mr./ Mrs/Miss...?	ขอแนะนำให้รู้จักคุณ...?	kǒr náih nam hâi róo jàk
John, this is Mr/Mrs/ Miss...	จอห์น นี่คุณ...	jorn née kun
My name is...	ผม(ดิฉัน)ชื่อ...	pǒm (di chán) chêur
Pleased to meet you!	ยินดีที่รู้จัก	yin dee têe róo jàk
What's your name?	คุณชื่ออะไร?	kun chêur arai
How are you?	เป็นยังไงบาง?	(b)pehn yang ngai bârng
Fine, thanks. And you?	สบายดี ขอบคุณ แล้วคุณละ?	sa bai dee kòrp kun láiw kun lâ
Where are you going?	ไปไหน	(b)pai nǎi
I'm going out.	ไปเที่ยว	(b)pai têaw
Where have you been?	ไปไหนมา	(b)pai nǎi mar
I've been out.	ไปเที่ยวมา	(b)pai têaw mar

Follow up   ติดตามคุณ

How long have you been here?	อยู่ที่นี่นานแค่ไหนแล้ว?	kun yòo têe née narn kâir nǎi láiw
We've been here a week.	เราอยู่ที่นี่ได้อาทิตย์ หนึ่งแลว	row yòo têe née dâi ar tít nèuhng láiw

Is this your first visit?	นี่เป็นครั้งแรกที่คุณมาที่นี่หรือเปล่า?	nêe (b)pehn krâng ráirk têe kun mar têe nêe rĕua (b)plòw
No, we came here last year.	ไม่ใช่ เราเคยมาที่นี่แล้วเมื่อปีที่แล้ว	mâi châi row koey mar têe nêe láiw mêua (b)pee têe láiw
Are you enjoying your stay?	อยู่ที่นี่ชอบไหม?	yòo têe nêe chôrp măi
Yes, I like it very much.	ชอบ ผม(ดิฉัน)ชอบมาก	chôrp pŏm (di chán) chôrp mârk
Where do you come from?	คุณมาจากไหน?	kun mar jàrk năi
I'm from...	ผม(ดิฉัน)มาจาก...	pŏm (di chán) mar jàrk
What nationality are you?	คุณเป็นคนชาติอะไร?	kun (b)pehn kon chârt arai
I'm...	ผมเป็นคน...	pŏm (b)pehn kon
American	อเมริกัน	a mey rí gan
British	อังกฤษ	ang grìt
Canadian	แคนาดา	kâir nar dar
English	อังกฤษ	ang grìt
Irish	ไอริช	ai rít
Where are you staying?	คุณพักที่ไหน?	kun pák têe năi
Are you on your own?	มาเที่ยวคนเดียวเหรอ?	mar têaw kon deaw rĕr
I'm with my...	ผม(ดิฉัน)มากับ...ของผม(ดิฉัน)	pŏm (di chán) mar gàp...kŏrng pŏm (di chán)
wife	ภรรยา	pan ra yar
husband	สามี	săr mee
family	ครอบครัว	krôrp krua
children	ลูกๆ	lôok lôok
parents	พ่อแม่	pôr mâir
boyfriend/girlfriend	แฟน	fairn

father/mother	พ่อ/แม่	pôr/mâir
son/daughter	ลูกชาย/ลูกสาว	lôok chai/lôok sŏw
brother/sister	พี่(น้อง)ชาย/พี่(น้อง)สาว	pêe (nórng) chai/pêe (nórng) sŏw
uncle/aunt	ลุง/ป้า	lung/(b)pâr
nephew/niece	หลานชาย/หลานสาว	lărn chay/lărn sŏw
cousin	ญาติ	yârt

COUNTRIES, see page 146

ทำความรู้จักกันและกัน

Are you married/ single?	คุณแต่งงานแล้วหรือยัง/ เป็นโสดอยู่หรือเปล่า?	kun tàihng ngarn láiw rěua yang/(b)pehn sòet yòo rěua (b)plòw
Do you have children?	คุณมีลูกแล้วหรือยัง?	kun mee lôok láiw rěua yang
What do you do?	คุณทำงานอะไร?	kun tam ngan arai
I'm a student.	ผม(ดิฉัน)เป็นนักศึกษา	pǒm (di chán) (b)pehn nák sèuhk sǎr
What are you studying?	คุณกำลังศึกษาด้านไหน?	kun gam lang sèuhk sǎr dârn nǎi
I'm here on a business trip/on holiday.	ผม(ดิฉัน)มาธุระ/ เที่ยวพักผอน	pǒm (di chán) mar tu rá/têaw pák pòrn
Do you travel a lot?	คุณเดินทาง ทองเที่ยวมากไหม?	kun dern tarng (d)tôrng têaw mârk mǎi
Do you play cards/ chess?	คุณเล่นไพ่/ หมากรุกเป็นไหม?	kun lêhn pâi/màrk rúk (b)pehn mǎi

The weather อากาศ

What a lovely day!	วันนี้อากาศดีจัง	wan née ar gàrt dee jang
What awful weather!	อากาศแย่จังเลย	ar gàrt yâir jang loey
Isn't it cold/ hot today?	วันนี้หนาว/ร้อนนะ?	wan née nǒw/rórn ná
Do you think it's going to ... tomorrow?	คิดว่าพรุ่งนี้...ไหม?	kit wâr prung née...mǎi
be a nice day	อากาศดี	ar gàrt dee
rain	ฝนตก	fǒn (d)tòk
What's the weather forecast?	พยากรณ์อากาศ วายังไงบาง?	pa yar gorn ar gàrt wâr yang ngai bâng

cloud	เมฆ	mêyk
fog	มีหมอก	mee mòrk
frost	น้ำค้างแข็ง	nárm kárng kǎihng
lightning	ฟ้าแลบ	fár lâirp
monsoon	มรสุม	mo ra sǔm
rain	ฝนตก	fǒn (d)tòk
thunder	ฟ้าร้อง	fár rórng
thunderstorm	ฝนฟ้าคะนอง	fǒn fár ka norng
wind	ลม	lom

Invitations คำเชื้อเชิญ

Would you like to have dinner with us on…?	มากินอาหารเย็นกับเรา...ไหม?	mar gin ar hårn yehn gàp row…mǎi
May I invite you to lunch?	อยากชวนไปกินอาหารเที่ยงด้วย?	yàrk chuan (b)pai gin ar hårn têarng dûay
Can you come round for a drink this evening?	แวะมาดื่มด้วยกันได้ไหมเย็นนี้?	wáih mar dèurm dûay gan dâi mǎi yehn née
There's a party. Are you coming?	มีงานปาร์ตี้ มาได้ไหม?	mee ngarn (b)par têe. mar dâi mǎi
That's very kind of you.	คุณใจดีจังเลย	kun jai dee jang loey
Great. I'd love to come.	ดีมาก ผม(ดิฉัน)อยากไปมาก	dee mârk. pǒm (di chán) yàrk (b)pai mârk
What time shall we come?	เราควรไปกี่โมง?	row kuan (b)pai gèe moeng
May I bring a friend?	ผม(ดิฉัน)พาเพื่อนไปด้วยคนหนึ่งได้ไหม?	pǒm (di chán) par pêuan (b)pai dûay kon nèuhng dâi mǎi
I'm afraid we have to leave now.	ขอโทษ เราต้องกลับแล้วละ	kǒr tôet row (d)tôrng glàp láiw lá
Next time you must come to visit us.	คราวหน้าคุณต้องมาเยี่ยมเรานะ	krow nâr kun (d)tôrng mar yêarm row ná
Thanks for the evening. It was great.	ขอบคุณสำหรับงานเลี้ยงเย็นนี้ ดีมากเลย	kòrp kun sǎm ráp ngarn léarng yehn née. dee mârk loey

Dating นัดหมาย

Do you mind if I smoke?	คุณจะรังเกียจไหมถ้าผม(ดิฉัน)จะสูบบุหรี่?	kun ja rang gèart mǎi târ pǒm (di chán) ja sòop bu rèe
Would you like a cigarette?	บุหรี่ไหม?	bu rèe mǎi
Do you have a light, please?	มีไฟแช็กไหม?	mee fai cháihk mǎi
Why are you laughing?	คุณหัวเราะอะไรเหรอ?	kun hǔa ró arai rěr
Is my Thai that bad?	ภาษาไทยของผม(ดิฉัน)แย่ขนาดนั้นเลยเหรอ?	par sǎr tai kǒrng pǒm (di chán) yâir ka nàrt nán loey rěr

DAYS OF THE WEEK, see page 151

Can I get you a drink?	ผม(ดิฉัน)ไปเอา เครื่องดื่มให้เอาไหม?	pŏm (di chán) (b)pai ow krèuang dèurm hâi ow măi
Are you waiting for someone?	รอใครอยู่หรือเปล่า?	ror krai yòo rĕua (b)plòw
Are you free this evening?	คุณว่างไหมเย็นนี้?	kun wârng măi yehn née
Would you like to go out with me tonight?	อยากออกไปเที่ยวข้างนอก กับผม(ดิฉัน)ไหม?	yàrk òrk (b)pai têaw kârng nòrk gàp pŏm (di chán) măi
Would you like to go dancing?	อยากออกไปเต้นรำไหม?	yàrk òrk (b)pai (d)têhn ram măi
I know a good discotheque.	ผม(ดิฉัน)รู้จักดิสโก้เธคดีๆ อยู่ที่หนึ่ง	pŏm (di chán) róo jàk dit sa gôe téhk dee dee têe nèuhng
Where shall we meet?	เราจะเจอกันที่ไหนดี?	row ja jer gan têe năi dee
I'll call for you at 8.	ผม(ดิฉัน)จะแวะ ไปหาตอนสองทุ่ม	pŏm (di chán) ja wáih (b)pai hăr d(t)orn sŏrng tûm
May I take you home?	เดี๋ยวผม(ดิฉัน) ไปส่งที่บ้านให้นะ?	dĕaw pŏm (di chán) (b)pai sòng têe bârn hâi ná
Can I see you again tomorrow?	ผม(ดิฉัน)จะเจอคุณ อีกทีพรุ่งนี้ได้ไหม?	pŏm (di chán) ja jer kun èek tee prûng née dâi măi
I hope we'll meet again.	ผม(ดิฉัน)หวังว่าเราจะ ได้เจอกันอีก	pŏm (di chán) wăng wâr row ja dâi jer gan èek

... and you might answer: ผม(ดิฉัน)สนใจมาก

I'd love to, thank you.	ขอบคุณ	pŏm (di chán) sŏn jai mârk kòrp kun
Thank you, but I'm busy.	ขอบคุณ แต่ว่าผม (ดิฉัน)ยุ่งมาก	kòrp kun (d)tàir wâr pŏm (di chán) yûng mârk
No, I'm not interested, thank you.	ไมละ ผม(ดิฉัน)ไม่สนใจ ขอบคุณ	mâi lâ pŏm (di chán) mâi sŏn jai kòrp kun
Leave me alone, please!	ขอร้อง อย่ายุ่งได้ไหม	kŏr rórng yàr yûng dâi măi
Thank you, it's been a wonderful evening.	ขอบคุณ งานเลี้ยง เย็นนี้เยี่ยมจริงๆ	kòrp kun ngarn léarng yehn née yêarm jing jing
I've enjoyed myself.	ผม(ดิฉัน)รู้สึกสนุกมาก	pŏm (di chán) róo sèuhk sa nùk mârk

Shopping Guide

This shopping guide is designed to help you find what you want with ease, accuracy and speed. It features:

1. A list of all major shops, stores and services (p. 98).
2. Some general expressions required when shopping to allow you to be specific and selective (p. 100).
3. Full details of the shops and services most likely to concern you. Here you'll find advice, alphabetical lists of items and conversion charts listed under the headings below.

LAUNDRY, see page 29/HAIRDRESSER'S, see page 30

Shops, stores and services ร้านค้าและบริการ

Large department stores and shopping centres have shot up all over Bangkok and most provincial capitals. These stores open seven days a week, usually from 10am to 9pm or sometimes later. Traditional shop-houses which open onto the street are usually owned by Chinese Thais and are also open seven days a week, from early morning to last thing at night.

Local fresh food markets are at their busiest in the early morning and may only be open from 5am to 9am in smaller country towns. At night time the market place becomes a place for eating and drinking at food stalls and barrows, although curios, cassette tapes, clothes and so on may also be on sale. City pavements also become lined with stalls selling clothing, luggage and watches. The rock-bottom prices indicate that many of the goods are imitations of the brand names they bear.

Whenever you purchase goods (with the exception of food) from roadside stalls or markets, the price you are quoted will include an allowance for you to bargain down. As a general rule you can expect to purchase the item at 50–75% of the first price quoted to you. If you are not sure what the going rate is, shop around and enquire from several stallholders. However, it is not appropriate to bargain for goods in department stores or hotels.

Where's the nearest...?	...ที่ใกล้ที่สุดอยู่ที่ไหน?	...têe glâi têe sùt yòo têe nǎi
antique shop	ร้านขายโบราณวัตถุ	rárn kǎi boe rarn wát tù
art gallery	หอศิลป์	hǒr sǐn
baker's	ร้านขายขนมปัง	rárn kǎi ka nǒm (b)pang
bank	ธนาคาร	ta nar karn
barber's	ร้านตัดผม	rárn (d)tàt pǒm
beauty salon	ร้านเสริมสวย	rárn sěrm sǔay
bookshop	ร้านหนังสือ	rárn nǎng sěur
butcher's	ร้านขายเนื้อ	rárn kǎi néua
camera shop	ร้านขายกล้องถ่ายรูป	rárn kǎi glôrng tài rôop
chemist's	ร้านขายยา	rárn kǎi yar
dentist	ร้านหมอฟัน	rárn mǒr fan

department store	ห้างสรรพสินค้า	hârng sáp pa sĭn kár
drugstore	ร้านขายยา	rárn kăi yar
dry cleaner's	ร้านซักแห้ง	rárn sák hâirng
electrical goods shop	ร้านขายเครื่องไฟฟ้า	rárn kăi krêuang fai fár
fishmonger's	ร้านขายปลา	rárn kăi (b)plar
florist's	ร้านขายดอกไม้	rárn kăi dòrk mái
grocer's	ร้านขายของชำ	rárn kăi kŏng cham
hairdresser's (ladies/ men)	ร้านทำผม	rárn tam pŏm
hardware store	ร้านขายเครื่องโลหะ	rárn krêuang loe hà
hospital	โรงพยาบาล	roeng pa yar barn
ironmonger's	ร้านขายเครื่องเหล็ก	rárn kăi krêuang lèhk
jeweller's	ร้านขายเครื่องประดับ	rárn kăi krêuang (b)pra dàp
launderette	ร้วนซักผ้า	rárn sák pâr
library	ห้องสมุด	hôrng sa mùt
market	ตลาด	(d)ta làrt
newsstand	แผงขายหนังสือพิมพ์	păirng kăi năng sĕur pim
optician	ร้านตัดแว่น	rárn (d)tàt wâihn
pastry shop	ร้านขายขนม	rárn kăi ka nŏm
photographer	ร้านถ่ายรูป	rárn tài rôop
police station	สถานีตำรวจ	sa tăr nee (d)tam rùat
post office	ไปรษณีย์	(b)prai sa nee
shoemaker's (repairs)	ร้านซ่อมรองเท้า	rárn sôrm rorng tów
shoe shop	ร้านขายรองเท้า	rárn kăi rorng tów
shopping centre	ศูนย์การค้า	sŏon garn kár
souvenir shop	ร้านขายของที่ระลึก	rárn kăi kŏng têe ra léuhk
sporting goods shop	ร้านขายเครื่องกีฬา	rárn kăi krêuang gee lar
stationer's	ร้านขายเครื่องเขียน	rárn kăi krêuang kĕarn
supermarket	ซุปเปอร์มาร์เก็ต	súp (b)per mar gêht
sweet shop	ร้านเขายขนมหวาน	rárn kăi ka nŏm wărn
tailor's	ร้านตัดเสื้อ	rárn (d)tàt sêua
telegraph office	ที่ทำการโทรเลข	têe tam garn toe ra léyk
toy shop	ร้านขายของเล่น	rárn kăi kŏng lêhn
travel agency	เอเยนต์ท่องเที่ยว	ey yêyn tôrng têaw
vegetable store	ร้านขายผัก	rárn kăi pàk
veterinarian	สัตวแพทย์	sàt pâirt

ทางเข้า	ENTRANCE
ทางออก	EXIT
ทางออกฉุกเฉิน	EMERGENCY EXIT

General expressions *การแสดงออกทั่วไป*

Where? *ที่ไหน?*

Where's there a good...?	มี...ที่ดีที่ไหนบ้าง?	mee... têe dee têe nǎi bârng
Where can I find a...?	ผม(ดิฉัน)จะ หา...ได้ที่ไหน?	pǒm (di chán) ja hǎr... dâi têe nǎi
Where's the main shopping area?	ย่านการค้าสำคัญ อยู่ที่ไหน?	yârn garn kár sǎm kan yòo têe nǎi
Is it far from here?	ไกลจากที่นี่ไหม?	glai jàrk têe nêe mǎi
How do I get there?	ผม(ดิฉัน)จะไปที่นั่น ได้ยังไง?	pǒm (di chán) ja (b)pai têe nân dâi yang ngai

ลดราคา
SALE

Service *บริการ*

Can you help me?	ช่วยผม(ดิฉัน) หน่อยได้ไหม?	chûay pǒm (di chán) nòy dâi mǎi
I'm just looking.	ดูเฉยๆ	doo chǒey chǒey
Do you sell...?	คุณมี...ขายไหม?	kun... kǎi mǎi
I'd like to buy...	ผม(ดิฉัน)อยากซื้อ...	pǒm (di chán) yàrk séur
I'd like...	ผม(ดิฉัน)ต้องการ...	pǒm (di chán) (d)tôrng garn
Can you show me some...?	ขอดู...หน่อยได้ไหม?	kǒr doo... nòy dâi mǎi
Do you have any...?	คุณมี...ไหม?	kun mee... mǎi
Where's the...?	...อยู่ที่ไหน?	... yòo têe nǎi
... department	แผนก...	pa nàirk
escalator	บันไดเลื่อน	ban dai lêuan
lift	ลิฟท์	lif

That one อันนั้น

Can you show me...?	ขอดู...หน่อยได้ไหม?	kŏr doo ... nòy dâi mǎi
this/that	อันนี้/อันนั้น	an née/an nán
the one in the window/in the display case	อันที่อยู่ในตู้โชว์/ที่โชว์อยู่	an têe yòo nai (d)tôo choe/ têe choe yòo

Defining the article อธิบายเกี่ยวกับสิ่งของ

I'd like a ... one.	ผมต้องการอัน...	pǒm (di chán) (d)tôrng garn an
big	ใหญ่	yài
cheap	(ที่)ราคาถูก	(têe) rar kar tòok
dark	สีเข้ม	sěe kêhm
good	(ที่)ดี	(têe) dee
heavy	(ที่)หนัก	(têe) nàk
large	ใหญ่	yài
light (weight)	(ที่น้ำหนัก)เบา	(têe nárm nàk) bow
light (colour)	สีอ่อน	sěe òrn
oval	รูปไข่	rôop kài
rectangular	สี่เหลี่ยมผืนผ้า	sěe lèarm pěurn pâr
round	กลม	glom
small	เล็ก	léhk
square	สี่เหลี่ยมจัตุรัส	sěe lèarm jàt (d)tù rát
sturdy	(ที่)แข็งแรงทนทาน	(têe) kǎihng rairng ton tarn
I don't want anything too expensive.	ผม(ดิฉัน)ไม่อยากได้ อะไรที่แพงเกินไป	pǒm (di chán) mâi yàrk dâi arai têe pairng gern (b)pai

Preference ความชอบ

Can you show me some others?	ขอดูอันอื่น อีกหน่อยได้ไหม?	kŏr doo an èurn èek nòy dâi mǎi
Don't you have anything...?	คุณมีอะไรที่...ไหม?	kun mee arai têe... mǎi
cheaper/better	ถูกกว่า/ดีกว่า	tòok gwàr/dee gwàr
larger/smaller	ใหญ่กว่า/เล็กกว่า	yài gwàr/léhk gwàr

How much? เท่าไหร่

How much is this?	อันนี้เท่าไหร่?	an née tôw rài
How much are they?	เท่าไหร่?	tôw rài
I don't understand.	ผม(ดิฉัน)ไม่เข้าใจ	pǒm (di chán) mâi kôw jai
Please write it down.	ช่วยเขียนให้ดูหน่อย	chûay kěarn hâi doo nòy

COLOURS, see page 113

I don't want to spend more than ... baht.	ผม(ดิฉัน) ไม่อยากจ่ายมากกว่า...บาท	pŏm (di chán) mâi yàrk jài mârk gwàr ... bàrt
I'm afraid that's too much.	แพงไป	pairng (b)pai
OK, let's say ... baht.	ตกลง ...บาทก็แล้วกัน	(d)tòk long ... bàrt gôr láiw gan

Decision การตัดสินใจ

It's not quite what I want.	มันไม่ใช่สิ่งที่ผม(ดิฉัน) ต้องการเลยทีเดียว	man mâi châi sìng têe pŏm (di chán) (d)tôrng garn loey tee deaw
No, I don't like it.	ไม่ ผม(ดิฉัน)ไม่ชอบอันนี้เลย	mâi pŏm (di chán) mâi chôrp an née loey
I'll take it.	ผม(ดิฉัน)เอาอันนี้ล่ะ	pŏm (di chán) ow an née lâ

Ordering การสั่ง

| Can you order it for me? | คุณช่วยสั่งให้ผม(ดิฉัน)หน่อยได้ไหม? | kun chûay sàng hâi pŏm (di chán) nòy dâi mǎi |
| How long will it take? | จะใช้เวลานานแค่ไหน? | ja chái wey lar narn kâir nǎi |

Delivery การส่ง

I'll take it with me.	ผม(ดิฉัน)จะเอาไปเอง	pŏm (di chán) ja ow (b)pai eyng
Deliver it to the ... Hotel.	ช่วยส่งไปที่โรงแรม...ด้วย	chûay sòng (b)pai têe roeng rairm ... dûay
Please send it to this address.	ช่วยส่งไปตามที่อยู่นี้ด้วย	chûay sòng (b)pai (d)tarm têe yòo née dûay
Will I have any difficulty with the customs?	ผม(ดิฉัน)จะมีปัญหายุ่งยากกับทางศุลกากรไหม?	pŏm (di chan) ja mee (b)pan hǎr yûng yârk gàp tarng sǔn la gar gorn mǎi

Paying การจ่ายเงิน

How much is it?	เท่าไหร่?	tôw rài
Can I pay by traveller's cheque?	จ่ายด้วยเช็คเดินทางได้ไหม?	jài dûay chéhk dern tarng dâi mǎi
Do you accept dollars/pounds?	รับเงินดอลลาร์/ปอนด์ไหม?	ráp ngern dor lar/(b)porn mǎi
Do you accept credit cards?	รับบัตรเครดิตไหม?	ráp bàt krey dìt mǎi

Anything else? *รับอะไรอีกไหม?*

No, thanks, that's all.	ไม่ ขอบคุณ พอแล้ว	mâi kòrp kun por láiw
Yes, I'd like...	ครับ(คะ) ผม(ดิฉัน) อยากได้...	kráp (kâ) pŏm (di chán) yàrk dâi
Can you show me...?	ช่วยบอก...หน่อยได้ไหม	chûay bòrk...nòy dâi măi
May I have a bag, please?	ผม(ดิฉัน) ขอถุงหน่อยได้ไหม?	pŏm (di chán) kŏr tŭng nòy dâi măi
Could you wrap it up for me, please?	ช่วยห่อให้หน่อยได้ไหม?	chûay hòr hâi nòy dâi măi
May I have a receipt?	ขอใบเสร็จรับเงิน หน่อยได้ไหม?	kŏr bai sèht ráp ngern nòy dâi măi

Dissatisfied? *ไม่พอใจ?*

Can you exchange this, please?	ขอเปลี่ยนอันนี้ได้ไหม?	kŏr (b)plèarn an née dâi măi
I want to return this.	ผม(ดิฉัน)อยากคืนอันนี้	pŏm (di chán) yàrk keurn an née
I'd like a refund. Here's the receipt.	ขอเงินคืน นี่ใบเสร็จรับเงิน	kŏr ngern keurn. nêe bai sèht ráp ngern

---

มีอะไรจะให้รับใช้ไหม?	Can I help you?
คุณอยากได้อะไร?	What would you like?
คุณต้องการ...อะไร(แบบไหน)?	What ... would you like?
สี / รูปร่าง(แบบไหน)/ คุณภาพ(แบบไหน)	colour/shape/quality
ขอโทษด้วย เราไม่มีของเลย	I'm sorry, we don't have any.
ตอนนี้ไม่มีของเหลือเลย	We're out of stock.
จะให้เราสั่งของให้คุณไหม?	Shall we order it for you?
คุณจะเอาไปเองหรือจะ ให้เราส่งไปให้?	Will you take it with you or shall we send it?
รับอะไรอีกไหม?	Anything else?
อันนั้น...บาท	That's ... baht, please.
ที่จ่ายเงินอยู่ที่โน่น	The cash desk is over there.

Bookshop—Stationer's ร้านหนังสือ   ร้านขายเครื่องเขียน

Newspapers and magazines are for sale at bookshops as well as
at some grocers' shops and stationers'. The two main English
language newspapers—the *Bangkok Post* and the *Nation*—are
not usually sold by roadside vendors. A number of publishing
houses have begun to produce news and feature magazines in
English.

Where's the nearest…?	…ที่ใกล้ที่สุดอยู่ที่ไหน?	…têe glâi têe sùt yòo têe nǎi
bookshop	ร้านหนังสือ	rárn nǎng sěur
stationer's	ร้านขายเครื่องเขียน	rárn kǎi krêuang kěarn
newsstand	แผงขายหนังสือพิมพ์	pǎirng kǎi nǎng sěur pim
Where can I buy an English-language newspaper?	ผม(ดิฉัน)จะหาซื้อหนังสือพิมพ์ภาษาอังกฤษได้ที่ไหน?	pǒm (di chán) ja hǎr séur nǎng sěur pim par sǎr ang grìt dâi têe nǎi
Where's the guide-book section?	แผนกหนังสือคู่มืออยู่ที่ไหน?	pa nàirk nǎng sěur kôo meur yòo têe nǎi
Where do you keep the English books?	ชั้นหนังสือภาษาอังกฤษอยู่ที่ไหน?	chán nǎng sěur par sǎr ang grìt yòo têe nǎi
Have you any of…'s books in English?	คุณมีหนังสือของ…เป็นภาษาอังกฤษบางไหม?	kun mee nǎng sěur kǒrng…. (b)pehn par sǎr ang grìt bârng mǎi
Do you have second-hand books?	คุณมีหนังสือมือสองบางไหม?	kun mee nǎng sěur meur sǒrng bârng mǎi
I want to buy a/an/some…	ผม(ดิฉัน)อยากซื้อ…	pǒm (di chán) yàrk séur
address book	สมุดจดที่อยู่	sa mùt jòt têe yòo
adhesive tape	เทปกาว	téyp gow
ball-point pen	ปากกาลูกลื่น	(b)pàrk gar lôok lêurn
book	หนังสือ	nǎng sěur
calendar	ปฏิทิน	pa tì tin
carbon paper	กระดาษอัดสำเนา	gra dàrt àt sǎm now
crayons	ดินสอสี	din sǒr sěe
dictionary	พจนานุกรม	po ja nar nú grom
Thai-English	ไทย–อังกฤษ	tai - ang grìt
pocket	ฉบับกระเป๋า	cha bàp gra (b)pǒw
drawing paper	กระดาษวาดเขียน	gra dàrt wârt kěarn

drawing pins	เข็มหมุดสำหรับวาดเขียน	kěhm mùt săm ràp wârt kěarn
envelopes	ซองจดหมาย	sorng jòt măi
eraser	ยางลบ	yarng lóp
exercise book	สมุดแบบฝึกหัด	sa mùt bàirp fèukk hàt
felt-tip pen	ปากกาเมจิก	(b)pàrk gar mey jìk
fountain pen	ปากกาหมึกซึม	(b)pàrk gar mèuhk seuhm
glue	กาว	gow
grammar book	หนังสือไวยากรณ์	náng sěur wai yar gorn
guidebook	หนังสือคู่มือ	náng sěur kôo meur
ink	หมึก	mèuhk
black/red/blue	ดำ/แดง/น้ำเงิน	dam/dairng/nárm ngern
(adhesive) labels	ป้ายสติ๊กเกอร์	(b)pâi sa (d)tík ger
magazine	วารสาร	wa ra sărn
map	แผนที่	păirn têe
street map	แผนที่ถนน	păirn têe ta nŏn
road map of...	แผนที่ถนนของ...	păirn têe ta nŏn kŏrng
mechanical pencil	ดินสอกด	din sŏr gòt
newspaper	หนังสือพิมพ์	náng sěur pim
American/English	อเมริกัน/อังกฤษ	a mey ri gan/ang grìt
notebook	สมุดโน้ต	sa mùt nóht
note paper	กระดาษจดบันทึก	gra dàrt jòt ban téuhk
paintbox	กล่องสี	glòrng sěe
paper	กระดาษ	gra dàrt
paperback	หนังสือปกอ่อน	náng sěur (b)pòk òrn
paperclips	กิ๊ปหนีบกระดาษ	gíp nèep gra dàrt
paper napkins	กระดาษเช็ดปาก	gra dàrt chéht (b)pàrk
paste	แป้งเปียก	(b)pâirng (b)pèark
pen	ปากกา	(b)pàrk gar
pencil	ดินสอ	din sŏr
pencil sharpener	ที่เหลาดินสอ	têe lŏw din sŏr
playing cards	ไพ่	pâi
postcard	โปสการ์ด	(b)poe sa gàrt
propelling pencil	ดินสอกด	din sŏr gòt
refill (for a pen)	หมึก	mèuhk
rubber	ยางลบ	yarng lóp
ruler	ไม้บรรทัด	mái ban tát
staples	ที่เก็บกระดาษ	têe yóhp gra dàrt
string	เข็มเย็บกระดาษ	kěhm yéhp gra dàrt
thumbtacks	เป๊กติดกระดาษ	(b)péhk (d)tìt gra dàrt
travel guide	หนังสือคู่มือ	náng sěur kôo meur
typewriter ribbon	ผ้าเทปพิมพ์ดีด	pâr téyp pim dèet
typing paper	กระดาษพิมพ์ดีด	gra dàrt pim dèet
writing pad	กระดาษเขียนหนังสือ	gra dàrt kěarn náng sěur

Camping and sports equipment แค้มป์ปิ้งและเครื่องกีฬา

I'd like a/an/some ...	ผม(ดิฉัน)อยากได้...	pŏm (di chán) yàrk dâi
I'd like to hire a(n)/ some ...	ผม(ดิฉัน)อยากเช่า...	pŏm (di chán) yàrk chôw

air bed (mattress)	ที่ปูนอน	têe (b)poo norn
backpack	เป้หลัง	(b)pêy lăng
butane gas	กาซบิวเทน	gárt biw teyn
campbed	เตียงสนาม	(d)tearng sa nărm
(folding) chair	เก้าอี้(พับ)	gôw ée (páp)
charcoal	ถาน	tàrn
compass	เข็มทิศ	kěhm tít
cool box	กระติกน้ำแข็ง	gra (d)tìk nárm kăihng
deck chair	เก้าอี้ผ้าใบ	gôw ée pâr bai
fire lighters	เครื่องจุดไฟ	krêuang jùt fai
fishing tackle	คันเบ็ดชนิดมีรอก	kan bèht cha nít mee rôrk
flashlight	ไฟกระพริบ	fai gra príp
groundsheet	ผ้ายางปูพื้น	pâ yarng (b)poo péurn
hammock	เปลญวน	(b)pley yuan
ice pack	น้ำแข็ง	nárm kăihng
insect spray (killer)	ยาฉีดกันยุง	yar chèet gan yung
kerosene	น้ำมันกาด	nám man gárt
lamp	ตะเกียง	(d)ta gearng
lantern	โคมไฟ	koem fai
mallet	ฆ้อนไม้	kórn mái
matches	ไม้ขีด	mái kèet
(foam rubber) mattress	ที่นอน(ยาง)	têe norn (yarng)
mosquito net	มุ้ง	múng
paraffin	น้ำมันก๊าด	nám man gárt
picnic basket	ตะกร้าปิคนิค	(d)ta grâr (b)pìk ník
pump	ที่สูบลม	têe sòop lom
rope	เชือก	chêuak
rucksack	เป้หลัง	(b)pêy lăng
screwdriver	ไขควง	kăi kuang
skin-diving equipment	เครื่องประดาน้ำ	krêuang (b)pra dar nárm
sleeping bag	ถุงนอน	tŭng norn
(folding) table	โต๊ะ(พับ)	(d)tóh (páp)
tent	เตนท	(d)têyn
tent pegs	หมุดปักเต้นท์	mùt (b)pàk (d)têyn
tent pole	เสาเต้นท	sŏw (d)têyn
torch	ไฟฉาย	fai chăi
windsurfer	กระดานโต้คลื่น	gra darn (d)tôe klêurn
water flask	กระติกน้ำ	gra (d)tìk nárm

Chemist's (drugstore) ร้านขายยา

Chemist's, like other shop-houses, are open seven days a week from early morning till late at night. There are few laws restricting across-the-counter sales of drugs in Thailand and antibiotics, penicillin etc. do not require a prescription. If you purchase drugs from a shop within a department store or shopping complex you are more likely to receive the advice of a qualified chemist. The word for a chemists' shop is *rárn yar* or *rárn kăi yar*.

General ทั่วไป

Where's the nearest (all-night) chemist's?	ร้านขายยา(ที่เปิดตลอด คืน)ที่ใกล้ที่สุดอยู่ที่ไหน?	rárn kăi yar (tĕe (b)pèrt (d)ta lòrt keurn) tée glâi tée sùt yòo têe năi
What time does the chemist's open/ close?	ร้านขายยาเปิด/ ปิดกี่โมง?	rárn kăi yar (b)pèrt/(b)pìt gèe moeng

1—Pharmaceutical เกี่ยวกับยา

I'd like something for...	ผม(ดิฉัน)อยากได้ยา สำหรับแก้...	pŏm (di chán) yàrk dâi yar săm ràp gâir...
a cold/a cough	หวัด/ไอ	wàt/ai
hay fever	โรคแพ้อากาศ	rôek páir ar gàrt
insect bites	แมลงกัดต่อย	ma lairng gàt (d)tòy
sunburn	แดดเผา	dàirt pŏw
travel/altitude sickness	เมารถเมาเรือ/ แพ้ความสูง	mow rót mow reua/páir kwarm sŏong
an upset stomach	ท้องเสีย	tórng sĕar
Can you prepare this prescription for me?	ช่วยเขียนใบสั่งยานี้ ให้หน่อยได้ไหม?	chûay kĕarn bai sàng yar née hâi nòy dâi măi
Can I get it without a prescription?	ผม(ดิฉัน)ซื้อยานี้ โดยไม่ใช้ใบสั่งยาได้ไหม?	pŏm (di chán) séur yar née doy mâi chái bai sàng yar dâi măi
Shall I wait?	ให้ผม(ดิฉัน)คอยไหม?	hâi pŏm (di chán) koy măi

Can I have a/an/some ...?	ขอซื้อ...หน่อย?	kŏr séur ... nòy
adhesive plaster	พาสเต้อร์	plar sa (d)têr
analgesic	ยาแก้ปวด	yar gâir (b)pùat
antiseptic cream	ครีมแก้อักเสบ	kreem gâir àk sèyp
aspirin	แอสไพริน	àirt sa pai rin
bandage (elastic)	ผ้าพันแผล	pâr pan plâir
Band-Aids®	พลาสเตอร์ปิดแผล	plar sa (d)ter (b)pèet plâir
condoms	ถุงยางอนามัย	tŭng yarng a nar mai
contraceptives	คุมกำเนิด	kum gam nért
corn plasters	พาสเตอร์สำหรับติดตาปลา	plar sa (d)têr sǎm ràp (d)tit (d)tar (b)plar
cotton wool (absorbent cotton)	สำลี	sǎm lee
cough drops	ยาแก้ไอ	yar gâir ai
disinfectant	ยาฆ่าเชื้อ(สำหรับใช้กับสิ่งของ)	yar kâr chéua (sǎm ràp chái gàp sìng kǒrng)
ear drops	ยาหยอดหู	yar yòrt hǒo
eye drops	ยาหยอดตา	yar yòrt (d)tar
first-aid kit	เครื่องมือปฐมพยาบาล	krêuang meur (b)pa tom pa yar barn
gauze	ผ้าก๊อซ	pâr gòrs
insect repellent/spray	ยากันแมลง/สเปรย์ฉีดกันแมลง	yar gan ma lairng/sa (b)prey chèet gan ma lairng
iodine	ไอโอดีน	ai oe deen
laxative	ยาระบาย	yar ra bai
mouthwash	น้ำยาบ้วนปาก	nárm yar bûan (b)pàrk
nose drops	ยาหยอดจมูก	yar yòrt ja mòok
sanitary towels (napkins)	ผ้าอนามัย	pâr a nar mai
sleeping pills	ยานอนหลับ	yar norn làp
suppositories	ยาเหน็บทวาร	yar nèhp ta warn
... tablets	...เม็ด	... méht
tampons	ผ้าอนามัยชนิดสอด	pâr a nar mai cha nít sod
thermometer	ปรอท	(b)pròrt
throat lozenges	ยาอม	yar om
tranquillizers	ยากล่อมประสาท	yar glòrm (b)pra sàrt
vitamin pills	วิตามิน	wi (d)tar min

ยาพิษ	POISON
สำหรับใช้ภายนอกเท่านั้น	FOR EXTERNAL USE ONLY

DOCTOR, see page 137

2—Toiletry เครื่องใช้ในห้องน้ำ

I'd like a/an/some …	ผม(ดิฉัน)อยากได้…	pŏm (dì chán) yàrk dâi
after-shave lotion	โลชั่นสำหรับทาหลังโกนหนวด	loe chân săm ràp tar lăng goen nùat
astringent	ยาสมาน	yar sa mărn
blusher (rouge)	รูชทาแก้ม	rôot tar gâirm
bubble bath	บับเบิ้ลบาธ	báp bêrl bàrt
cream	ครีม	kreem
cleansing cream	ครีมล้างหน้า	kreem lárng nâr
foundation cream	ครีมรองพื้น	kreem rorng péurn
moisturizing cream	ครีมบำรุงผิว	kreem bam rung pĭw
night cream	ครีมบำรุงผิวตอนกลางคืน	kreem bam rung pĭw (d)torn glarng keurn
cuticle remover	ที่แต่งโคนเล็บ	têe (d)tàihng koen léhp
deodorant	ยาดับกลิ่นตัว	yar dàp glìn (d)tua
emery board	ตะไบเล็บ(ไม้)	(d)ta bai léhp (mái)
eyebrow pencil	ดินสอเขียนคิ้ว	din sŏr kĕarn kíw
eyeliner	ที่เขียนขอบตา	têe kĕarn kòrp (d)tar
eye shadow	ที่ทาตา	têe tar (d)tar
face powder	แป้งผัดหน้า	(b)pâihng pàt nâr
foot cream	ครีมทาเท้า	kreem tar tów
hand cream	ครีมทามือ	kreem tar meur
lipsalve	ขี้ผึ้งทาปาก	kêe pêuhng tar (b)pàrk
lipstick	ลิปสติก	líp sa (d)tìk
make-up remover pads	แผ่นเช็ดเครื่องสำอางค์	pàirn chéht krêuang săm arng
mascara	ที่ปัดขนตา	têe (b)pat kŏn (d)tar
nail brush	แปรงขัดเล็บ	(b)prairng kàt léhp
nail clippers	กรรไกรขลิบเล็บ	gan grai klip léhp
nail file	ตะไบขัดเล็บ	(d)ta bai kàt léhp
nail polish	ยาทาเล็บ	yar tar léhp
nail polish remover	น้ำยาล้างเล็บ	nárm yar lárng léhp
nail scissors	กูรไกรตัดเล็บ	gan grai (d)tàt léhp
perfume	น้ำหอม	nárm hŏrm
powder	แป้ง	(b)pâirng
powder puff	แป้งพลัฟ	(b)pâirng plap
razor	มีดโกน	mêet goen
razor blades	ใบมีดโกน	bai mêet goen
rouge	รูช	rôot
safety pins	เข็มกลัด	kĕhm glàt
shaving brush	แปรงสำหรับโกนหนวด	(b)prairng săm ràp goen nùat
shaving cream	ครีมสำหรับโกนหนวด	kreem săm ràp goen nùat

soap	สบู่	sa bòo
sponge	ฟองน้ำขัดตัว	forng nárm kàt (d)tua
sun-tan cream	ครีมกันแดด	kreem gan dàirt
sun-tan oil	น้ำมันกันแดด	nám man gan dàirt
talcum powder	แป้งโรยตัว	(b)pâirng roey (d)tua
tissues	กระดาษทีขชุ	gra dàrt tít sôo
toilet paper	กระดาษชำระ	gra dàrt cham rá
toilet water	โอดิโคโลญจ์	oe di koe loen
toothbrush	แปรงสีฟัน	(b)praing sěe fan
toothpaste	ยาสีฟัน	yar sěe fan
towel	ผ้าขนหนู	pâr kŏn nŏo
tweezers	แหนบ	nàirp

For your hair สำหรับเส้นผม

bobby pins	กิ๊บ	gíp
colour shampoo	แชมพูย้อมผม	chairm poo yórm pŏm
comb	หวี	wěe
curlers	เครื่องมือดัดผม	krêuang meur dàt pŏm
dry shampoo	แชมพูผง	chairm poo pŏng
dye	ยาย้อมผม	yar yórm pŏm
hairbrush	หวีแปรงผม	wěe (b)prairng pŏm
hair gel	เยลใส่ผม	yeyl sài pŏm
hairgrips	กิ๊บติดผม	gíp (d)tìt pŏm
hair lotion	โลชั่นใส่ผม	loe chân sài pŏm
hairpins	ปิ่นปักผม	(b)pìn (b)pàk pŏm
hair spray	สเปรย์ฉีดผม	sa (b)prěy chèet pŏm
setting lotion	โลชั่นสำหรับเซ็ทผม	loe chân săm ràp séht pŏm
shampoo	แชมพู	chairm poo
for dry/greasy (oily) hair	สำหรับผมแห้ง/ผมมัน	săm ràp pŏm hâirng/ pŏm man
tint	ยาย้อมผม	yar yórm pŏm
wig	วิกผม	wík pŏm

For the baby สำหรับเด็กอ่อน

baby food	อาหารเด็ก	ar hǎrn dèhk
dummy (pacifier)	จุกนม	jùk nom
feeding bottle	ขวดคุ่น้ำ	kùat nárm
nappies (diapers)	ผ้าอ้อม	pâr ôrm

Clothing เสื้อผ้า

If you want to buy something specific, prepare yourself in advance. Look at the list of clothing on page 115. Get some idea of the colour, material and size you want. They're all listed on the next few pages.

General ทั่วไป

I'd like ...	ผม(ดิฉัน)อยากได้...	pŏm (di chán) yàrk dâi
I'd like ... for a 10-year-old boy/girl.	ผม(ดิฉัน)อยากได้...สำหรับเด็กผู้ชาย/เด็กผู้หญิงอายุ ๑๐ขวบ	pŏm (di chán) yàrk dâi ... săm ràp dèhk pôo chai/ dèhk pôo yĭng ar yú sìp kùap
I'd like something like this.	ผม(ดิฉัน)อยากได้อะไรเหมือนกับอันนี้	pŏm (di chán) yàrk dâi arai mĕuan gàp an née
I like the one in the window.	ผม(ดิฉัน)อยากได้อันที่อยู่ในตู้โชว์	pŏm (di chán) yàrk dâi an têe yòo nai (d)tôo choe
How much is that per metre?	อันนี้เมตรละเท่าไหร่?	an née méht la tôw rài

1 centimetre (cm)	= 0.39 in.	1 inch	= 2.54 cm
1 metre (m)	= 39.37 in.	1 foot	= 30.5 cm
10 metres	= 32.81 ft.	1 yard	= 0.91 m.

Colour สี

I'd like something in ...	ผม(ดิฉัน)อยากได้สี...	pŏm (di chán) yàrk dâi sĕe
I'd like a darker/lighter shade.	ผม(ดิฉัน)อยากได้สีเข้มกว่านี้/ออนกว่านี้	pŏm (di chán) yàrk dâi sĕe kêhm gwàr née/òrn gwàr née
I'd like something to match this.	ผม(ดิฉัน)อยากได้อันที่เขากับอันนี้	pŏm (di chán) yàrk dâi an têe kôw gàp an née
I don't like the colour.	ผม(ดิฉัน)ไม่ชอบสีเลย	pŏm (di chán) mâi chôrp sĕe loey

beige	สีทราย	sĕe sai
black	สีดำ	sĕe dam
blue	สีน้ำเงิน	sĕe nárm ngern
brown	สีน้ำตาล	sĕe nárm (d)tarn
fawn	สีเทาแกมเหลือง	sĕe tow gairm lĕuang
golden	สีทอง	sĕe torng
green	สีเขียว	sĕe kĕaw
grey	สีเทา	sĕe tow
mauve	สีม่วงสด	sĕe mûang sòt
orange	สีส้ม	sĕe sôm
pink	สีชมพู	sĕe chom poo
purple	สีม่วง	sĕe mûang
red	สีแดง	sĕe dairng
scarlet	สีเลือดหมู	sĕe lêuat mŏo
silver	สีเงิน	sĕe ngern
turquoise	สีเทอร์คอยส์	sĕe ter koyt
white	สีขาว	sĕe kŏw
yellow	สีเหลือง	sĕe lĕuang
light...	สี...อ่อน	sĕe... òrn
dark...	สี...เข้ม	sĕe... kêhm

สีเรียบ	ลายทาง	ลายจุด	ลายหมากรุก	ลวดลาย
(rêarp)	(lai tarng)	(lai jùt)	(lai màr krúk)	(lûat lai)

Fabric เนื้อผ้า

Do you have any-thing in ...?	คุณมีอะไร ที่ทำด้วยผ้า...ไหม?	kun mee arai têe tam dûay pâr... măi
Is that ...?	นั่น...ใช่ไหม?	nân... châi mâi
handmade	ทำด้วยมือ	tam dûay meur
imported	นำเข้าจากต่างประเทศ	nam kôw jàrk (d)tàrng (b)pra téyt
made here	ทำที่นี่	tam têe nêe
I'd like something thinner.	ผม(ดิฉัน)อยากได้ ที่บางกว่านี้	pŏm (di chán) yàrk dâi têe barng gwàr née
Do you have anything of better quality?	คุณมีอะไรที่ คุณภาพดีกว่านี้ไหม?	kun mee arai têe kun a pârp dee gwàr née măi
What's it made of?	อันนี้ทำด้วยอะไร?	an née tam dûay arai

cambric	ผ้าลินินขาว	pâr li nin kŏw
camel-hair	ขนอูฐ	kŏn òot
chiffon	แพร์ชีฟอง	prair chee forng
corduroy	ผ้าลูกฟูก	pâr ríw
cotton	ผ้าฝ้าย	pâr fâi
crepe	แพรยน	prair yòn
denim	ผ้ายีนส์	pâr yeen
felt	ผ้าสักหลาด	pâr sàk làrt
flannel	ผ้าสักหลาดอ่อน	pâr sàk làrt òrn
gabardine	ผ้าลายสูงหน้าเดียว	pâr lai sŏrng nâr deaw
lace	ผ้าลูกไม้	pâr lôok mái
leather	หนัง	nǎng
linen	ผ้าลินิน	pâr li nin
poplin	ผ้าแพรป๊อปปลิน	pâr prair (b)pohp lin
satin	ผ้าซาติน	pâr sar (d)tin
silk	ผ้าไหม	pâr mǎi
suede	หนังกลับ	nǎng glàp
towelling	ผ้าขนหนู	pâr kŏn nŏo
velvet	ผ้ากำมะหยี่	pâr gam ma yòe
velveteen	ผ้ากำมะหยี่เทียม	pâr gam ma yèe tearm
wool	ผ้าขนแกะ	pâr kŏn gàih
worsted	ไหมพรม	mǎi prom

Is it...?	อันนี้...หรือเปล่า?	an née...rěur (b)plòw
pure cotton/wool	ผ้าฝ้าย/ผ้าขนแกะแท้	pâr fâi/ pâr kŏn gàih táir
synthetic	ผ้าใยสังเคราะห์	pâr yai sǎng kró
colourfast	สีตก	sěe (d)tòk
crease (wrinkle) resistant	กันยับ	gan yáp
Is it hand washable/Is it machine washable?	อันนี้ซักด้วยมือ/อันนี้ใช้ ด้วยเครื่องซักผ้าได้ไหม?	an née sák dûay meur/an née sák dûay krêuang sák pâr dâi mǎi
Will it shrink?	มันจะหดหรือเปล่า?	man ja hòt rěur (b)plòw

Size ขนาด

I take size 38.	ผม(ดิฉัน)เอาเบอร์ ๓๘	pŏm (di chàn) ow ber sǎrm sìp pàirt
Could you measure me?	ช่วยวัดตัวผม(ดิฉัน) หน่อยได้ไหม?	chûay wát (d)tua pŏm (di chán) nòy dâi mǎi
I don't know the Thai sizes.	ผม(ดิฉัน)ไม่รู้จัก ขนาดของไทย	pŏm (di chán) mâi róo jàk ka nàrt kŏrng tai

NUMBERS, see page 147

คู่มือช้อปปิ้ง

Sizes can vary somewhat from one manufacturer to an-other, so be sure to try on shoes and clothing before you buy.

small (S)	เล็ก	léhk
medium (M)	กลาง	glarng
large (L)	ใหญ่	yài
extra large (XL)	ใหญ่พิเศษ	yài pi sèyt
larger/smaller	ใหญ่กว่า / เล็กกว่า	yài gwàr/ léhk gwàr

A good fit? พอดีไหม?

Can I try it on?	ขอลองหน่อยได้ไหม?	kŏr lorng nòy dâi măi
Where's the fitting room?	ห้องลองอยู่ที่ไหน?	hôrng lorng yòo têe năi
Is there a mirror?	มีกระจกไหม?	mee gra jòk măi
It fits very well.	กำลังพอดี	gam lang por dee
It doesn't fit.	มันไม่พอดี	man mâi por dee

Tailor—Dressmaker ช่างตัดเสื้อผ้า

I'd like to have a... made.	ผม(ดิฉัน) อยากตัด...สักตัว	pŏm (dichán) yàrk (d)tàt... sàk (d)tua
dress	ชุดเสื้อกระโปรงติดกัน	chút sêua gra(b)proeng (d)tìt gan
shirt	เสื้อเชิ้ต	sêua chért
suit	สูท	sòot
Can I see some patterns?	ขอดูแบบหน่อย	kŏr doo bàirp nòi
I'd like it the same... as this.	อยากได้...เหมือนตัวนี้	yàrk dâi....mĕuan (d)tua née
colour	สี	sĕe
style	สไตล์	sa(d)tai
When can I collect it?	จะให้มารับได้เมื่อไหร่	ja hâi mar ráp dâi mêua rài
Will it be ready by Wednesday?	วันพุธจะเสร็จไหม	wan pút ja sèht mái
It's too...	มัน...เกินไป	man... gern (b)pai
short/long	สั้น / ยาว	sân/yow
tight/loose	คับ / หลวม	káp/lŭam
How long will it take to alter?	ใช้เวลาแก้นานแค่ไหน?	chái wey lar gâir narn kâir năi

Clothes and accessories *เสื้อผ้าและของที่ไปกับเสื้อผ้า*

I would like a/an/ some...	ผม(ดิฉัน)อยากได้...	pŏm (di chán) yàrk dâi
bathing cap	หมวกอาบน้ำ	mùak àrp nárm
bathing suit	ชุดว่ายน้ำ	chút wâi nárm
bathrobe	เสื้อคลุมอาบน้ำ	sêua klum àrp nárm
blouse	เสื้อผู้หญิง	sêua pôo yĭng
bow tie	หูกระต่าย	hŏo gra (d)tài
bra	ยกทรง	yók song
braces	สายโยงกางเกง	săi yoeng garng geyng
cap	หมวกแกป	mùak gáihp
cardigan	คาร์ดิกัน	kar di gan
coat	เสื้อโค้ท	sêua kóet
dress	เสื้อกระโปรงชุด	sêua gra (b)proeng chùt
with long sleeves	แขนยาว	kăirn yow
with short sleeves	แขนสั้น	kăirn sân
sleeveless	ไม่มีแขน	mâi mee kăirn
dressing gown	เสื้อคลุมอาบน้ำ	sêua klum àrp nárm
evening dress (woman's)	ชุดราตรี	chút rar (d)tree
girdle	เข็มขัด/ ผ้าคาดเอว	kĕhm kàt/ pâr kârt ew
gloves	ถุงมือ	tŭng meur
handbag	กระเป๋าถือ	gra (b)pŏw tĕur
handkerchief	ผ้าเช็ดหน้า	pâr chéht nâr
hat	หมวก	mùak
jacket	เสื้อแจ็กเก็ต	sêua jàirk gèht
jeans	ยีนส์	yeens
jersey	เสื้อไหมพรม	sêua măi prom
jumper (Br.)	เสื้อไหมพรม	sêua măi prom
kneesocks	ถุงเท้ายาวถึงเข่า	tŭng tów yow tĕuhng kòw
nightdress	ชุดนอน	chút norn
pair of...	...คู่	... kôo
panties	กางเกงรัดรูป	garng geyng rát rôop
pants (Am.)	กางเกงขายาว	garng geyng kăr yow
panty girdle	ถุงนอง	tŭng nông
panty hose	ถุงนอง	tŭng nông
pullover	เสื้อไหมพรม	sêua măi prom
polo (turtle)-neck	คอโปโล	kor (b)poe loe
round-neck	คอกลม	kor glom
V-neck	คอวี	kor wee
with long/short sleeves	แขนยาว/ แขนสั้น	kăirn yow/kăirn sân
mee kăirn	มีแขน	mee kăirn
without sleeves	ไม่มีแขน	mâi mee kăirn

pyjamas	เสื้อกางเกงนอน	sêua garng geyng norn
raincoat	เสื้อกันฝน	sêua gan fõn
scarf	ผ้าพันคอ	pâr pan kor
shirt	เสื้อเชิ้ต	sêua chért
shorts	กางเกงขาสั้น	garng geyng kǎr sân
skirt	กระโปรง	gra (b)proeng
slip	กางเกงอาบน้ำผู้ชาย	garng geyng àrp nárm pôo chai
socks	ถุงเท้า	tǔng tów
stockings	ถุงน่อง	tǔng nông
suit (man's)	ชุดสากล(ของผู้ชาย)	chút sǎr gon (kǒrng pôo chai)
suit (woman's)	ชุดสากล(ของสุภาพสตรี)	chút sǎr gon (kǒrng sǔ pârp sa (d)trêe)
suspenders (Am.)	สายที่แขวนกางเกง	sǎi têe kwǎirn garng geyng
sweater	เสื้อไหมพรม	sêua mǎi prom
sweatshirt	เสื้อกีฬาคอกลมแขนยาว	sêua gee lar kor glom kǎirn yow
swimming trunks	กางเกงว่ายน้ำ	garng geyng wâi nárm
swimsuit	ชุดว่ายน้ำ	chút wâi nárm
T-shirt	เสื้อคอกลม	sêua kor glom
tie	เนคไท	néhk tai
tights	ถุงน่อง	tǔng nông
tracksuit	ชุดวอร์ม	chút worm
trousers	กางเกงขายาว	garng geyng kǎr yow
umbrella	ร่ม	rôm
underpants	กางเกงใน	garng geyng nai
undershirt	เสื้อยืด	sêua yêurt
vest (Am.)	เสื้อกั๊ก	sêua gák
vest (Br.)	เสื้อกล้าม	sêua glârm
waistcoat	เสื้อกั๊ก	sêua gák

belt	เข็มขัด	kěhm kàt
buckle	หัวเข็มขัด	hǔa kěhm kàt
button	กระดุม	gra dum
collar	คอเสื้อ	kor sêua
pocket	กระเป๋า	gra (b)pǒw
press stud (snap fastener)	แปะติดเสื้อ	(b)páih (d)tit sêua
zip (zipper)	ซิป	síp

Shoes รองเท้า

I'd like a pair of...	ผม(ดิฉัน)อยากได้...คู่หนึ่ง	pŏm (di chán) yàrk dâi... kôo nèuhng
boots	รองเท้าบู๊ท	rorng tów bôot
plimsolls (sneakers)	รองเท้าผ้าใบ	rorng tów pâr bai
sandals	รองเท้าแตะ	rorng tów (d)tàih
shoes	รองเท้า	rorng tów
flat	พื้นราบ	péurn rârp
with (high) heels	ส้นสูง	sôn sŏong
with leather soles	พื้นหนัง	péurn năng
with rubber soles	พื้นยาง	péurn yarng
slippers	รองเท้าแตะ	rorng tów (d)tàih
These are too...	มัน...เกินไป	man ... gern (b)pai
narrow/wide	แคบ/กว้าง	kâirp/gwârng
big/small	ใหญ่/เล็ก	yài/léhk
Do you have a larger/ smaller size?	คุณมีขนาดใหญ่กว่า/ เล็กกว่านี้ไหม?	kun mee ka nàrt yâi gwàr/ léhk gwar née mái
Do you have the same in black?	มีสีดำแบบเดียวกันนี้?	mee sĕe dam bàirp deaw gan née
cloth	ผ้า	pâr
leather	หนัง	năng
rubber	ยาง	yarng
suede	หนังกลับ	năng glàp
Is it real leather?	อันนี้หนังแท้หรือเปล่า?	an née năng táir rĕur (b)plòw
I need some shoe polish/shoelaces.	ผม(ดิฉัน)อยากได้ยาง ขัดรองเท้า/ เชือกผูกรองเท้า	pŏm (di chán) yàrk dâi yarng kàt rorng tów/chêuak pòok rorng tów

Shoes worn out? Here's the key to getting them fixed again:

Can you repair these shoes?	ช่วยซ่อมรองเท้า คู่นี้ได้ไหม?	chûay sôrm rorng tów kôo née dâi mái
Can you stitch this?	ช่วยเย็บอันนี้ ให้หน่อยได้ไหม?	chûay yéhp an née hâi nòy dâi mái
I want new soles and heels.	ช่วยเปลี่ยนพื้นและส้น รองเท้าให้หน่อย	chûay (b)plèarn péurn láih sôn rorng tów hâl nòy
When will they be ready?	จะเสร็จเมื่อไหร่?	ja sèht mêua rài

COLOURS, see page 113

Electrical appliances เครื่องใช้ไฟฟ้า

The standard current is 220 volts, 50-cycle AC with two-pin plugs and sockets. Most hotels have a point for shavers.

What's the voltage?	ที่นี่ใช้ไฟฟ้ากี่โวลท์?	têe nêe chái fai fár gèe woel
Do you have a battery for this?	คุณมีถ่านไฟฉายสำหรับอันนี้ไหม?	kun mee tàrn fai chǎi sǎm ràp an née mǎi
This is broken. Can you repair it?	อันนี้มันเสีย ช่วยซ่อมให้หน่อยได้ไหม?	an née man sěar. chûay sôrm hâi nòy dâi mǎi
Can you show me how it works?	ช่วยแสดงให้ดูหน่อย ว่ามันทำงานยังไง?	chûay sa dairng hâi doo nòy wâr man tam ngarn yang ngai
I'd like (to hire) a video cassette.	ผม(ดิฉัน)อยากได้ (อยากเช่า)ม้วนเทปวีดีโอ	pǒm (di chán) yàrk dâi (yàrk chôw) múan téyp wee dee oe
I'd like a/an/ some...	ผม(ดิฉัน)อยากได้...	pǒm (di chán) yàrk dâi
adaptor	ปลั๊กแปลงไฟฟ้า	blák (b)plairng fai fár
amplifier	เครื่องขยายเสียง	krêuang ka yǎi sěarng
bulb	หลอดไฟฟ้า	lòrt fai fár
CD player	เครื่องเลนซีดี	krêuang lêhn see dee
clock-radio	วิทยุ-นาฬิกา	wít ta yú - nar lí gar
electric toothbrush	แปรงสีฟันไฟฟ้า	(b)prairng sěe fan fai fár
extension lead (cord)	สายต่อ(ไฟฟ้า)	sǎi (d)tòr (fai fár)
hair dryer	เครื่องเป่าผม	krêuang (b)pòw pǒm
headphones	หูฟัง	hǒo fang
(travelling) iron	เตารีด(สำหรับเดินทาง)	(d)tow rêet (sǎm ràp dern tarng)
lamp	โคมไฟ	koem fai
plug	ปลั๊ก	(b)plák
portable...	...กระเป๋าหิ้ว	... gra (b)pǒw hîw
radio	วิทยุ	wít ta yú
car radio	วิทยุรถยนต์	wít ta yú rót yon
(cassette) recorder	เครื่องอัดเทป	krêuang àt téyp
record player	เครื่องเลนแทป	krêuang lêhn téyp
shaver	เครื่องโกนหนวดไฟฟ้า	krêuang goen nùat fai fár
speakers	ลำโพง	lam poeng
(colour) television	โทรทัศน์(สี)	toe ra tát (sěe)
transformer	หม้อแปลงไฟฟ้า	môr (b)plairng fai fár
video-recorder	เครื่องอัดวีดีโอ	krêuang àt wee dee oe

Grocery ร้านขายของชำ

Thais measure in kilograms and kilometres. They have a 100g measure too, called a *kèet*— ขีด .

I'd like some bread, please.	ผม(ดิฉัน)อยากได้ขนมปัง	pŏm (di chán) yàrk dâi ka nŏm (b)pang
What sort of cheese do you have?	คุณมีเนยแข็งแบบไหนบ้าง?	kun mee noey kǎihng bàirp nǎi bârng
A piece of...	...ชิ้นหนึ่ง	... chín nèuhng
that one	อันนั้น	an nán
the one on the shelf	อันที่อยู่บนชั้นนั้น	an têe yòo bon chán nán
I'll have one of those, please.	ผม(ดิฉัน)อยากได้อันนั้น อันหนึ่ง	pŏm (di chán) yàrk dâi an nán an nèuhng
May I help myself?	ผม(ดิฉัน)หยิบเองได้ไหม?	pŏm (di chán) yìp eyng dâi mǎi
I'd like...	ผม(ดิฉัน)อยากได้...	pŏm (di chán) yàrk dâi
a kilo of oranges	ส้มหนึ่งกิโล	sôm nèuhng gi loe
half a kilo of tomatoes	มะเขือเทศครึ่งกิโล	ma kěua téyt krêuhng gi loe
100 grams of chillies	พริกขีดหนึ่ง/๑๐๐กรัม	prík kèet nèuhng/rói gram
a litre of milk	นมหนึ่งลิตร	nom nèuhng lít
half a dozen eggs	ไข่ครึ่งโหล	kài krêuhng lǒe
4 slices of ham	แฮมสี่แผ่น	hairm sèe pàirn
a packet of tea	ชาหนึ่งกล่อง	char nèuhng glòrng
a jar of jam	แยมหนึ่งขวด	yairm nèuhng kùat
a tin (can) of peaches	ลูกท้อหนึ่งกระป๋อง	lôok tór nèuhng gra (b)pŏrng
a box of chocolates	ช็อคโกแล็ตหนึ่งกล่อง	chôk goe lâiht nèuhng glòng

---

1 kilogram or kilo (kg.) = 1000 grams (g.)	
100 g. = 3.5 oz.	½ kg. = 1.1 lb.
200 g. = 7.0 oz.	1 kg. = 2.2 lb.
1 oz. = 28.35 g.	
1 lb. = 453.60 g.	

---

1 litre (l.) = 0.88 imp. quarts = 1.06 U.S. quarts	
1 imp. quart = 1.14 l.	1 U.S. quart = 0.95 l.
1 imp. gallon = 4.55 l.	1 U.S. gallon = 3.8 l.

FOOD, see also page 63

Household articles ของใช้ในบ้าน

bottle opener	ที่เปิดขวด	têe (b)pèrt kùat
bucket (pail)	ถังน้ำ	tǎng nárm
can opener	ที่เปิดกระป๋อง	têe (b)pèrt gra (b)pǒrng
candles	เทียน	tearn
clothes pegs (pins)	ไม้หนีบผ้า	mái nèep pâr
dish detergent	น้ำยาล้างจาน	nám yar lárng jarn
food box	อาหารกล่อง	ar hǎrn glòng
frying pan	กะทะแบน	gà tá bairn
matches	ไม้ขีด	mái kèet
paper napkins	กระดาษเช็ดปาก	gra dàrt chéht (b)pàrk
plastic bags	ถุงพลาสติก	tǔng plar sa (d)tìk
saucepan	หม้อ	môr
tin opener	ที่เปิดกระป๋อง	têe (b)pèrt gra (b)pǒrng
tea towel	ผ้าเช็ดจาน	pâr chéht jarn
vacuum flask	กระติกสุญญากาศ	gra (d)tìk sǒon yar gàrt
washing powder	ผงซักฟอก	pǒng sák fôrk
washing-up liquid	น้ำยาล้างจาน	nám yar lárng jarn

Tools เครื่องมือ

hammer	ฆ้อน	kórn
nails	ตะปู	(d)tà (b)poo
penknife	มีดพับ	mêet páp
pliers	คีม	keem
scissors	กรรไกร	gan grai
screws	ตะปูควง	(d)tà (b)poo kuang
screwdriver	ไขควง	kǎi duang
spanner	กุญแจเลื่อน	gun jair lêuan

Crockery ถ้วยชาม

cups	แก้ว	gâiw
mugs	เหยือก	yèuak
plates	จาน	jarn
saucers	จานรองถ้วย	jarn rorng tûay
tumblers	ถ้วยแก้ว	tûay gâiw

Cutlery (flatware) ช้อน-ส้อม

forks	ส้อม	sôrm
knives	มีด	mêet
spoons	ช้อน	chórn
teaspoons	ช้อนชา	chórn char

Jeweller's—Watchmaker's ร้านขายเครื่องรูปพรรณ ร้านนาฬิกา

Could I see that, please?	ขอดูอันนั้นหน่อยได้ไหม?	kŏr doo an nán nòy dâi măi
Do you have anything in gold?	มีอะไรที่ทำจากทองไหม?	mee arai têe tam jàrk torng măi
How many carats is this?	อันนี้กี่กะรัต?	an née gèe ga rát
Is this real silver?	อันนี้เงินแท้หรือเปล่า?	an née ngern táir rĕur (b)plòw
Can you repair this watch?	ช่วยซ่อมนาฬิกาเรือนนี้ หน่อยได้ไหม?	chûay sôrm nar lí gar reuan née nòy dâi măi
I'd like a/an/some...	ผม(ดิฉัน)อยากได้...	pŏm (di chán) yàrk dâi

alarm clock	นาฬิกาปลุก	nar lí gar (b)pluk
bangle	กำไล	gam lai
battery	ถ่านไฟฉาย	tàrn fai chăi
bracelet	สร้อยข้อมือ	sôy kôr meur
chain bracelet	สร้อยข้อมือ	sôy kôr meur
charm bracelet	สร้อยข้อมือ ที่มีเครื่องราง	sôy kôr meur têe mee krêuang rarng
brooch	เข็มกลัด	kĕhm glàt
chain	สร้อย	sôy
charm	เครื่องราง	krêuang rarng
cigarette case	ตลับใส่บุหรี่	(d)ta làp sài bu rèe
cigarette lighter	ไฟแช็ก	fai cháihk
clip	เข็มกลัดหนีบ	kĕhm glàt nèep
clock	นาฬิกา	nar lí gar
cross	ไม้กางเขน	mái garng kĕyn
cuckoo clock	นาฬิกานกร้อง	nar lí nok rórng
cuff-links	กระดุมข้อมือเสื้อ	gra dum kôr meur sêua
earrings	ตุ้มหู	(d)tûm hŏo
gem	เพชรพลอย	péht ploy
jewel box	ตู้เครื่องเพชร	(d)tôo krêuang péht
mechanical pencil	ดินสอกด	din sŏr gòt
music box	กล่องดนตรี	glòrng don (d)tree
necklace	สร้อยคอ	sôy kor
pendant	จี้	jêe
pin	เข็มหมุด	kĕhm mùt
pocket watch	นาฬิกาพก	nar lí gar pók
powder compact	ตลับแป้ง	(d)ta làp (b)pâirng
propelling pencil	ดินสอกด	din sŏr gòt

ring	แหวน	wăirn
engagement ring	แหวนหมั้น	wăirn mân
signet ring	แหวนรุน	wăirn rûn
wedding ring	แหวนแต่งงาน	wăirn (d)tàirng ngarn
rosary	ลูกประคำ	lôok (b)pra kam
silverware	เครื่องเงิน	krêuang ngern
tie clip	ที่หนีบเนคไท	têe nèep néyk tai
tie pin	เข็มกลัดเนคไท	kăihm glàt néyk tai
watch	นาฬิกาข้อมือ	nar lí gar kôr meur
automatic	อัตโนมัติ	àt noe mát
digital	ดิจิตอล	(d)ti jí (d)torn
quartz	ควอทซ์	kwôrt
with a second hand	มือสอง	meur sŏrng
waterproof	กันน้ำ	gan nárm
watchstrap	สายนาฬิกาข้อมือ	săy na lí gar kôr meur
wristwatch	นาฬิกาข้อมือ	nar lí gar kôr meur

amber	อำพัน	am pan
amethyst	เขียวหนุมาน	kêaw ha nŭ marn
chromium	โครเมี่ยม	kroe mêarm
copper	ทองแดง	torng dairng
coral	หินปะการัง	hĭn (b)pà gar rang
crystal	แก้วผลึก/คริสตัล	gâiw plèuhk/kri sa (d)tăn
cut glass	แก้วเจียรไน	gâiw jea ra nai
diamond	เพชร	péht
emerald	มรกต	mo ra gòt
enamel	ลงยา/เคลือบ	long yar/klêuap
gold	ทองคำ	torng kam
gold plate	ชุบทอง	chúp torng
jade	หยก	yòk
onyx	หินจำพวกโมรา	hĭn jam pûak moe rar
pearl	ไข่มุก	kài múk
pewter	พิวเตอร์	piw (d)ter
platinum	แพลตตินั่ม	plairt (d)ti nâm
ruby	ทับทิม	táp tim
sapphire	ไพลิน/บุษราคัม/มรกต	pai lin/bùt rar kam/mo ra gòt
silver	เงิน	ngern
silver plate	ชุบเงิน	chúp ngern
stainless steel	สแตนเลส	sa (d)tăirn léyt
topaz	บุษราคัม	bùt sa rar kam
turquoise	เทอรคอยส์/พลอยสีฟ้า	ter kŏyt/ploy sĕe fár

Optician ร้านตัดแว่น

I've broken my glasses.	แว่นผม(ดิฉัน)แตก	wâirn pŏm (di chán) (d)tàirk
Can you repair them for me?	ช่วยซ่อมแว่นให้ผม(ดิฉัน) หน่อยได้ไหม?	chûay sôrm wâirn hâi pŏm (di chán) nòy dâi măi
When will they be ready?	จะเสร็จเมื่อไหร่?	ja sèht mêua rài
Can you change the lenses?	ช่วยเปลี่ยนเลนส์ ให้หน่อยได้ไหม?	chûay (b)plìarn leyns hâi nòy dâi măi
I'd like tinted lenses.	เลนส์สี	leyns sĕe
The frame is broken.	กรอบแว่นหัก	gròrp wâirn hàk
I'd like a spectacle case.	ผม(ดิฉัน)อยากได้ ซองใส่แว่น	pŏm (di chán) yàrk dâi sorng sài wâirn
I'd like to have my eyesight checked.	ช่วยตรวจสายตาให้ผม (ดิฉัน)หน่อย	chûay (d)trùat săi (d)tar pŏm (di chán) nòy
I'm short-sighted/ long-sighted.	สายตาผม(ดิฉัน)สั้น/ยาว	săi (d)tar pŏm (di chán) sân/yow
I'd like some contact lenses.	ผม(ดิฉัน)อยากได้ คอนแท็กต์เลนส์	pŏm (di chán) yàrk dâi korn táihk leyns
I've lost one of my contact lenses.	คอนแท็กต์เลนส์ผม(ดิฉัน) หายไปข้างหนึ่ง	korn táihk leyns pŏm (di chán) hăi (b)pai kârng nèuhng
Could you give me another one?	ขอซื้อข้างเดียวได้ไหม?	kŏr séur kârng deaw dâi măi
I have...	ผม(ดิฉัน)ใช้ประเภท...	pŏm (di chán) chái (b)pra péyt
hard/soft lenses	ฮาร์ทเลนส์/ซอฟเลนส์	hárt leyns/sóf leyns
Do you have any contact-lens fluid?	มีน้ำยาล้างคอนแท็กต์ เลนส์ไหม?	mee nám yar láryng korn táihk leyns măi
I'd like to buy a pair of sunglasses.	ผม(ดิฉัน)อยากจะ ได้แว่นตาดำ	pŏm (di chán) yàrk ja dâi wâirn (d)tar dam
May I look in a mirror?	ขอดูกระจกหน่อยได้ไหม?	kŏr doo gra jòk nòy dâi măi
I'd like to buy a pair of binoculars.	ผม(ดิฉัน)อยากได้ กล้องสองทางไกล	pŏm (di chán) yàrk dâi glôrng sòrng tarng glai

Photography *การถ่ายรูป*

I'd like a(n) ... camera.	ผม(ดิฉัน)อยากได้ กล้องถ่ายรูป... ตัวหนึ่ง	pŏm (di chán) yàrk dâi glôrng tài rôop... (d)tua nèuhng
automatic	อัตโนมัติ	àt noe mát
inexpensive	ไม่แพง	mâi pairng
simple	แบบธรรมดา	bàirp tam ma dar
Can you show me some..., please?	ขอดู...หน่อยได้ไหม?	kŏr doo....nòy dây mãi
cine (movie) cameras	กล้องถ่ายหนัง	glôrng tài năng
video cameras	กล้องวีดีโอ	glôrng wee dee oe
I'd like to have some passport photos taken.	ผม(ดิฉัน) อยากถ่ายรูปขนาดติด พาสปอรต/ หนังสือเดินทาง	pŏm (di chán) yàrk tài rôop ka nàrt (d)tit par sa (b)pòrt/năng sěur dern tarng

Film *ฟิล์ม*

I'd like a film for this camera.	ผม(ดิฉัน)อยากได้ฟิล์ม สำหรับกล้องตัวนี้สักม้วน	pŏm (di chán) yàrk dâi feem sǎm ràp glôrng (d)tua née sàk múan
black and white	ขาวดำ	kŏw dam
colour	สี	sěe
colour negative	ฟิล์มสีที่ล้างแล้ว	feem sěe têe lárng láiw
colour slide	ฟิล์มสไลด์	feem sa lai
cartridge	กล้องฟิล์มขนาดใหญ่	glôrng feem ka nàrt yài
disc film	ฟิล์มดิสลับ	feem (d)ta làp
roll film	ฟิล์มม้วน	feem múan
video cassette	ม้วนเทปวีดีโอ	múan téyp wee dee oe
24/36 exposures	๒๔/๓๖ รูป	yêe sìp sèe/ sǎrm sìp hòk rôop
this size	ขนาดนี้	ka nàrt née
this ASA/DIN number	เอเอสเอ/ ความไวแสงของฟิล์มเท่านี้	ey eys ey/kwarm wai sǎirng kŏrng feem tôw née
artificial light type	ชนิดแสงไม่ธรรมชาติ	cha nít sǎirng mâi tam ma chârt
daylight type	ชนิดแสงธรรมชาติ	cha nít sǎirng tam ma chârt
fast (high-speed)	ความเร็วสูง	kwarm rehw sŏong
fine grain	เนื้อละเอียด	néua lá èart

Processing การล้างรูป

How much do you charge for processing?	ค่าล้างรูปที่นี่คิดเท่าไหร่?	kâr lárng rôop têe née kít tôw rài
I'd like... prints of each negative.	ผม(ดิฉัน)อยากได้รูป...ชุด	pŏm (dì chán) yàrk dâi rôop ... chút
with a matt finish	กระดาษด้าน	gra dàrt dârn
with a glossy finish	กระดาษมัน	gra dàrt man
Will you enlarge this, please?	ช่วยขยายรูปนี้ให้หน่อยได้ไหม?	chûay ka yăi rôop née hâi nòy dâi măi
When will the photos be ready?	รูปจะเสร็จเมื่อไหร่?	rôop ja sèht mêua rài

Accessories and repairs อุปกรณ์ถ่ายรูปและการซ่อม

I'd like a/an/some...	ผม(ดิฉัน)อยากได้...	pŏm (dì chán) yàrk dâi
battery	แบตเตอรี่	bàirt (d)ter rêe
cable release	สายกดชัตเตอร์	săi gòt chát (d)ter
camera case	กระเป๋าใส่กล้อง	gra (b)pŏw sài glôrng
(electronic) flash	แฟลช	flâirt
filter	ฟิลเตอร์	fil (d)ter
for black and white	สำหรับฟิล์มขาวดำ	săm ràp feem kŏw dam
for colour	สำหรับฟิล์มสี	săm ràp feem sĕe
lens	เลนส์	leyns
telephoto lens	เลนส์เทเล	leyns tey lêy
wide-angle lens	เลนส์มุมกว้าง	leyns mum gwârng
lens cap	ฝาครอบเลนส์	făr krôrp leyns
Can you repair this camera?	ช่วยซ่อมกล้อง ถ่ายรูปนี้ให้หน่อย ได้ไหม?	chûay sôrm glôrng tài rôop née hâi nòy dâi măi
The film is jammed.	ฟิล์มเลื่อนไม่ไป	feem lêuan mâi (b)pai
There's something wrong with the...	มีปัญหาบางอย่างกับ...	mee (b)pan hăr barng yàrng gàp
exposure counter	ที่บอกจำนวนรูปที่ถ่าย	têe bòrk jam nuan rôop têe tài
film windor	ตัวขึ้นฟิล์ม	(d)tua kêuhn feem
flash attachment	แป้นแฟลช	(b)pâirn flâirt
lens	เลนส์	leyns
light meter	เครื่องวัดแสง	krêuang wát săirng
rangefinder	เครื่องวัดระยะ	krêuang wát rá yá
shutter	ชัตเตอร์	chát (d)ter

NUMBERS, see page 147

Tobacconist's ร้านขายบุหรี่และยาสูบ

Thai cigarettes and tobacco are on sale at most general purpose stores and at restaurants. The most commonly smoked are the filtered *krorng típ* although mentholated cigarettes called *săi fŏn* are also available. International cigarettes are more costly and can be bought in department stores and from roadside vendors.

A packet of cigarettes, please.	ขอบุหรี่ซองหนึ่ง	kŏr bu rèe sorng nèuhng
Do you have any... cigarettes?	คุณมีบุหรี่...ไหม?	kun mee bu rèe... măi
American/English	อเมริกัน/ อังกฤษ	a mey ri gan/ang grìt
I'd like a carton.	ผม(ดิฉัน)อยากได้ บุหรี่คอตตอนหนึ่ง	pŏm (di chán) yàrk dâi bu rèe kârt (d)torn nèuhng
Give me a/some..., please.	ผม(ดิฉัน)อยากได้...	pŏm (di chán) yàrk dâi
candy	ลูกกวาด	lôok gwàrt
chewing gum	หมากฝรั่ง	màrk fa ràng
chewing tobacco	ยาเส้น	yar sêhn
chocolate	ช็อกโกแล็ต	chôk goe láiht
cigarette case	ตลับบุหรี่	(d)ta làp bu rèe
cigarette holder	ที่คาบบุหรี่	têe kârp bu rèe
cigarettes	บุหรี่	bu rèe
filter-tipped/ without filter	กันกรอง/ไม่มีกันกรอง	gôn grorng/ mâi mee gôn grorng
light/dark tobacco	ยาเส้นอ่อน/ เข้ม	yar sêhn òrn/ kêym
mild/strong	รสอ่อน/ จัด	rót òrn/jàt
menthol	รสเมนทอล	rót meyn torl
cigars	ชิการ์	si gar
lighter	ไฟแช็ก	fai châihk
matches	ไม้ขีด	mái kèet
pipe	ไปป์	(b)pai
pipe cleaners	ที่ทำความสะอาด ไปป์	têe tam kwarm sa àrt (b)pai
pipe tobacco	ยาเส้นสำหรับไปป์	yar sêyn săm ràp (b)pai
postcard	โปสการ์ด	(b)poe sa gàrt
snuff	ยานัตถุ์	yar nát
stamps	แสตมป์	sa (d)tairm
sweets	ลูกกวาด	lôok gwàrt
wick	ไส้ตะเกียง	sâi (d)tà gearng

Miscellaneous   เบ็ดเตล็ด

Souvenirs   ของที่ระลึก

Thailand is an emporium of handicrafts which makes souvenir
shopping an irresistible temptation. The country is famed for its
silk, most of which comes from the North-East, and tends to be
rather thick and heavy. It can be bought from the roll or made
up by one of Bangkok's speedy and efficient tailoring services
concentrated along the Sukumwit Road and in most shopping
arcades.

Other souvenirs include antiques (export permission is required
for genuine antiques), hand-made flowers, bronze, niello and
lacquer ware, wooden elephants, brightly coloured kites, dolls
in hill tribe costume, hill tribe clothes and fabrics, gemstones,
jewellery and ceramics. It is illegal to take Buddha images out
of Thailand unless prior permission had been sought.

ของเก่า	kŏrng gòw	antiques
ดอกไม้ประดิษฐ์	dòrk mái (b)pra dìt	hand-made flowers
ทองสัมฤทธิ์	torng sǎm rít	bronze ware
เครื่องถม	krêuang tòm	niello ware
เครื่องเขิน	krêuang kĕrn	lacquer ware
ว่าวสีสด	wôw sĕe sòt	brightly coloured kites
อัญมณี	an ya ma nee	gemstones
เครื่องรูปพรรณ	krêuang rôop pan	jewellery
พระพุทธรูป	prá pút tá rôop	Buddha images
เครื่องเงิน	krûeang ngern	silver ware
ผ้าไหม	pâr mǎi	silk
ช้างไม้	chárng mái	wooden elephant
ชุดชาวเขา	chút chow kŏw	hill tribe clothes
เซรามิค	sey rar mík	ceramics

Records—Cassettes   แผ่นเสียง เทปคาทเซ็ท

I'd like a...	ผม(ดิฉัน)อยากได...	pŏm (dì chán) yàrk dâi
cassette	เทปคาทเซ็ท	téyp kârt séht
video cassette	ม้วนเทปวีดีโอ	múan téyp wee dee oe
compact disc	ซีดี	see dee

L.P.(33 rpm)	แผ่นเสียง(๓๓รอบ ต่อนาที)	pàirn sěarng (sǎrm sìp rôrp (d)tòr nar tee)
E.P.(45 rpm)	แผ่นเสียง(๔๕รอบ ต่อนาที)	pàirn sěarng (sèe sìp hâr rôrp (d)tòr nar tee)
single	แผ่นซิงเกิ้ล	pàirn sing gêrl

Do you have any records by ...?	มีแผ่นเสียงของ...ไหม?	mee pàirn sěarng kŏrng ... mǎi
Can I listen to this record?	ขอฟังแผ่นนี้ หน่อยได้ไหม?	kŏr fang pàirn née nòy dâi mǎi
classical music	ดนตรีคลาสสิค	don (d)tree klârt sìk
folk music	ดนตรีพื้นบ้าน	don (d)tree péurn bârn
folk song	เพลงพื้นบ้าน/โฟล์คซองวี	pleyng péurn bârn/fôek sorng
jazz	แจ๊ส	jáiht
light music	ดนตรีเบาๆ	don (d)tree bow bow
orchestral music	ดนตรีออเคสต้า	don (d)tree or key sa (d)trǎr
pop music	ดนตรีป๊อบ	don (d)tree (b)pôrp

Toys ของเล่น

I'd like a toy/game...	ผม(ดิฉัน)อยากได้ ของเล่น/เกม	pǒm (di chán) yàrk dâi kŏrng lêhn/ geym
for a boy	สำหรับเด็กผู้ชาย	sǎm ràp dèhk pôo chai
for a 5-year-old girl	สำหรับเด็กผู้หญิงอายุ ๕ขวบ	sǎm ràp dèhk pôo yǐng ar yú hâr kùap
(beach) ball	ลูกบอลชายหาด	lôok born (chai hàrt)
bucket and spade (pail and shovel)	ถังและพลั่ว	tǎng láih plûa
card game	ไพ่	pâi
chess set	หมากรุก	màrk rúk
colouring book	สมุดระบายสี	sa mùt ra bai sěe
doll	ตุ๊กตา	(d)túk a (d)tar
electronic game	เกมไฟฟ้า	geym fai fár
hill tribe doll	ตุ๊กตาชาวเขา	(d)túk a (d)tar chow kŏw
roller skates	สเก็ต	sa gèht
snorkel	ท่อดำน้ำ	tôr dam nárm
teddy bear	ตุ๊กตาหมี	(d)túk a (d)tar měe
toy car	รถของเล่น	rót kŏrng lêhn

Your money: banks—currency

Banks are open between 8.30am and 3.30pm from Monday to Friday but their currency exchanges often stay open for longer hours, seven days a week.

The unit of Thai currency is the baht (บาท—*bàrt*). The smallest coins are the copper 25 and 50 satang (หัตางค์ —*sa (d)tàrng*) pieces and there are 100 satang in one baht. Silver coins are used for 1, 5 and 10 baht, while bank notes cover 10 (brown), 20 (green), 50 (blue), 100 (red) and 500 (purple) baht denominations.

Thais do not tend to pay for goods by cheque but credit cards and traveller's cheques will be accepted as a method of payment in most large restaurants and hotels.

Where's the nearest bank?	ธนาคารที่ใกล้ ที่สุดอยู่ที่ไหน?	ta nar karn têe glâi têe sùt yòo têe năi
Where's the nearest currency exchange office?	ที่รับแลกเงินที่ใกล้ ที่สุดอยู่ที่ไหน?	têe ráp lâirk ngern têe glâi têe sùt yòo têe năi

At the bank *ที่ธนาคาร*

I want to change some dollars/pounds.	ผม(ดิฉัน)อยากแลก เงินดอลลาร์/ ปอนด์หน่อย	pŏm (di chán) yàrk lâirk ngern dorn lar/(b)porn nòy
I want to cash a traveller's cheque.	ผม(ดิฉัน)อยากแลก เช็คเดินทางเป็นเงินสด	pŏm (di chán) yàrk lâirk chéhk dern tarng (b)pehn ngern sòt

What's the exchange rate?	อัตราแลกเปลี่ยนเท่าไหร่?	at (d)tra lâirk (b)plèarn tôw rài
How much commission do you charge?	คิดค่าบริการเท่าไหร่?	kìt kàr boe ri garn tôw rài
Can you cash a personal cheque?	เช็คส่วนตัว ใช้เบิกเงินสดได้ไหม?	chéhk sùan tua chái bèrk ngern sòt dâi mǎi
Can you telex my bank in London?	ช่วยเทเล็กซ์ไปที่ ธนาคารของผม(ดิฉัน) ที่ลอนดอนได้ไหม?	chûay tey léhk (b)pai têe ta nar karn kǒng pǒm (di chán) têe lorn dorn dâi mǎi
I have a/an/some...	ผม(ดิฉัน)มี...	pǒm (di chán) mee
credit card	บัตรเครดิต	bàt krey dìt
Eurocheques	ยูโรเช็ค	yoo roe chéhk
letter of credit	แอล.ซี.	airl see
I'm expecting some money from New York. Has it arrived?	ผม(ดิฉัน) คอยเงินจากนิวยอร์กอยู่ ไม่ทราบว่ามาถึงแล้วยัง?	pǒm (di chán) koy ngern jàrk niw yôrk yòo mâi sarp wâr mar těuhng láiw yang
Please give me... notes (bills) and some small change.	ขอเป็นแบงค์/ใบ...และ เงินย่อยอีกนิดหน่อย	kǒr (b)pehn bairng/bai... láih ngern yôy èek nít nòy
Give me... large notes and the rest in small notes.	ขอเป็นแบงค์ใหญ่...ใบ และที่เหลือเป็นแบงค์ย่อย	kǒr (b)pehn bairng yài...bai láih têe lěua (b)pehn bairng yôy

Deposits—Withdrawals ฝาก ถอน

I want to...	ผม(ดิฉัน)อยากจะ...	pǒm (di chán) yàrk ja
open an account	เปิดบัญชี	(b)pèrt ban chee
withdraw... baht	ถอนเงิน...บาท	tǒrn ngern...bàrt
Where should I sign?	เซ็นชื่อตรงไหน?	sehn chêur (d)trong nǎi
I'd like to pay this into my account.	ผม(ดิฉัน)อยากจะ ให้จ่ายเข้าบัญชี ของผม(ดิฉัน)	pǒm (di chán) yàrk ja hâi jài kôw ban chee kǒrng pǒm (di chán)

NUMBERS, see page 147

Business terms เงื่อนไขทางธุรกิจ

My name is...	ผมชื่อ...	pŏm chêur
Here's my card.	นี่นามบัตรของผม(ดิฉัน)	nêe narm bàt kŏrng pŏm (di chán)
I have an appointment with...	ผม(ดิฉัน)มีนัดกับ...	pŏm (di chán) mee nát gàp
Can you give me an estimate of the cost?	ช่วยประเมินค่าใช้จ่ายคราวๆได้ไหม?	chûay (b)pra mern kâr chái jài krôw krôw dâi măi
What's the rate of inflation?	อัตราเงินเฟ้อเท่าไหร่?	a (d)tra ngern fér tôw rài
Can you provide me with...?	ช่วยจัดหา...ให้หน่อย?	chûay jàt hăr ... hâi nòy
an interpreter	ล่าม	lârm
a personal computer	คอมพิวเตอร์(พี.ซี.)	korm piw (d)ter (pee see)
a secretary	เลขานุการ	lêy kăr nú garn
Where can I make photocopies?	ผม(ดิฉัน)จะถ่ายเอกสารได้ที่ไหน?	pŏm (di chán) ja tài èyk ga sărn dâi têe năi

amount	จำนวน	jam nuan
balance	ดุล	dun
capital	ทุน	tun
cheque	เช็ค	chéhk
contract	สัญญา	săn yar
discount	ส่วนลด	sùan lót
expenses	ค่าใช้จ่าย	kâr chái jài
interest	ดอกเบี้ย	dòrk bêar
investment	การลงทุน	garn long tun
invoice	ใบเรียกเก็บเงิน	bai rêark gèhp ngern
loss	ขาดทุน	kàrt tun
mortgage	จำนอง	jam norng
payment	จ่าย	jài
percentage	เปอร์เซนเต์	(b)per sehn
profit	กำไร	gam rai
purchase	ซื้อ	séur
sale	ขาย	kăi
share	หุ้น	hûn
transfer	โอนเงิน	oen ngern
value	มูลค่า	moon kâr

At the post office

Bangkok's Central Post Office on Charoen Krung Road is open from 8am to 8pm on weekdays and from 8am to 1pm at weekends and on public holidays. It operates a busy but efficient poste restante service and a packing and parcelling service for those wishing to send excess luggage home.

Branch post offices are open from 8am to 6pm on weekdays and from 8am to 1pm on Saturdays.

Mail can be posted in the red letter boxes along the roadside but it is more reliable to post your mail at the post office itself as box collections are sometimes irregular.

The Central Post Office in Bangkok has a 24-hour international telephone exchange although since the introduction of direct dialling international calls can now be made from some branch post offices.

Where's the nearest post office?	ที่ทำการไปรษณีย์ที่ใกล้ที่สุดอยู่ที่ไหน?	têe tam garn (b)prai sa nee têe glâi têe sùt yòo têe năin
What time does the post office open/close?	ที่ทำการไปรษณีย์เปิด/ปิดกี่โมง?	têe tam garn (b)prai sa nee (b)pèrt/(b)pìt gèe moeng
A stamp for this letter/postcard please.	ขอซื้อแสตมป์สำหรับจดหมาย/ไปสการ์ดอันนี้	kŏr séur sa (d)tairm săm ràp jòt măi/(b)pòe sa gàrt an née
A...-baht stamp, please.	ขอแสตมป์...บาทดวงหนึ่ง	kŏr sa (d)tairm ... bàrt duang nèuhng
What's the postage for a letter to London?	ค่าแสตมป์เท่าไหร่สำหรับจดหมายส่งไปลอนดอน?	kâr sa (d)tairm tôw rài săm ràp jòt măi sòng (b)pai lorn dorn
What's the postage for a postcard to Los Angeles?	ค่าแสตมป์เท่าไหร่สำหรับโปสการ์ดส่งไปลอสแองเจลิส?	kâr sa (d)tairm tôw rài săm ràp (b)pòe sa gàrt sòng (b)pai lót airng jeh lít
Where's the letter box (mailbox)?	ตู้ไปรษณีย์อยู่ที่ไหน?	(d)tôo (b)prai sa nee yòo têe năi
I want to send this parcel.	ผม(ดิฉัน)อยากส่งพัสดุห่อนี้	pŏm (di chán) yàrk sòng pát sa du hòr née

I'd like to send this (by)...	ผม(ดิฉัน)อยากส่ง อันนี้ทาง/โดย...	pǒm (di chán) yàrk sòng an née tarng/doey
airmail	ไปรษณีย์อากาศ	(b)prai sa nee ar gàrt
express (special delivery)	ไปรษณีย์ด่วน	(b)prai sa nee dùan
registered mail	ลงทะเบียน	long ta bearn
At which counter can I cash an international money order?	ผม(ดิฉัน)จะเอาตั๋ว แลกเงินระหว่างประเทศ ไปขึ้นเงินได้ที่ช่องไหน?	pǒm (di chán) ja ow (d)tǔa lâirk ngern ra wàrng (b)pra têyt (b)pai kêuhn ngern dâi tée chông nǎi
Where's the poste restante (general delivery)?	ส่งทั่วไปช่องไหน?	sòng tûa (b)pai chông nǎi
Is there any post (mail) for me? My name is...	มีจดหมายมาถึงผม (ดิฉัน)บ้างไหม? ผมชื่อ...	mee jòt mǎi mar těuhng pǒm (di chán) bârng mǎi. pǒm chêur

แสตมป์/ดวงตราไปรษณียากร	STAMPS
พัสดุ	PARCELS
ตั๋วแลกเงิน/ธนาณัติ	MONEY ORDERS

Telegrams—Telex—Fax โทรเลข เทเล็กซ์ แฟ็กซ์

Telegrams and facsimile messages can be sent from Bangkok's Central Post Office. Telegrams can also be sent from branch post offices. Most large hotels and shops specializing in communications also have fax facilities.

I'd like to send a telegram/telex.	ผม(ดิฉัน)อยากส่ง โทรเลข/เทเล็กซ์	pǒm (di chán) yàrk sòng toe ra lêyk/tey léhk
May I have a form, please?	ขอแบบฟอร์มหน่อย?	kǒr bàirp form nòy
How much is it per word?	ค่าส่งเท่าไหร่คะคำ?	kâr sòng tôw rài (d)tòr kam
How long will a cable to Boston take?	โทรเลขไปบอสตัน ใช้เวลานานแค่ไหน?	toe ra lêyk (b)pai bòrt sa (d)tan chái wey lar narn kâir nǎi
How much will this fax cost?	ค่าแฟ็กซ์อันนี้เท่าไหร่?	kâr fáihk an née tôw rài

Telephoning โทรศัพท์

Most roadside telephone booths have red telephones and are for local calls only. The boxes take 1-baht coins. Booths for long distance internal calls (including Malaysia) also exist, and have turquoise telephones taking 5-baht coins. In addition airports and some department stores and shopping complexes have telephones taking phone cards which can be used for direct dialling overseas. Telephone cards can be purchased from special desks in department stores.

Where's the telephone?	โทรศัพท์อยู่ที่ไหน?	toe ra sàp yòo têe nǎi
I'd like a telephone card.	ขอซื้อการ์ดโฟนหน่อย	kǒr séur gàrt foen nòy
Where's the nearest telephone booth?	ตู้โทรศัพท์ที่ใกล้ ที่สุดอยู่ที่ไหน?	(d)tôo toe ra sàp têe glâi têe sùt yòo têe nǎi
May I use your phone?	ขอใช้โทรศัพท์ หน่อยได้ไหม?	kǒr chái toe ra sàp nòy dâi mǎi
Do you have a telephone directory for Chiang Mai?	คุณมีสมุดโทรศัพท์สำหรับ เชียงใหม่ไหม?	kun mee sa mùt toe ra sàp sǎm ràp chearng mài mǎi
I'd like to call ... in England.	ผมอยากจะโทรถึง... ที่อังกฤษ	pǒm yàrk ja toe těuhng...têe ang grìt
What's the dialling (area) code for	รหัสพื้นที่ของ...รหัสอะ ไร?	ra hàt péurn têe kǒng...ra hàt arai
How do I get the international operator?	โอเปอเรเตอร์ระหว่าง ประเทศ หมายเลขอะไร?	oe (b)per rey (d)têr ra wàrng (b)pra têyt mǎi lêyk arai

Operator โอเปอเรเตอร์

I'd like Khon Khan 23 45 67.	ช่วยต่อขอนแก่น หมายเลข ๒๓ ๔๕ ๖๗ ให้หน่อย	chûay (d)tòr kǒrn gàihn mǎi lêyk sǒrng sǎrm sèe hâr hòk jèht
Can you help me get this number?	ช่วยต่อหมายเลข นี้ให้หน่อย?	chûay (d)tòr mǎi lêyk née hâi nòy

NUMBERS, see page 147

| I'd like to place a personal (person-to-person) call. | ผม(ดิฉัน)อยากจะ ขอโทรสวนตัวหนอย | pŏm (di chán) yàrk ja kŏr toe sùan (d)tua nòy |
| I'd like to reverse the charges (call collect). | ผม(ดิฉัน)อยากขอ โทรเก็บเงินปลายทาง | pŏm (di chán) yàrk kŏr toe gèh ngern (b)plai tarng |

Speaking กำลังพูด

Hello. This is...	สวัสดี/ฮัลโหล นี่...	sa wàt dee/hăn lŏe. nêe
I'd like to speak to...	ขอพูดกับคุณ...	kŏr pôot gàp kun
Extension...	ตอหมายเลข...	(d)tòr măi lêyk
Speak louder/more slowly, please.	ช่วยพูดดังขึ้น/ช้าลง หนอยได้ไหม	chûay pôot dang kêuhn/ chár long nòy dâi măi

Bad luck โชคไม่ดี

Would you try again later, please?	กรุณาโทรมาใหมอี กครั้ง?	ga ru nar toe mar mài èek kráng
Operator, you gave me the wrong number.	โอเปอเรเด้อร์ คุณ ตอใหผม(ดิฉัน)ผิด	oe (b)per rey (d)têr kun (d)tòr hâi pŏm (di chán) pit
Operator, we were cut off.	โอเปอเรเด้อร์ สายมันขาด	oe (b)per rey (d)têr săi man kàrt

Not there ไม่อยู่ที่นั่น

When will he/she be back?	เขา/เธอจะกลับ มาตอนไหน?	kŏw/ter ja glàp mar (d)torn năi
Will you tell him/her I called? My name is...	ฝากบอกเขา/ เธอดวยวาผม(ดิฉัน) โทรมา ผม(ดิฉัน)ชื่อ...	fàrk bòrk kŏw/ter dûay wâr pŏm (di chán) toe mar. pŏm (di chán) chêur
Would you ask him/her to call me? My number is...	ฝากบอกใหเขา/ เธอโทรกลับดวย หมายเลข...?	fàrk bòrk hâi kŏw/ter toe glàp dûay. măi lêyk

| Would you take a message, please. | ฝากข้อความถึงเขา/เธอได้ไหม | fàrk kôr kwarm těuhng kǒw/ter dâi mǎi |

Charges ค่าโทรศัพท์

| What was the cost of that call? | ค่าโทรศัพท์เมื่อสักครู่เท่าไหร่? | kâr toe ra sàp mêua sàk krôo tôw rài |

| I want to pay for the call. | ขอจ่ายค่าโทรศัพท์เมื่อสักครู่ | kǒr jài kâr toe ra sàp mêua sàk krôo |

มีโทรศัพท์ถึงคุณ	There's a telephone call for you.
คุณจะโทรไปหมายเลขอะไร?	What number are you calling?
สายไม่ว่าง	The line's engaged.
ไม่มีคนรับ	There's no answer.
คุณโทรผิด	You've got the wrong number.
โทรศัพท์เสีย	The phone is out of order.
รอเดี๋ยว	Just a moment.
กรุณารอสักครู่	Hold on, please.
ตอนนี้เขา/เธอไม่อยู่	He's/She's out at the moment.

Doctor

Health care is not free in Thailand and you are strongly advised to take out health insurance before travelling. Clinics are often open 24 hours a day and since they are private there is no need to register with any particular one.

Be careful of having injections as many doctors, especially in the provinces, rely upon sterilizing needles in boiling water rather than using disposable ones and rates of HIV infection are very high in Thailand.

General ทั่วไป

Can you get me a doctor?	ช่วยตามหมอมาให้หน่อยได้ไหม?	chûay (d)tarm mŏr mar hâi nòy dâi măi
Where can I find a doctor who speaks English?	ผมจะหาหมอที่พูดภาษาอังกฤษได้ที่ไหน?	pŏm ja hăr mŏr têe pôot par săr ang grìt dâi têe năi
Where's the surgery (doctor's office)?	คลีนิคหมออยู่ที่ไหน?	klee ník mŏr yòo têe năi
What are the surgery (office) hours?	เวลาทำการของคลีนิคหมอกี่โมงถึงกี่โมง?	wey lar tam garn kŏng klee ník mŏr gèe moeng tĕuhng gèe moeng
Could the doctor come to see me here?	ให้หมอมาที่นี่ได้ไหม?	hâi mŏr mar têe nêe dâi măi
What time can the doctor come?	หมอจะมาได้กี่โมง?	mŏr ja mar dâi gèe moeng
Can you recommend a/an ...?	คุณช่วยแนะนำ ...ให้หน่อยได้ไหม?	kun chûay náih nam...hâi nòy dâi măi
general practitioner	หมอ/แพทย์	mŏr/pâirt
children's doctor	กุมารแพทย์	gu marn a pâirt
eye specialist	จักษุแพทย์	jàk sù pâirt
gynaecologist	นรีแพทย์	na ree pâirt
Can I have an appointment...?	ขอนัด...ได้ไหม?	kŏr nát...dâi măi
tomorrow	พรุ่งนี้	prûng née
as soon as possible	เร็วที่สุดเท่าที่จะเร็วได้	rehw têe sùt tôw têe ja rehw dâi

CHEMIST'S, see page 107

Parts of the body *ส่วนต่างๆของร่างกาย*

appendix	ไส้ติ่ง	sâi (d)tìng
arm	แขน	kǎirn
back	หลัง	lǎng
bladder	กระเพาะปัสสาวะ	gra po (b)pàt sǎr wá
bone	กระดูก	gra dòok
bowel	ภายในช่องท้อง	pai nai chông tórng
breast	หน้าอก	nâr òk
chest	หน้าอก	nâr òk
ear	หู	hǒo
eye(s)	ตา	(d)tar
face	หน้า	nâr
finger	นิ้ว	níw
foot	เท้า	tów
genitals	อวัยวะเพศ	a way a wá péyt
gland	ต่อม	(d)tòrm
hand	มือ	meur
head	หัว	hǔa
heart	หัวใจ	hǔa jai
jaw	ขากรรไกร	kǎr gan grai
joint	ข้อต่อ	kôr (d)tòr
kidney	ไต	(d)tai
knee	เข่า	kòw
leg	ขา	kǎr
ligament	เอ็น	ehn
lip	ริมฝีปาก	rim fěe (b)pàrk
liver	ตับ	(d)tàp
lung	ปอด	(b)pòrt
mouth	ปาก	(b)pàrk
muscle	กล้ามเนื้อ	glârm néua
neck	คอ	kor
nerve	เส้นประสาท	sêhn (b)pra sàrt
nose	จมูก	ja mòok
rib	ซี่โครง	sêe kroeng
shoulder	ไหล่	lài
skin	ผิวหนัง	pǐw nǎng
spine	กระดูกสันหลัง	gra dòok sǎn lǎng
stomach	ท้อง	tórng
tendon	เอ็นในร่างกาย	ehn nai râng gai
thigh	ต้นขา/ ขาอ่อน	(d)tôn kǎr/kǎr òrn
throat	ลำคอ	lam kor
thumb	นิ้วหัวแม่มือ	níw hǔa mâir meur
toe	นิ้วเท้า	níw tów
tongue	ลิ้น	lín
tonsils	ต่อมทอนซิล	(d)tòrm torn sin
vein	เส้นเลือด	sêhn lêuat

Accident—Injury อุบัติเหตุ บาดเจ็บ

There's been an accident.	เกิดอุบัติเหตุ	gèrt u bàt (d)tì hêyt
My child has had a fall.	ลูกผม(ดิฉัน)ตกจากที่สูง/ หกล้ม	lôok pŏm (di chán) (d)tòk jàrk têe sŏong/hòk lóm
He/She has hurt his/ her head.	เขา/เธอได้รับบาดเจ็บ ที่หัว	kŏw/ter dâi ráp bàrt jèhp têe hŭa
He's/She's un- conscious.	เขา/เธอหมดสติ	kŏw/ter mòt sa (d)tì
He's/She's bleeding (heavily).	เลือดเขา/เธอออก(มาก)	lêuat kŏw/ter òrk (mârk)
He's/She's (serious- ly) injured.	เขา/เธอได้รับ บาดเจ็บ(ร้ายแรง)	kŏw/ter dâi ráp bàrt jèhp (rái rairng)
His/Her arm is broken.	แขนเขา/เธอหัก	kăirn kŏw/ter hàk
His/Her ankle is swollen.	ข้อเท้าเขา/เธอบวม	kôr tów kŏw/ter buam
I've been stung.	ผม(ดิฉัน)ถูกแมลงต่อย	pŏm (di chán) (d)tòok ma lairng (d)tòy
I've got something in my eye.	มีอะไรเข้าไปในตาของผม (ดิฉัน)	mee arai kôw (b)pai nai (d)tar kŏrng pŏm (di chán)
I've got a/an ...	ผม(ดิฉัน)มีปัญหา...	pŏm (di chán) mee (b)pan hăr
boil	ถูกน้ำร้อนลวก	(d)tòok nárm rórn lûak
bruise	เป็นรอยช้ำ	(b)pehn roy chám
burn	ถูกไฟไหม้	tòok fai mâi
cut	ถูกมีดบาด	tòok mêet bàrt
graze	เป็นแผลถลอก	(b)pehn plăir ta lòrk
insect bite	ถูกแมลงต่อย	tòok ma lairng (d)toy
lump	บวม/โน	buam/noe
rash	เป็นผื่นคัน	(b)pehn pèurn kan
sting	ถูกแมลงต่อย	tòok ma lairng (d)tòy
swelling	บวม	buam
wound	ได้รับบาดเจ็บ	dâi ráp bàrt jèhp
Could you have a look at it?	ช่วยดูให้หน่อยได้ไหม?	chûay doo hâi nòy dâi măi
I can't move my ...	ผม(ดิฉัน)ขยับ...ไม่ได้	pŏm (di chán) ka yàp...mâi dâi
It hurts.	มันเจ็บ	man jèhp

เจ็บตรงไหน?	Where does it hurt?
เจ็บแบบไหน?	What kind of pain is it?
เจ็บไม่มาก/ แปลบ/ตุ๊บๆ	dull/sharp/throbbing
ตลอดเวลา/เป็นๆ หายๆ	constant/on and off
มัน...	It's...
หัก/ เคล็ด	broken/sprained
เคลื่อน/ ฉีก	dislocated/torn
ผม(ดิฉัน)อยากให้คุณ ฉายเอ็กซเรย์	I'd like you to have an X-ray.
เราจะต้องใส่เฝือก	We'll have to put it in plaster.
มันติดเชื้อ	It's infected.
คุณได้ฉีดวัคซีนป้องกัน บาดทะยักหรือเปล่า?	Have you been vaccinated against tetanus?
ผม(ดิฉัน)จะให้ยาแก้ปวดคุณ	I'll give you a painkiller.

Illness *เจ็บป่วย*

I'm ill.	ผม(ดิฉัน)ไม่สบาย	pǒm (di chán) mâi sabay
I feel ...	ผม(ดิฉัน)รู้สึก...	pǒm (di chán) róo sèuhk
dizzy	เวียนศีรษะ	wearn sěe sà
nauseous	คลื่นไส้	klêurn sâi
shivery	หนาวสั่น	nǒw sàn
I have a temperature (fever).	เป็นไข้	(b)pehn kâi
My temperature is 38 degrees.	อุณหภูมิของผมสูง ๓๘ องศา	un a poom kǒrng pǒm sǒong sǎrm sìp (b)pàirt ong sǎr
I've been vomiting.	ผม(ดิฉัน)เพิ่งอาเจียนมา	pǒm (di chán) pêuhng ar jearn mar
I'm constipated/ I've got diarrhoea.	ผม(ดิฉัน) มีอาการท้องผูก/ ผม(ดิฉัน)มีอาการท้องร่วง	pǒm (di chán) mee ar gàrn tórng pòok/pǒm (di chán) mee ar gàrn tórng rûang
My ... hurt(s).	...ของผม(ดิฉัน)เจ็บ	... kǒrng pǒm (di chán) jèhp

I've got (a/an)...	ผม(ดิฉัน)เป็น...	pǒm (di chán) (b)pehn
asthma	เป็นโรคหืด	(b)pehn rôek hèurt
backache	เป็นโรคปวดหลัง	(b)pehn rôek (b)pùat lǎng
cold	เป็นหวัด	(b)pehn wàt
cough	ไอ	ai
cramps	เป็นตะคริว	(b)pehn (d)ta kriw
earache	ปวดหู	(b)pùat hǒo
hay fever	แพ้อากาศ	páir ar gàrt
headache	ปวดหัว	(b)pùat hǔa
indigestion	ท้องผูก	tórng pòok
nosebleed	เลือดกำเดาไหล	lêuat gam dow lǎi
palpitations	ใจสั่น	jai sàn
rheumatism	เป็นโรคปวดในข้อ	(b)pehn rôek (b)pùat nai kôr
sore throat	เจ็บคอ	jèhp kor
stiff neck	คอแข็ง	kor kǎihng
stomach ache	ปวดท้อง	(b)pùat tórng
sunstroke	เป็นลมแดด	(b)pehn lom dàirt
I have difficulties breathing.	หายใจขัดๆ	hǎi jai kàt kàt
I have chest pains.	เจ็บที่หน้าอก	jèhp têe nâr òk
My blood pressure is...	ความดันโลหิตของ ผม(ดิฉัน)...	kwarm dan loe hìt kǒng pǒm (di chán)
too high/too low	สูงเกินไป/ต่ำเกินไป	sǒong gern (b)pai/(d)tàm gern (b)pai
I'm allergic to...	ผม(ดิฉัน)แพ้...	pǒm (di chán) páir
I'm diabetic.	ผม(ดิฉันเป็นโรค เบาหวาน	pǒm (di chán) (b)pehn rôek bow wǎrn

Women's section ส่วนที่เกี่ยวกับผู้หญิง

I have period pains.	ดิฉันปวดประจำเดือน	di chán (b)pùat (b)pra jam deuan
I have a vaginal infection.	ดิฉันติดเชื้อที่อวัยวะเพศ	di chán (d)tìt chéua têe a way ya wá péyt
I'm on the pill.	ดิฉันกินยาคุมอยู่	di chán gin yar kum yòo
I haven't had a period for 2 months.	ประจำเดือนของดิฉัน ไม่มาสองเดือนแล้ว	(b)pra jam deuan kǒng di chán mâi mar sǒrng deuan láiw
I'm (3 months') pregnant.	ดิฉันตั้งท้อง(สามเดือน) แล้ว	di chán (d)tâng tórng (sǎrm deuan) láiw

คุณรู้สึกอย่างนี้มานานเท่าไหร่แล้ว?	How long have you been feeling like this?
นี่เป็นครั้งแรกหรือเปล่าที่คุณเป็นโรคนี้?	Is this the first time you've had this?
ผม(ดิฉัน)จะวัดอุณหภูมิ/ความดันดูหน่อย	I'll take your temperature/blood pressure.
ถลกแขนเสื้อขึ้นหน่อย	Roll up your sleeve, please.
ช่วยถอดเสื้อออกด้วย	Please undress (down to the waist).
ช่วยนอนราบลงตรงนั้นด้วย	Please lie down over here.
อ้าปากหน่อย	Open your mouth.
หายใจลึกๆ	Breathe deeply.
ไอให้ฟังหน่อย	Cough, please.
เจ็บที่ตรงไหน?	Where does it hurt?
คุณเป็น...	You've got (a/an)...
โรคไส้ติ่งอักเสบ	appendicitis
กระเพาะปัสสาวะอักเสบ	cystitis
โรคกระเพาะอักเสบ	gastritis
ไข้	flu
...อักเสบ	inflammation of...
อาหารเป็นพิษ	food poisoning
โรคดีซ่าน	jaundice
กามโรค	venereal disease
ปอดบวม	pneumonia
โรคหัด	measles
มัน(ไม่)เป็นโรคติดต่อ	It's (not) contagious.
มันเป็นโรคภูมิแพ้	It's an allergy.
ผม(ดิฉัน)จะฉีดยาให้เข็มหนึ่ง	I'll give you an injection.
ผมอยากได้ตัวอย่างเลือด/อุจจาระ/ปัสสาวะของคุณ	I want a specimen of your blood/stools/urine.
คุณจะต้องนอนพักสัก... วัน	You must stay in bed for... days.
ผม(ดิฉัน)อยากให้คุณไปโรงพยาบาลเพื่อตรวจเช็คร่างกาย	I want you to go to the hospital for a general check-up.

Prescription—Treatment ใบสั่งยา การรักษา

This is my usual medicine.	นี่เป็นยาที่ผม(ดิฉัน) กินเป็นประจำ	nêe (b)pehn yar têe pŏm (di chán) gin (b)pehn (b)pra jam
Can you give me a prescription for this?	ช่วยเขียนใบสั่งยา ตัวนี้ให้ผม(ดิฉัน) หน่อยได้ไหม?	chûay kĕarn bai sàng yar (d)tua née hâi pŏm (di chán) nòy dâi măi
Can you prescribe a/an/some...?	ช่วยสั่ง...ให้หน่อยได้ไหม?	chûay sàng...hâi nòy dâi măi
antidepressant	ยาบรรเทาอาการหดหู่	yar ban tow ar garn hòt hòo
sleeping pills tranquillizer	ยานอนหลับ ยากล่อมประสาท	yar norn làp yar glòm (b)pra sàrt
Are you using a sterilized needle?	คุณใช้เข็มฉีดยาที่ฆ่าเชื้อ หรือเปล่า	kun chái kĕhm chèet yar têe kâr chéua rĕua (b)plòw
I'm allergic to...	ผม(ดิฉัน)แพ้...	pŏm (di chán) páir
certain antibiotics/ penicillin	ยาปฏิชีวนะบางตัว/ เพนนิซิลิน	yar (b)pa (d)tí chi wa ná barng (d)tua/peyn ni si lin
How many times a day should I take it?	ต้องกินวันละกี่ครั้ง?	(d)tôrng gin wan lá gèe kráng

ตอนนี้คุณกินยาอะไรอยู่?	What medicine are you taking?
ฉีดหรือกิน?	By injection or orally?
กินยานี้...ช้อนชา	Take... teaspoons of this medicine...
กินยานี้หนึ่งเม็ด กับน้ำหนึ่งแก้ว	Take one pill with a glass of water...
ทุก...ชั่วโมง	every... hours
วันละ...ครั้ง	... times a day
ก่อน/ หลังอาหาร	before/after each meal
ตอนเช้า/ตอนกลางคืน	in the morning/at night
ถ้ามีอาการเจ็บ	if there is any pain
เป็นเวลา...วัน	for... days

CHEMIST'S, see page 107

Fee ค่ารักษา

How much do I owe you?	เท่าไหร่?	tôw rài
May I have a receipt for my health insurance?	ขอใบเสร็จรับเงิน ไปให้ประกันสุขภาพ ด้วยได้ไหม?	kŏr bai sèht ráp ngern (b)pai hâi (b)pra gan sùk ka pârp dâi măi
Can I have a medical certificate?	ขอใบรับรองแพทย์ หน่อยได้ไหม?	kŏr bai ráp rorng pâirt nòy dâi măi
Would you fill in this health insurance form, please?	ช่วยกรอกแบบฟอร์ม ประกันสุขภาพนี้ด้วย ได้ไหม?	chûay gròrk bairp form (b)pra gan sùk ka pârp née dûay dâi măi

Hospital โรงพยาบาล

Please notify my family.	ช่วยแจ้งให้ครอบครัว ของผม(ดิฉัน)ทราบด้วย	chûay jâirng hâi krôrp krua kŏrng pŏm (di chán) sârp dûay
What are the visiting hours?	เวลาเปิดทำการ จากกี่โมงถึงกี่โมง?	wey lar (b)pèrt tam garn jàrk gèe moeng tĕung gèe moeng
When can I get up?	เมื่อไหร่ผม(ดิฉัน) ถึงจะลุกได้?	mêua rài pŏm (di chán) tĕuhng ja lúk dâi
When will the doctor come?	คุณหมอจะมาเมื่อไหร่?	kun mŏr ja mar mêua rài
I'm in pain.	ผม(ดิฉัน)รู้สึกปวดมาก	pŏm (di chán) róo sèuhk (b)pùat mârk
I can't eat/sleep.	ผม(ดิฉัน)กินไม่ได้/ นอนไม่หลับ	pŏm (di chán) gin mái dâi/norn mâi làp
Where is the bell?	กระดิ่งอยู่ที่ไหน?	gra dìng yòo têe năi

nurse	พยาบาล	pa yar barn
patient	คนไข้	kon kâi
anaesthetic	ยาชา	yar char
blood transfusion	การถ่ายเลือด	garn tài lêuat
injection	ฉีดยา	chèet yar
operation	ผ่าตัด	pàr (d)tàt
bed	เตียง	(d)tearng
bedpan	กระโถนปัสสาวะ	gra tŏen (b)pàt săr wá
thermometer	ปรอท	(b)pròrt

Dentist หมอฟัน/ทันตแพทย์

Dental treatment is available on a private basis either at dental clinics or in hospitals. Costs vary according to the standard of clinic attended. Again, be wary of inadequately sterilized dental equipment.

Can you recommend a good dentist?	ช่วยแนะนำหมอฟันดีๆ	chûay náih nam mŏr fan dee dee
Can I make an (urgent) appointment to see Dr...?	ขอนัดเจอหมอ... (เป็นการด่วน)ได้ไหม?	kŏr nát jer mŏr... ((b)pehn garn dùan) dâi mǎi
Couldn't you make it earlier?	นัดเร็วกว่านี้หน่อย ได้ไหม?	nát rehw gwar née dâi mǎi
I have a broken tooth.	ฟันผม(ดิฉัน)หัก	fan pŏm (di chán) hàk
I have toothache.	ผม(ดิฉัน)ปวดฟัน	pŏm (di chán) (b)pùat fan
I have an abscess.	ผม(ดิฉัน)เป็นเหงือก	pŏm (di chán) (b)pehn nŏrng
This tooth hurts.	ปวดฟันซี่นี้	(b)pùat fan sêe née
at the top	ด้านบน	dârn bon
at the bottom	ด้านล่าง	dârn lârng
at the front	ด้านหน้า	dârn nâr
at the back	หน้าหลัง	nâr lǎng
Can you fix it temporarily?	ช่วยอุดชั่วคราวได้ไหม?	chûay ùt chûa krow dâi mǎi
I don't want it pulled out.	ผม(ดิฉัน)ไม่อยากให้ถอน	pŏm (di chán) mâi yàrk hâi tŏrn
Could you give me an anaesthetic?	ช่วยให้ยาชาผม (ดิฉัน)ได้ไหม?	chûay hâi yar char pŏm (di chán) dâi mǎi
I've lost a filling.	ที่อุดหลุดหายไป	têe ùt lùt hǎi (b)pai
My gums ...	เหงือกผม(ดิฉัน)...	ngèuak pŏm (di chán)
are very sore	ปวดมาก	(b)pùat mârk
are bleeding	เลือดไหล	lêuat lǎi
I've broken my dentures.	ฟันปลอมของผม(ดิฉัน)หัก	fan (b)plorm kŏrng pŏm (di chán) hàk
Can you repair my dentures?	ช่วยซ่อมฟันปลอม ของผม(ดิฉัน) หน่อยได้ไหม?	chûay sôrm fan (b)plorm kŏrng pŏm (di chán) nòy dâi mǎi
When will they be ready?	จะเสร็จเมื่อไหร่?	ja sèht mêua rài

Reference section

Where do you come from? คุณมาจากไหน?

Africa	อาฟริกา	ar fri gar
Asia	เอเชีย	ey sear
Australia	ออสเตรเลีย	or sa (d)trey lear
Europe	ยุโรป	yu roep
North America	อเมริกาเหนือ	a mey rí gar nĕua
South America	อเมริกาใต้	a mey rí gar (d)tâi
Austria	ออสเตรีย	òrt sa (d)trear
Belgium	เบลเยียม	ben yêarm
Canada	แคนาดา	kair nar dar
China	จีน	jeen
Denmark	เดนมาร์ก	deyn mârk
England	อังกฤษ	ang grìt
Finland	ฟินแลนด์	fin lairn
France	ฝรั่งเศส	fa ràng sèyt
Germany	เยอรมันนี	yer ra man nee
Great Britain	อังกฤษ/สหราชอาณาจักร	ang grìt/sa hăr rârt cha ar nar jàk
Greece	กรีซ	grèek
India	อินเดีย	in dear
Indonesia	อินโดนีเซีย	in doe nee sear
Ireland	ไอรแลนด์	ai lairn
Israel	อิสราเอล	it sa rar eyn
Italy	อิตาลี	it (d)tar lee
Japan	ญี่ปุ่น	yêe (b)pùn
Laos	ลาว	low
Luxembourg	ลักเซมเบิร์ก	lák seym bèrk
Myanmar	พม่า	pa mâr
Netherlands	เนเธอรแลนด์	ney ter lairn
New Zealand	นิวซีแลนด์	niw see lairn
Norway	นอรเวย์	nor wey
Philippines	ฟิลิปปินส์	fi li peen
Portugal	โปรตุเกส	(b)poer (d)tù gèyt
Russia	รัสเซีย	rát sear
Scotland	สกอตแลนด์	sa gót lairn
South Africa	อาฟริกาใต้	ar frík gar (d)tâi
Spain	สเปน	sa (b)peyn
Sweden	สวีเดน	sa wĕe deyn
Switzerland	สวิตเซอรแลนด์	sa wít ser lairn
Thailand	ไทย	tai
United States	สหรัฐ	sa hăr rát
Vietnam	เวียดนาม	wêart narm
Wales	เวลส	weyl

Numbers ตัวเลข

0	๐	sŏon
1	๑	nèuhng
2	๒	sŏrng
3	๓	sărm
4	๔	sèe
5	๕	hâr
6	๖	hòk
7	๗	jèht
8	๘	(b)pàirt
9	๙	gôw
10	๑๐	sìp
11	๑๑	sìp èht
12	๑๒	sìp sŏrng
13	๑๓	sìp sărm
14	๑๔	sìp sèe
15	๑๕	sìp hâr
16	๑๖	sìp hòk
17	๑๗	sìp jèht
18	๑๘	sìp (b)pàirt
19	๑๙	sìp gôw
20	๒๐	yêe sìp
21	๒๑	yêe sìp èht
22	๒๒	yêe sìp sŏrng
23	๒๓	yêe sìp sărm
24	๒๔	yêe sìp sèe
25	๒๕	yêe sìp hâr
26	๒๖	yêe sìp hòk
27	๒๗	yêe sìp jèht
28	๒๘	yêe sìp (b)pàirt
29	๒๙	yêe sìp gôw
30	๓๐	sărm sìp
31	๓๑	sărm sìp èht
32	๓๒	sărm sìp sŏrng
33	๓๓	sărm sìp sărm
40	๔๐	sèe sìp
41	๔๑	sèe sìp èht
42	๔๒	sèe sìp sŏrng
43	๔๓	sèe sìp sărm
50	๕๐	hâr sìp
51	๕๑	hâr sìp èht
52	๕๒	hâr sìp sŏrng
53	๕๓	hâr sìp sărm
60	๖๐	hòk sìp
61	๖๑	hòk sìp èht
62	๖๒	hòk sìp sŏrng

63	๖๓	hòk sìp sǎrm
70	๗๐	jèht sìp
71	๗๑	jèht sìp èht
72	๗๒	jèht sìp sǒrng
73	๗๓	jèht sìp sǎrm
80	๘๐	(b)pàirt sìp
81	๘๑	(b)pàirt sìp èht
82	๘๒	(b)pàirt sìp sǒrng
83	๘๓	(b)pàirt sìp sǎrm
90	๙๐	gôw sìp
91	๙๑	gôw sìp èyt
92	๙๒	gôw sìp sǒrng
93	๙๓	gôw sìp sǎrm
100	๑๐๐	róy
101	๑๐๑	róy èht
102	๑๐๒	róy sǒrng
110	๑๑๐	róy sìp
120	๑๒๐	róy yêe sìp
130	๑๓๐	róy sǎrm sìp
140	๑๔๐	róy sèe sìp
150	๑๕๐	róy hâr sìp
160	๑๖๐	róy hòk sìp
170	๑๗๐	róy jèht sìp
180	๑๘๐	róy (b)pàirt sìp
190	๑๙๐	róy gôw sìp
200	๒๐๐	sǒrng róy
300	๓๐๐	sǎrm róy
400	๔๐๐	sèe róy
500	๕๐๐	hâr róy
600	๖๐๐	hòk róy
700	๗๐๐	jèyt róy
800	๘๐๐	(b)pàirt róy
900	๙๐๐	gôw róy
1000	๑๐๐๐	pan
1100	๑๑๐๐	pan nèuhng róy
1200	๑๒๐๐	pan sǒrng róy
2000	๒๐๐๐	sǒrng pan
5000	๕๐๐๐	hâr pan
10,000	๑๐,๐๐๐	mèurn
50,000	๕๐,๐๐๐	hâr mèurn
100,000	๑๐๐,๐๐๐	sǎirn
1,000,000	๑,๐๐๐,๐๐๐	lárn

first	ที่หนึ่ง	têe nèuhng
second	ที่สอง	têe sŏrng
third	ที่สาม	têe sărm
fourth	ที่สี่	têe sèe
fifth	ที่ห้า	têe hâr
sixth	ที่หก	têe hòk
seventh	ที่เจ็ด	têe jèht
eighth	ที่แปด	têe (b)pàirt
ninth	ที่เก้า	têe gôw
tenth	ที่สิบ	têe sìp
once/twice	ครั้งหนึ่ง/สองครั้ง	kráng nèuhng/sŏrng kráng
three times	สามครั้ง	sărm kráng
a half	ครึ่งหนึ่ง	krêuhng nèuhng
half a...	ครึ่ง...	krêuhng
half of...	ครึ่งหนึ่งของ...	krêuhng nèuhng kŏrng
half (adj.)	ครึ่ง	krêuhng
a quarter/one third	หนึ่งในสี่/หนึ่งในสาม	nèuhng nai sèe/nèuhng nai sărm
a pair of	หนึ่งคู่	nèuhng kôo
a dozen	หนึ่งโหล	nèuhng lŏe
one per cent	หนึ่งเปอร์เซนต์/ร้อยละหนึ่ง	nèuhng (b)per seyn/róy la nèuhng
3.4%	ร้อยละ๓.๔	róy la sărm jùt sèe

Year and age ปีและอายุ

1981	๑๙๘๑	pan gôw róy jèht sìp èht
1993	๑๙๙๓	pan gôw róy gôw sìp sărm
2005	๒๐๐๕	sŏrng pan hâr
year	ปี	(b)pee
leap year	ปีอธิกสุรทิน	(b)pee ar tí gà sù ra tin
decade	ทศวรรษ	tót sa wát
century	ศตวรรษ	sà ta wát
this year	ปีนี้	(b)pee née
last year	ปีที่แล้ว	(b)pee têe láiw
next year	ปีหน้า	(b)pee nâr
each year	แต่ละปี	(d)tàir lá (b)pee
2 years ago	๒ปีที่แล้ว	sŏrng (b)pee têe láiw
in one year	ในหนึ่งปี	nai nèuhng (b)pee
in the eighties	ในทศวรรษที่ ๘๐	nai tót sa wát têe (b)pàirt sìp
in the 20th century	ในศตวรรษที่ ๒๐	sà ta wát têe yêe sìp

How old are you?	คุณอายุเท่าไหร่?	kun ar yú tôw rài
I'm 30 years old.	ผม(ดิฉัน)อายุ ๓๐ปี	pŏm (di chán) ar yú sărm sìp (b)pee
He/She was born in 1960.	เขาเกิดปี ๑๙๖๐	kŏw gèrt (b)pee pan gôw róy hòk sìp
What is his/her age?	เขาอายุเท่าไหร่?	kŏw ar yú tôw rài
Children under 16 are not admitted.	เด็กอายุต่ำกว่า ๑๖ปีห้ามเข้า	déhk ar yú (d)tàm gwàr sìp hòk (b)pee hârm kôw

Seasons ฤดู/หน้า

spring/summer	ใบไม้ผลิ/ร้อน	bai mái plì/rórn
autumn/winter	ใบไม้รวง/หนาว	bai mái rûang/nŏw
in spring	ในฤดูใบไม้ผลิ	nai ri doo bai mái plì
during the summer	ในช่วงฤดูร้อน	nai chûang ri doo rórn
in autumn (fall)	ในฤดูใบไม้รวง	nai ri doo bai mái rûang
during the winter	ในช่วงฤดูหนาว	nai chûang ri doo nŏw
high season	ฤดูท่องเที่ยว	ri doo tông têaw
low season	นอกฤดูท่องเที่ยว	nôrk ri doo tông têaw

Months เดือน

January	มกราคม	mók ga rar kom
February	กุมภาพันธ์	gum par pan
March	มีนาคม	mee nar kom
April	เมษายน	mey săr yon
May	พฤษภาคม	prút sa pår kom
June	มิถุนายน	mí tu nar yon
July	กรกฎาคม	ga rák ga (d)tar kom
August	สิงหาคม	sĭng hăr kom
September	กันยายน	kan yar yon
October	ตุลาคม	(d)tu lar kom
November	พฤศจิกายน	prút sa jìk gar yon
December	ธันวาคม	tan war kom
in September	ในเดือนกันยายน	nai deuan gan yar yon
since October	ตั้งแต่เดือนตุลาคมเป็นต้นมา	(d)tâng tàir deuan (d)tu lar kom (b)pehn (d)tôn mar
the beginning of January	ต้นเดือนมกราคม	(d)tôn deuan mók ga rar kom
the middle of February	กลางเดือนกุมภาพันธ์	glarng deuan gum par pan
the end of March	ปลายเดือนมีนาคม	(b)plai deuan mee nar kom

Days and date วันและวันที่

What day is it today?	วันนี้วันอะไร?	wan née wan arai
Sunday	วันอาทิตย์	wan ar tìt
Monday	วันจันทร์	wan jan
Tuesday	วันอังคาร	wan ang karn
Wednesday	วันพุธ	wan pút
Thursday	วันพฤหัสบดี	wan pá rú hàt
Friday	วันศุกร์	wan sùk
Saturday	วันเสาร์	wan sŏw
It's...	มันเป็น/ คือ...	man (b)pehn/keur
July 1	วันที่ ๑ กรกฎาคม	wan têe nèuhng ga rák ga (d)tar kom
March 10	วันที่ ๑๐ มีนาคม	wan têe sìp mee nar kom
in the morning	เวลาเช้า	wey lar chów
during the day	เวลากลางวัน	wey lar glarng wan
in the afternoon	เวลาบ่าย	wey lar bài
in the evening	เวลาเย็น	wey lar yehn
at night	เวลากลางคืน	wéy lâr giarng keurn
the day before yesterday	เมื่อวานซืน	mêua warn seurn
yesterday	เมื่อวาน	mêua warn
today	วันนี้	wan née
tomorrow	พรุ่งนี้	prûng née
the day after tomorrow	มะรืนนี้	ma reurn née
the day before	วันก่อน	wan gòrn
the next day	วันถัดไป	wan tàt (b)pai
two days ago	สองวันก่อน	sŏrng wan gòrn
in three days' time	ในอีกสามวันข้างหน้า	nai èek sǎrm wan kârng nâr
last week	อาทิตย์ที่แล้ว	ar tìt têe láiw
next week	อาทิตย์หน้า	ar tìt nâr
for a fortnight (two weeks)	เป็นเวลาสองอาทิตย์	(b)pehn wey lar sǒrng ar tìt
birthday	วันเกิด	wan gèrt
day off	วันหยุด	wan yùt
holiday	วันหยุดพักผ่อน	wan yùt pák pòrn
holidays/vacation	วันหยุดพักผ่อน	wan yùt pák pòrn
week	อาทิตย์/ สัปดาห์	ar tìt/sàp pa dar
weekend	สุดสัปดาห์	sùt sàp pa dar
working day	วันทำงาน	wan tam ngarn

Public holidays *วันหยุดประจำปี*

The dates for some public holidays differ each year since they are calculated by the lunar calendar. Although banks and government offices close on these days, shops remain open and public transport is unaffected. Chinese New Year, which is not a national holiday, does mean that many of the smaller shops close for two or three days, but department stores are largely unaffected.

วันขึ้นปีใหม่	wan kéuhn (b)pee mài	New Year's Day
วันจักรี	wanjàkgree	April 6, Chakri Day, in memory of Rama I
สงกรานต์	sŏng grarn	April 13–15, Songkran, or the traditional Thai New Year
วันแรงงาน	wan rairng ngarn	May 1, Labour Day
วันฉัตรมงคล	wan chàt mongkon	May 5, Coronation Day, in memory of the coronation in 1946 of the present king, Rama IX
วันเฉลิมพระชนมพรรษา สมเด็จพระบรมราชินีนาถ	wan chalěrm práchanom pansăr	August 12, H.M. Queen's Birthday (Mother's Day)
วันปิยะมหาราช	wan (b)pee-yámahăr rârt	October 23, Chulalongkorn Day, in memory of King Rama V
วันเฉลิม พระชนมพรรษา พระบาทสมเด็จ พระเจ้าอยู่หัว	wan chalěrm práchanom pansăr prábàrt sŏmdèht prá jôw yoo hŭa	December 5, H.M. King's Birthday (National Day)
วันรัฐธรรมนูญ	wan rát-tá-tam-má-noon	December 10, Constitution Day

Movable holidays

มาฆบูชา
(marká boochar)

February, commemorating the day which the Buddha taught the key tenets of Buddhism. Thais celebrate this with a *wearn tearn* ceremony in which people walk round the temple chapel with lighted candles.

วิสาขบูชา
(wisárkà boochar)

May, commemorating the Buddha's birth, enlightenment and death with a *wearn tearn* ceremony.

อาสาฬหบูชา
(arsárláhà boochar)

July, commemorating the first sermon of the Buddha.

เข้าพรรษา
(kôw pansár)

Late July, the first day of Buddhist Lent and the time when Thai men traditionally become ordained as monks.

ลอยกระทง
(loi gratong)

The Festival of Lights. Praise is given to the Goddess of the Waters, *mâir pá kongkǎr*, in the form of banana leaf (or polystyrene) boats filled with flowers, incense and candles.

Greetings and wishes *คำทักทายและอวยพร*

Merry Christmas!	สุขสันต์วันคริสต์มาส	sùk sǎn wan krít sa mârt
Happy New Year!	สวัสดีปีใหม่	sa wàt dee (b)pee mài
Happy birthday!	สุขสันต์วันเกิด	sùk sǎn wan gèrt
Best wishes!	โชคดี	chôek dee
Congratulations!	ขอแสดงความยินดีด้วย	kǒr sa dairng kwarm yin dee dûay
Good luck/ All the best!	โชคดี	chôek dee
Have a good trip!	เที่ยวให้สนุก	têaw hâi sa nùk
Have a good holiday!	พักผ่อนให้สนุก	pák pòrn hâi sa nùk
Best regards from ...	ด้วยความปรารถนาดีจาก...	dûay kwarm (b)pràt ta nǎr dee jàrk
My regards to ...	ฝากความคิดถึง/เคารพถึง...	fàrk kwarm kít těuhng/kow róp těuhng

What time is it? *ตอนนี้กี่โมง/เวลาเท่าไหร่?*

Telling the time in Thai can be a complicated business. The twenty four hours of the day and night are divided into four six-hour time periods, as follows: midnight to 6am (ตี —(d) tee), 7am to 1pm (เช้า —chów), 1pm to 6pm(บ่าย —bai) and 7pm to midnight (ทุ่ม —tûm). Each time span begins again at one, so that 7am becomes not "seven hours morning" but "'one hour morning". The word "one" is often omitted.

Excuse me. Can you tell me the time?	ขอโทษ ตอนนี้เวลา เท่าไหร่?	kŏr tôet (d)torn née wey lar tôw rài
It's...	ตอนนี้...	(d)torn née
five past one (13.05)	บ่ายโมงห้านาที	bài moeng hâr nar tee
ten past two (14.10)	บ่ายสองโมงสิบนาที	bài sŏrng moeng sìp nar tee
a quarter past three (15.15)	บ่ายสามโมงสิบห้านาที	bài sărm moeng sìp hâr nar tee
twenty past four (16.20)	บ่ายสี่โมงยี่สิบนาที	bài sèe moeng yêe sìp nar tee
twenty-five past five (17.25)	ห้าโมงยี่สิบห้านาที	hâr moeng yêe sìp hâr nar tee
half past six (18.30)	หกโมงครึ่ง	hòk moeng krêuhng
twenty-five to seven (18.35)	หกโมงสามสิบห้านาที	hòk moeng sărm sìp hâr nar tee
twenty to eight (19.40)	ทุ่มสี่สิบนาที	tûm sèe sìp nar tee
a quarter to nine (20.45)	สองทุ่มสี่สิบห้านาที	sŏrng tûm sèe sìp hâr nar tee
ten to ten (21.50)	สามทุ่มห้าสิบนาที	sărm tûm hâr sìp nar tee
five to eleven (22.55)	สี่ทุ่มห้าสิบห้านาที	sèe tûm hâr sìp hâr nar tee
twelve o'clock (noon/ midnight)	เที่ยงวัน/เที่ยงคืน	têarng wan/têarng keurn
in the morning	ตอนเช้า	(d)torn chów
in the afternoon	ตอนบ่าย	(d)torn bài
in the evening	ตอนเย็น	(d)torn yehn
The train leaves at ...	รถไฟออกเวลา...	rót fai òrk wey lar
13.04 (1.04 p.m.)	บ่ายโมงสี่นาที	bài moeng sèe nar tee
0.40 (0.40 a.m.)	เที่ยงคืนสี่สิบนาที	têarng keurn sèe sìp nar tee
in five minutes	ในอีกห้านาทีข้างหน้า	nai èek hâr nar tee kârng nâr

in a quarter of an hour	ในอีกสิบห้านาที	nai èek sìp hâr nar tee
half an hour ago	เมื่อครึ่งชั่วโมงที่แล้ว	mêua krèuhng chûa moeng têe láiw
about two hours	ประมาณสองชั่วโมง	(b)pra marn sŏrng chûa moeng
more than 10 minutes	กว่าสิบนาที	gwàr sìp nar tee
less than 30 seconds	ไม่ถึงสามสิบวินาที	mâi tĕuhng sărm sìp wí nar tee
The clock is fast/ slow.	นาฬิกาเดินเร็วไป/ช้าไป	nar li gar dern rehw (b)pai/ chár (b)pai

Common abbreviations คำย่อที่พบเห็นบ่อยๆ

พ.ศ.	พุทธศักราช	Buddhist Era*
ค.ศ.	คริสตศักราช	Christian Era, AD
กทม.	กรุงเทพมหานคร	Bangkok Metropolitan District
บขส.	บริษัทขนส่งจำกัด	The National Transport Company Limited
รฟท.	การรถไฟแห่งประเทศไทย	The National Railway of Thailand
ขสมก.	ขนส่งมวลชนกรุงเทพมหานคร	The Bangkok Metropolitan Public Transport Company
ก.ก.	กิโลกรัม	kilograms
ก.ม.	กิโลเมตร	kilometres
น.	นาฬิกา	o'clock
พ.ร.ก.	พระราชกำหนด	Decree
พ.ร.บ.	พระราชบัญญัติ	an Act of legislation
ด.ช.	เด็กชาย	boy
ด.ญ.	เด็กหญิง	girl
น.ส.	นางสาว	Miss
ดร.	ดอกเตอร์	Doctor of Philosophy
ส.ส.	สมาชิกสภาผู้แทนราษฎร	Member of Parliament
ครม.	คณะรัฐมนตรี	Cabinet

*The Thais count their years not from the birth of Christ but from the birth of the Buddha, 543 years earlier. They are consequently 543 years ahead of the West.

Signs and notices *เครื่องหมายและสัญญาน*

ระวังสุนัขดุ	Beware of the dog
รับ-จ่ายเงิน	Cash desk
โปรดระวัง	Caution
อันตราย(แก่ชีวิต)	Danger (of death)
โปรดอย่าจอดรถวางขวางประตู	Do not block entrance
ห้ามรบกวน	Do not disturb
ห้ามจับ	Do not touch
ลง	Down
ทางออกฉุกเฉิน	Emergency exit
เข้ามาได้โดยไม่ต้องเคาะประตู	Enter without knocking
ทางเข้า	Entrance
ทางออก	Exit
ให้เช่า	For hire
สำหรับขาย	For sale
ห้าม...	... forbidden
เข้าฟรี	Free admittance
สุภาพบุรุษ/ชาย	Gentlemen
ร้อน	Hot
ข้อมูล	Information
สุภาพสตรี/หญิง	Ladies
ลิฟท์	Lift
ห้ามเข้า	No admittance
ห้ามทิ้งขยะ	No littering
ห้ามสูบบุหรี่	No smoking
ไม่ว่าง	No vacancies
เปิด	Open
เต็ม/จองแล้ว	Occupied
เสีย	Out of order
โปรดกดกระดิ่ง	Please ring
โปรดรอ	Please wait
ถนนส่วนบุคคล	Private road
ดึง	Pull
ผลัก	Push
จอง	Reserved
ขาย/ลดราคา	Sale
ขายหมด	Sold out
ให้เช่า	To let
ห้ามบุกรุก	Trespassers will be prosecuted
ขึ้น	Up
ว่าง	Vacant
สีไม่แห้ง	Wet paint

Emergency ฉุกเฉิน

Call the police	ช่วยเรียกตำรวจให้หน่อย	chûay rêark (d)tam rûat hâi nòy
Consulate	กงสุล	gong sǔn
DANGER	อันตราย	an (d)ta rai
Embassy	สถานทูต	sa tǎrn tôot
FIRE	ไฟไหม้	fai mâi
Gas	กาซ	gárt
Get a doctor	เรียกหมอให้หน่อย	rêark mǒr hâi nòy
Go away	ไปให้พ้น	(b)pai hâi pón
HELP	ช่วยด้วย	chûay dûay
Get help quickly	หาคนมาช่วยเร็วเข้า	hǎr kon mar chûay rehw kôw
I'm ill	ผม(ดิฉัน)ป่วย	pǒm (di chán) (b)pùay
I'm lost	ผม(ดิฉัน)หลงทาง	pǒm (di chán) lǒng tarng
LOOK OUT	ระวัง	ra wang
Poison	ยาพิษ	yar pít
POLICE	ตำรวจ	(d)tam rùat
Stop that man/ woman	ช่วยหยุดคนนั้นด้วย	chûay yut kon nán dûay

Emergency telephone numbers หมายเลขโทรศัพท์ฉุกเฉิน

The all purpose emergency telephone number is 191. Hospitals and many clinics are open for emergencies 24 hours a day.

Lost property—Theft ของหาย ขโมย

Where's the...?	...อยู่ที่ไหน?	... yòo têe nǎi
lost property (lost and found) office	ฝ่ายจัดการเรื่องของหาย	fǎi jàt garn rêuang kǒrng hǎi
police station	สถานีตำรวจ	sa tǎr nee (d)tam rûat
I want to report a theft.	ผม(ดิฉัน)จะ ขอแจ้งความเรื่องขโมย	pǒm (di chán) ja kǒr jâirng kwarm rêuang ka mooy
My... has been stolen.	...ของผม(ดิฉัน)ถูกขโมย	... kǒrng pǒm (di chán) tòok ka moey
I've lost my...	...ของผม(ดิฉัน)หาย	... kǒrng pom (di chán) hǎi
handbag	กระเป๋ามือถือ	gra (b)pǒw meur těur
passport	หนังสือเดินทาง	nǎng sěur dern tarng
wallet	กระเป๋าใส่เงิน	gra (b)pǒw sài ngern

CAR ACCIDENTS, see page 78

Conversion tables

Centimetres and inches

To change centimetres into inches, multiply by .39.

To change inches into centimetres, multiply by 2.54.

	in.	feet	yards
1 mm	0.039	0.003	0.001
1 cm	0.39	0.03	0.01
1 dm	3.94	0.32	0.10
1 m	39.40	3.28	1.09

	mm	cm	m
1 in.	25.4	2.54	0.025
1 ft.	304.8	30.48	0.304
1 yd.	914.4	91.44	0.914

(32 metres = 35 yards)

Temperature

To convert Centigrade into degrees Fahrenheit, multiply Centigrade by 1.8 and add 32.

To convert degrees Fahrenheit into Centigrade, subtract 32 from Fahrenheit and divide by 1.8.

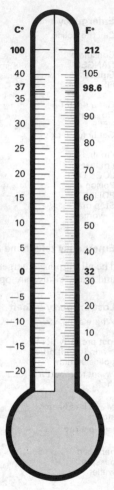

Kilometres into miles

1 kilometre (km.) = 0.62 miles												
km.	10	20	30	40	50	60	70	80	90	100	110	120	130
miles	6	12	19	25	31	37	44	50	56	62	68	75	81

Miles into kilometres

1 mile = 1.609 kilometres (km.)									
miles	10	20	30	40	50	60	70	80	90	100
km.	16	32	48	64	80	97	113	129	145	161

Fluid measures

1 litre (l.) = 0.88 imp. quart or 1.06 U.S. quart
1 imp. quart = 1.14 l.   1 U.S. quart = 0.95 l.
1 imp. gallon = 4.55 l.   1 U.S. gallon = 3.8 l.

litres	5	10	15	20	25	30	35	40	45	50
imp. gal.	1.1	2.2	3.3	4.4	5.5	6.6	7.7	8.8	9.9	11.0
U.S. gal.	1.3	2.6	3.9	5.2	6.5	7.8	9.1	10.4	11.7	13.0

Weights and measures

1 kilogram or kilo (kg.) = 1000 grams (g.)

100 g. = 3.5 oz.	½ kg. = 1.1 lb.
200 g. = 7.0 oz.	1 kg. = 2.2 lb.
1 oz. = 28.35 g.	
1 lb. = 453.60 g.	

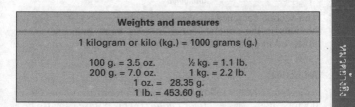

A very basic grammar

At first sight Thai appears to have very little in the way of strict grammar rules and it certainly cannot be explained in the terms we might use for European languages. There are no declensions of nouns or conjugations of verbs to remember and the simplest of rules are used to create past and future tenses. This can give the initial impression of Thai being a very simple language but the fact that sentences are structured in such a different way from English, with very little to follow for actual grammar rules, can end up making it much more difficult.

Parts of speech are not nearly so clearly defined in Thai as they are in Western languages. Nevertheless, a few helpful indicators can be given with reference to nouns, verbs and adjectives.

Nouns

There is no word for *the* or *a* in Thai so the word หมอ *(mŏr)*, for example, can mean "a doctor", "the doctor", "doctors" (in general) or "the doctors". The plural is *only* indicated when it is essential and not evident in the context. This can be done by the addition of the prefix พวก *(pûak)*, making พวกหมอ *(pûak mŏr)*. For example:

หมอไปทำงานที่กรุงเทพฯ	*mŏr (b)pai tam ngarn têe grung têyp*	The doctor went to work in Bangkok
พวกหมอไปทำงาน ที่กรุงเทพฯ	*pûak mŏr (b)pai tamngarn têe grungtêyp*	The doctors went to work in Bangkok

The second sentence above would only be used, if it was not obvious in the context that there was more than one doctor involved in going to work in Bangkok.

Adjectives

Adjectives always follow the noun. In order to say "the clever doctor", it is หมอฉลาด *(mŏr chalàrt)*. This phrase can also be a complete sentence, meaning "the doctor is clever". When adjectives are used with a noun the verb "to be" ((b)pehn) is dropped: Therefore:

| เขาฉลาด | *kŏw chalàrt* | He is clever. |

but

| เขาเป็นหมอ | *kŏw (b)pehn mŏr* | He is a doctor. |

Adjectives can be doubled for emphasis. Some adjectives lend themselves to this more readily than others. For example, ใกล้ *(glâi)* meaning "near" is often doubled to ใกล้ๆ *(glâi glâi)* meaning "quite near" or "close at hand", whereas ไกล *(glai)* meaning "far" is never doubled. Sometimes the tone changes on the first word of the pair double to give extra emphasis. For example,

| ช่วยสวย | *sùai suai* | extremely beautiful |
| ว้านหวาน | *wárn warn* | incredibly sweet |

Verbs

Verbs do not conjugate in Thai so whatever subject they are attached to they do not change in form.

The **past tense** can be indicated by the addition of either แล้ว *(láiw*—already) after the verb, or of ได้ *(dâi*—to get or receive) immediately in front of the verb. However, these are used only sparingly, and are not necessary if the past tense is implicit in the context. Sentences beginning with เมื่อ *(mêua*— when), for example, are automatically past tense.

The **future tense** is indicated by the addition of จะ *(ja)* immediately in front of the verb.
For example:

หมอไปทำงานแล้ว	*mŏr (b)pai tam ngarn láiw*	The doctor has gone to work (already).
หมอได้ไปทำงานที่กรุงเทพฯ	*mŏr dâi (b)pai tam ngarn têe grungtêyp*	The doctor went to work in Bangkok.
หมอจะไปทำงานที่กรุงเทพฯ	*mŏr ja (b)pai tam ngarn têe grungtêyp*	The doctor will go to work in Bangkok.

Classifiers

Counting nouns is a rather complicated process and involves the use of noun "classifiers". Each noun has a "classifier", which is a term of measurement appropriate to the noun in question. The word คน (*kon*), for example, is used to classify all nouns referring to people.

When the number of a certain noun is to be specified, the word order is as follows: noun + number + classifier. For example, หมอห้าคน (*mǒr hâr kon*) would mean "five doctors". The only exception to this rule occurs with the number one, in which case the word order is noun + classifier + one, for example: หมอคนหนึ่ง (*mǒr kon nèuhng*—one doctor).

A list of useful classifiers is given below:

คน	*kon*	for people
ตัว	*tua*	for animals, tables, chairs and items of clothing
ลูก	*lôok*	for fruit and eggs
ชิ้น	*chín*	meaning a "piece" can be used for anything served/sold in pieces, for example cake, sweetmeats, paper
ใบ	*bai*	for fruit, paper and banknotes
ฉบับ	*chabàp*	for letters and newspapers
เล่ม	*lêhm*	for books

Portions of food and drink are classified according to the dishes in which they are served. Therefore fried rice would be classified by the word plate, coffee by cup, noodle soup by bowl and so forth:

ข้าวผัดจานหนึ่ง	*kôw pàt jarn nèuhng*	one plate of fried rice
กาแฟถ้วยหนึ่ง	*gar fair tûay nèuhng*	one cup of coffee
ก๋วยเตี๋ยวชามหนึ่ง	*guáy-tĕaw charm nèuhng*	one bowl of noodles

Questions and Answers

There are a number of ways of asking questions.

1. The words ใช่ไหม (*châi mǎi*) or หรือ (*rěua*) can be placed at the end of a phrase or sentence to verify that the statement made is true. For example:

| คุณเป็นหมอ | *kun (b)pehn mǒr* | You are a doctor. |
| คุณเป็นหมอใช่ไหม | *kun (b)pehn mǒr châi mǎi* | You are a doctor, aren't you? |

This kind of question is answered in the positive with ใช่ (*châi*) and in the negative with ไม่ใช่ (*mâi châi*). There is no single word for "yes" in Thai. The word for "no" is ไม่ (*mâi*).

2. Questions can also be asked by adding *mǎi* to the end of a phrase. For example:

| คุณชอบอาหารไทยไหม | *kun chôrp ar hǎrn tai mǎi* | Do you like Thai food? |

With this kind of verbal based question the verb is repeated in the answer. In the case of the example it is either ชอบ (*chôrp*) for a positive answer or ไม่ชอบ (*mâi chôrp*) for a negative response. The word ไม่ (*mâi*) is used directly in front of the verb to negate its meaning.

หมอทำงานไหม	*mǒr tam ngarn mǎi*	Does the doctor work?
ทำงาน	*tam ngarn*	Yes.
ไม่ทำงาน	*mâi tam ngarn*	No.
หมอไม่ทำงาน	*mǒr mâi tam ngarn*	The doctor does not work.
เขาทำงานที่กรุงเทพฯ ใช่ไหม	*kǒw tam ngarn têe grungtêyp châi mǎi*	He works in Bangkok, doesn't he?
ใช่ เขาทำงาน ที่กรุงเทพฯ	*châi kǒw tam ngarn têe grungtêyp*	Yes, he works in Bangkok.
ไม่ใช่ เขาไม่ทำงาน ที่กรุงเทพฯ เขาทำงานที่ลอนดอน	*mâi châi kǒw mâi tam ngarn têe grungtêyp kǒw tam ngarn têe lorndorn*	No, he doesn't work in Bangkok, he works in London.

DICTIONARY

Dictionary
and alphabetical index

English—Thai

A

abbreviation คำย่อ kam yôr 155
about *(approximately)* ประมาณ (b)pra marn 155
above บน bon 15
abscess ฝี fĕe 145
absorbent cotton สำลี săm lee 108
accessories เครื่องประดับ krêuang (b)pra dàp 115, 125
accident อุบัติเหตุ u ba ti hèyt 79, 139
account บัญชี ban chee 130
ache ปวด (b)pùat 141
adaptor ปลั๊กแปลงไฟฟ้า (b)plàk (b)plairng fai fár 118
address ที่อยู่ têe yòo 21, 31, 77, 79, 102
address book สมุดจดที่อยู่ sa mùt jòt têe yòo 104
adhesive กาว gow 105
adhesive tape เทปกาว têyp gaw 104
admission ผ่านประตู pàrn (b)pra (d)too 82, 89
aeroplane เครื่องบิน krêuang bin 65
Africa อาฟริกา ar fri gar 146
after หลัง(จาก) lăng (jàrk) 15
after-shave lotion โลชั่นทาหลังโกนหนวด loe chǎn tar lǎng goen nùat 109
afternoon, in the ตอนบาย (d)torn bài 151; เวลาบ่าย, wey lar bài 153
again อีกครั้ง èek kráng 96, 135
against ต่อต้าน (d)tòr (d)tărn 140
age อายุ ar yú 149
ago ที่แล้ว têe láiw 149
air bed ที่นุ่นนอน têe (b)poo norn 106
air conditioning แอร์ air 23, 28
air mattress ที่นุ่นนอน têe (b)poo norn 106
airmail จดหมายอากาศ jot măi ar gàrt 133
airport สนามบิน sa nărm bin 21, 65
aisle seat ที่นั่งติดทางเดิน têe nâng (d)tìt tarng dern 65
alarm clock นาฬิกาปลุก nar lí gar (b)plòok 121
alcohol ยัลกอฮอล al gor hprl 38, 60
alcoholic เกี่ยวกับยัลกอฮอล gìaw gàp al

kor horl 60
allergic แพ้ páir 141, 143
almond ยัลมอนด a la morn 56
alphabet ยักขระ ak kạ rà 9
alter, to *(garment)* แก้ gâir 114
altitude sickness แพความสูง páir kwarm sŏong 107
amazing นาทึ่ง năr têuhng 84
amber อำพัน am pan 122
ambulance รถพยาบาล rót pa yar barn 79
American อเมริกัน a mey ri gan 93, 105, 126
American plan รวมอาหารทุกมื้อ ruam ar hărn túk méur 24
amethyst เขียวนนุมาณ kîaw ha nŭ marn 122
amount จำนวน jam nuan 131
amplifier เครื่องขยายเสียง krêuang ka yăi sĕarng 118
anaesthetic ยาชา yar char 144, 145
analgesic ยาแกปวด yar kǎir (b)puat 108
Ancient City เมืองโบราณ meung borarn 81
and และ láih 15
animal สัตว์ sàt 85
aniseed โปยกัก (b)póey gák 55
ankle ขอเท้า kôr tów 139
another อีก èek 60
answer ตอบ (d)tòrp 136
antibiotic ปฏิชีวนะ (b)pa (d)ti chee wa ná 143
antidepressant ยาบรรเทาอาการหดหู yar ban tao ar gạrn hòt hòo 143
antique shop รานขายของโบราณ rárn kǎi kŏrng bọe rarn 98
antiques โบราณวัตถุ bọp rarn wát tù 83
antiseptic cream ครีมแกอักเสบ kreem gǎir àk sèyp 108
anyone ใคร krai 11, 17
anything อะไร arai 18, 24, 25, 101, 112
anywhere ที่ไหน têp nǎi 90
apartment อพาร์ตเมนต a part méhnt 23
appendicitis ไสติ่ง sǎi (d)tìng 142

appetizer อาหารเรียกน้ำย่อย ar hărn rêark nárm yôi 42

apple แอปเปิ้ล áihp (b)pêrn 56, 64

appliance เครื่องใช้ krêuang chái 118

appointment นัดหมาย nát mǎi 131, 137, 145

April เมษายน mey săr yon 150

archaeology โบราณคดี boe rarn ka dee 83

architect สถาปนิก sa thăr (b)pa ník 83

area code รหัสพื้นที่ ra hàt péurn têe 134

arm แขน kǎirn 138, 139

arrival ขาเข้า kǎr kâo 16, 66

arrive, to มาถึง ma tĕuhng 65, 69

art ศิลปะ sĭn la (b)pa 83

art gallery หอศิลป์ hǒr sĭn 81, 98

article มาตรา mâr (d)tra 101

artificial light แสงเมธรรมชาติ sáirng măi tam ma chârt 124

artist ศิลปิน sĭn la (b)pin 83

ashtray หนึ่งไมล์รัง têe kèar bu rèe 37

Asia เอเชีย ey sear 146

ask for, to ขอ, kǒr, lèk 26

asparagus หน่อไมฝรั่ง nòr mái fa ràng 53

aspirin แอสไพริน àirt sa pai rin 108

asthma โรคหืด rôek hèurt 141

astringent ยาสมานแผล yar sa mǎrn 109

at ที่ têe 15

at least อย่างน้อย yàrng nói 24

aubergine มะเขือยาว ma kěua yow 53

August สิงหาคม sĭng hǎr kom 150

aunt ป้า (b)pâr 93

Australia ออสเตรเลีย òr sa (d)trey lear 146

Austria ออสเตรีย òrt sa (d)trear 146

automatic อัตโนมัติ àt noe mát 20, 122, 124

autumn ฤดูใบไม้ร่วง ri doo bai mái rûang 150

average เฉลี่ย cha lìa 91

awful แย่ yâir 84, 94

B

baby เด็กอ่อน dèhk òrn 24, 110

baby food อาหารเด็ก ar hărn dèhk 110

babysitter คนเลี้ยงเด็ก kon léang dèhk 27

back หลัง lăng 138

back, to be/to get กลับมา glàp mar 21, 80

backache ปวดหลัง (b)pùat lăng 141

backpack เป้หลัง (b)pêy lăng 106

bacon เบคอน bey korn 41

bacon and eggs เบคอนกับไข่ bey korn gàp kài 41

bad เลว lehw 14

bag กระเป๋า gra (b)pǒw 18

baggage check ตรวจกระเป๋า (d)trùat gra (b)pǒw 68, 71

baked อบ òb 46, 47

baker's ร้านขายขนมปัง rárn kǎi ka nŏm (b)pang 98

balance (finance) ดุล dun 131

balcony ระเบียง ra beang 23

ball (inflated) ลูกบอล lôok born 128

ball-point pen ปากกาลูกลื่น (b)pàrk gar lôok lêurn 104

ballet บัลเลต์ ban lêy 88

banana กล้วย glûay 56, 64

Band-Aid® พลาสเตอร์ปิดแผล plar sa (d)ter (b)pìt plǎir 108

bandage ผ้าพันแผล pâr pan plǎir 108

bangle กำไล gam lai 121

bangs ผมม้า pom mâr 30

bank (finance) ธนาคาร ta nar karn 98, 129, 130

barber's ร้านตัดผม rárn (d)tàt pŏm 30, 98

basil โหระพา hŏe ra par 55

basketball บาสเก็ตบอล bar sa gèht born 90

bath อาบน้ำ àrp nárm 23, 25, 27

bath towel ผ้าขนหนู pâr kŏn nŏo 27

bathing cap หมวกคลุมผมอาบน้ำ mùak klum pŏm àrp nárm 115

bathing hut ที่อาบน้ำ têe àrp nárm 91

bathing suit ชุดอาบน้ำ chút àrp nárm 115

bathrobe เสื้อคลุมอาบน้ำ sêua klum àrp nárm 115

bathroom ห้องอาบน้ำ hôrng àrp nárm 27

battery แบตเตอรี่ bairt ter rêe 75, 78, 125; ถ่านไฟฉาย tàrn fai chǎi 118, 121

beach หาดทราย hàrt sai 90

beach ball ลูกบอลชายหาด lôok born chai hàrt 128

bean ถั่ว tùa 53

beard เครา krow 31

beautiful สวย sǔay 14, 84

beauty salon ห้องเสริมสวย rórng sěrm sǔay 30, 98

bed เตียง (d)tearng 24, 28, 142, 144

bed and breakfast ค่าที่พักและอาหารเช้า kâr têe pák láir ar hărn chów 24

bedpan กระโถนปัสสาวะ gra tŏen (b)pàt sa wá 144

beef เนื้อ néua 47

beer เบียร์ bear 59, 64

before (time) ก่อน gòrn 15

beginning เริ่มต้น rêrm (d)tôn 150

behind หลัง lăng 15, 77

beige สีทราย sěe sai 112

Belgium เบลเยี่ยม ben yêarm 146

bell (electric) กระดิ่งไฟฟ้า gra dìng fai fár 144

bellboy เด็กรับไช้ dèk ráp chái 26

below ต่ำกว่า, ใต้ (d)tàm gwàr, (d) tâi 15

belt เข็มขัด kěhm kàt 116

bend (road) โค้ง kóeng 79

DICTIONARY

berth ที่นอน têe norn 70, 71
better ดีกว่า dee gwàr 14, 25, 101
between ระหว่าง ra wàrng 15
bicycle จักรยาน jàk ra yarn 74
big ใหญ่ yài 14, 101
bill ใบเสร็จ bai sèht 31, 63
bill *(banknote)* ธนบัตร ta na bàt 130
billion *(Am.)* พันล้าน pan lárn 148
binoculars กล้องสองทางไกล glông sòng tarng glai 123
bird นก nók 85
birth เกิด kèrt 25
birthday วันเกิด wan gèrt 151, 153
biscuit *(Br.)* ขนมปังกรอบ ka nŏm (b)pang gròrp 64
bitter ขม kŏm 62
black ดำ dam 112
black and white *(film)* ขาวดำ kŏw dam 124, 125
black coffee กาแฟดำ gar fair dam 41, 61
bladder กระเพาะปัสสาวะ gra po (b)pàt săr wa 138
blade ใบมีด bai mêet 109
blanket ผ้าห่ม pâr hòm 27
bleach กัดสีผม gàt sĕe pŏm 30
bleed, to เลือดออก lêuat òrk 139, 145
blind *(window shade)* มูลี่ môo lêe 29
blocked ตัน (d)tan 28
blood เลือด lêuat 142
blood pressure ความดันโลหิต kwarm dan loe hìt 141, 142
blood transfusion การถ่ายเลือด garn tài lêuat 144
blouse เสื้อผู้หญิง sêua pôo yĭng 115
blow-dry เป่า (b)pòw 30
blue น้ำเงิน nárm ngern 112
blusher รูจทาแก้ม rôot tar gâirm 109
boat เรือ reua 73, 74
bobby pin กิ๊บติดผม gíp (d)tìt pŏm 110
body ร่างกาย rârng gai 138
boiled egg ไขต้ม kài (d)tôm 41
bone กระดูก gra dòok 138
book หนังสือ náng sĕur, 12, 104
booking office ที่จองตัวล่วงหน้า têe jorng (d)tŭa lûang nâr 19, 67
bookshop ร้านหนังสือ rárn náng sĕur 98, 104
boot รองเท้าบูท rorng táw bóot 117
born เกิด gèrt 150
botanical gardens สวนพฤกษชาติ sŭan prúk sa chârt 81
botany พฤกษศาสตร์ prúk sa sàrt 83
bottle ขวด kùat 17, 59
bottle-opener ที่เปิดขวด têe (b)pèrt kùat 120
bottom ด้านล่าง dârn lârng 145
bow tie หูกระตาย hŏo gra (d)tai 115
bowel ภายในของท้อง pai nai chông tórng 138

box กล่อง glòng 120
boxing ชกมวย chók muay 90
boy เด็กชาย dèhk chai 111, 112, 128
boyfriend แฟนหนุ่ม fairn nùm 93
bra เสื้อยกทรง sêua yók song 115
bracelet สร้อยข้อมือ sôy kôr meur 121
braces *(suspenders)* สายโยงกางเกง săi yeong garng geyng 115
brake เบรก breyk 78
brake fluid น้ำมันเบรก nám man breyk 75
bread ขนมปัง ka nŏm (b)pang 37, 41, 64
break down, to เสีย sĕar 78
breakdown เสีย sĕar 78
breakdown van รถลาก rót lârk 79
breakfast อาหารเช้า ar hărn chów 24, 27, 35, 41
breast หน้าอก năr òk 138
breathe, to หายใจ hăi jai 141, 142
bridge สะพาน sa pan 85
British อังกฤษ ang grìt 93
broken เสีย sĕar 118; หัก hàk 123, 139, 140
brooch เข็มกลัด kĕhm glàt 121
brother พี่ชายน้องชาย pêe chai nórng chai 93
brown น้ำตาล nárm (d)tarn 112
brush แปรงผม (b)prairng pŏm 110
bubble bath บับเบิลบาธ báp bêrl bàrt 109
bucket ถัง táng 120, 128
buckle หัวเข็มขัด hŭa kĕhm kàt 116
Buddha image พระพุทธรูป pra pút tá rôop 127
build, to สร้าง sârng 83
building อาคาร ar karn 81, 83
bulb *(light)* หลอดไฟ lòrt fai 28, 76, 118
Burma *(Myanmar)* พม่า pa mâr 146
burn ไหม้ mâi 139
burn out, to *(bulb)* ไฟขาด fai kàrt 28
bus รถ rót 18, 19, 65, 72, 80
bus stop ป้าย(รถเมล์) (b)pâi (rót mey) 73
business ธุรกิจ tú ra gìt 16, 131
business class ชั้นธุรกิจ chán tú ra gìt 65
business district ย่านธุรกิจ yârn tú rá gìt 81
business trip ไปติดต่อธุระ (b)pai (d)tìt (d)tòr tú rá 94
busy ยุ่ง yûng 96
but แต่ (d)tàir 15
butane gas ก๊าซบิวเทน gárt biw teyn 32, 106
butcher's ร้านขายเนื้อ rárn kăi néua 98
butter เนย noey 37, 41, 64
button กระดุมเสื้อ gra dum sêua 29, 116
buy, to ซื้อ séur 82, 100, 104

DICTIONARY

C

cabana ที่อาบน้ำ tée àrp nárm 91
cabbage กระหล่ำ grà làm 53
cabin (ship) ห้องนอนในเรือ hông norn nai reua 74
cable release สายกดชัตเตอร์ săi gòt chát (d)têr 125
cake ขนมเค้ก ka nŏm kéhk 38, 64
calendar ปฎิทิน pa tì tin 104
call (phone) โทรศัพท์ toe.ra sàp 136
call, to (give name) เรียกว่า rêark wär 11; (phone) โทร toe 134, 136; (summon) เรียก rêark 79, 157
call back, to กลับไปใหม่ glàp (b)pai mài 136
calm สงบ sa ngòp 91
cambric ผ้าลินินขาว păr li nin kŏw 112
camel-hair ขนอูฐ kŏn òot 112
camera กล้องถ่ายรูป glôrng tài rôop 124, 125
camera case กระเป๋าใส่กล้อง gra (b)pŏw sài glông 125
camera shop ร้านขายกล้อง rárn kăi glôrng 98
camp site ที่ตั้งแคมป์ têe (d)tãng káirm ๐๒
camp, to ตั้งแคมป์ (d)tãng káirm 32
campbed เตียงสนาม (d)tearng sa nărm 106
camping แค้มป์ปิ้ง káirm (b)pîng 32
camping equipment เครื่องมือแคมป์ปิ้ง kreûang meur káirm (b)pîng 106
can (container) กระป๋อง gra (b)pŏrng 120
can opener ที่เปิดกระป๋อง tée tée(b)pèrt gra (b)pŏrng 120
Canada แคนาดา kair nar dar 146
Canadian แคนาดา kăir nar dar 93
cancel, to ยกเลิก yók lêrk 66
candle เทียน tearn 120
candy ลูกกวาด lôok gwàrt 126
cap หมวกแก๊ป mùak găihp 115
capital (finance) ทุน tun 131
car รถ rót 19, 20, 75, 78
car hire รถเช่า rót chôw 20
car park ที่จอดรถ tée jòrt rót 78
car racing แข่งรถ kàjîng rót 90
car radio วิทยุรถยนต์ wít ta yú rót yon 118
car rental รถเช่า rót chôw 20
carafe คาราฟ kar rârf 60
carat กะรัต ga rát 121
caravan รถบ้านเคลื่อนที่ jort rót norn 32
caraway ยี่หร่า yêe râr 55
carbon paper กระดาษอัดสำเนา gra dàrt àt sămnow 104
carbonated (fizzy) ชนิดที่มีก๊าซ cha nít tée mee gárt 61
carburettor คาร์บิวเรเตอร์ kar bi wrey têr 78

card นามบัตร narm bàt 131
card game ไพ่ pâi 128
cardigan คาร์ดีกัน kar dì gan 115
carrot แครอท kair rót 53
cart รถเข็น rót kĕhn 18
carton (of cigarettes) ห่อ hòr 17; คาร์ตตอน kàrt (d)torn 126
cartridge (camera) กล่องใส่ฟิล์มขนาดใหญ่ glông feem ka nàrt yài 124
case กระเป๋า gra (b)pŏw 125
cash desk ที่รับเงิน tée ráp ngern 103, 156
cash, to เบิกเงิน bèrk ngern 130, 133
cassette เทปคาสเซ็ท téyp kar sèht 118, 127
cassette recorder เครื่องอัดเทป krêuang àt téyp 118
castle ปราสาท (b)pra sàrt 81
catacombs อุโมงค์ u moeng 81
catalogue แคตตาล็อก kàirt (d)tar lòk 82
catfish ปลาดุก (b)plar dùk 45
cathedral วิหาร wi hărn 81
Catholic คาทอลิก kar tor lík 84
cauliflower กระหล่ำดอก gra làm dòrk 53
caution ระมัดระวัง rarmát rawang 156
cave ถ้ำ tâm 91
celery คื่นช่ายฝรั่ง kĕuhn chăi fa ràng 53
cemetery ป่าช้า (b)pàr chár 81
centimetre เซ็นติเมตร sehn (d)tí méht 111
centre ใจกลาง jai glarng 19, 21, 77, 81
century ศตวรรษ sàt tà wát 149
ceramics เซรามิก sey rar mík 83
cereal ซีเรียล see rearl 41
certificate ใบรับรองแพทย์ bai ráp rorng pàirt 144
chain (jewellery) สร้อย sôy 121
chain bracelet สร้อยข้อมือ sôy kôr meur 121
chair เก้าอี้ kôw êe 106
chamber music ดนตรีที่เล่นในห้อง don (d)tree tée lêhn nai hông 128
change, to เปลี่ยน (b)plèarn 62, 66, 68, 76, 123
change, to (money) แลกเงิน lâirk ngern 18, 129
change (money) แลกเงิน lâirk ngern 63, 129
chapel โรงสวด roeng sùat 81
charge คิดค่า kít kâr 20, 78, 90, 136
charge, to คิดค่า kít kâr 24, 130
charm (trinket) เครื่องราง krêuang rarng 121
charm bracelet สร้อยข้อมือที่มีเครื่องราง sôy kôr meur tée mee krêuang rarng 121
cheap ถูก tòok 14, 24, 25, 101
check (restaurant) เช็คเงิน gèhp ngern 63
check (bank) เช็ค chéhk 130, 131
check, to ตรวจ (d)trùat 123
check, to (luggage) ตรวจดู(กระเป๋า) fàrk

พจนานุกรม

(gra (b)pŏw) 71
check in, to *(airport)* เช็คอิน chéhk in 65
check out, to เช็คเอาท์ chéhk ŏw 31
check-up *(medical)* ตรวจร่างกาย (d)trùat
rârng gai 142
cheese เนยแข็ง noey káihng 64
chemist's ร้านขายยา rárn kǎi yar 98, 107
cheque เช็ค, chéhk 130, 131
cherry เชอร์รี่ cher rêe 56
chess หมากรุก màrk rúk 94
chess set หมากรุก màrk rúk 128
chest หน้าอก nâr ŏk 138, 141
chestnut เกาลัด gow lát 56
chewing gum หมากฝรั่ง màrk fa ràng 126
chewing tobacco ยาเส้น yar sêhn 126
chicken ไก่ gài 64
chicken breast อกไก่ ŏk gài 49
chiffon แพรชีฟอง prair chee forng 113
child เด็ก dèhk 24, 62, 82, 150
children's doctor กุมารแพทย์ gu marn
pâirt 137
China จีน jeen 146
chips มันทอด man tôrt 64
chocolate ช็อกโกแล็ต chók goe láiht 119,
126
chocolate (hot) ช็อกโกแล็ต(ร้อน) chók goe
láiht (rórn) 41, 61
chopstick ตะเกียบ (d)ta gèap 37
Christmas คริสต์มาส krít sa mârt 153
chromium โครเมียม kroe mêarm 122
church โบสถ์ bòet 81, 84
cigar ซิการ์ si gar 126
cigarette บุหรี่ bu rèe 17, 95, 126
cigarette case ตลับบุหรี่ (d)tal àp bu rèe
121, 126
cigarette holder ที่คาบบุหรี่ têe kârp bu rèe
126
cigarette lighter ไฟแช็ค fai cháihk 121,
126
cine camera กล้องถ่ายหนัง glôrng tài nǎng
124
cinema หนัง nǎng 86
cinnamon อบเชย òp choey 55
circle *(theatre)* ชั้นลอย chán loy 87, 88
city เมือง meuang 81
city centre ใจกลางเมือง jai glarng meuang
81
classical คลาสสิก klârt sìk 128
clean สะอาด sa àrt 62
clean, to ทั่วความสะอาด tam kwarm sa àrt
76; ซักแห้ง sák háirng 29
cleansing cream ครีมล้างหน้า kreem lárng
nâr 109
cliff หน้าผา nâr pǎr 85
clip เข็มกลัดหนีบ kěhm glàt nèep 121
cloakroom ห้องรับฝากของ hôrng ráp fàrk
kǒrng 88
clock นาฬิกา nar lí gar 121, 155

clock-radio วิทยุ-นาฬิกา wít ta yú nar lí
gar 118
close, to ปิด (b)pìt 107, 132
cloth ผ้า pâr 117
clothes เสื้อผ้า sêua pǎr 29, 115
clothes peg/pin ไม้หนีบผ้า mái nèep pǎr
120
clothing เสื้อผ้า sêua pǎr 111
cloud เมฆ mêyk 94
clove กานพลู garn ploo 55
coach *(bus)* รถทัวร์ rót tua 72
coat เสื้อโค้ท sêua kóet 115
coconut มะพร้าว ma prów 56
coffee กาแฟ gar fair 41, 61, 64
cognac *(brandy)* คอนยัค korn yák 60
coin เหรียญ(กษาปณ์) rearn (ga sàrp) 83
cold หนาว nǎw 25, 94; เย็น yehn 14, 61
cold *(illness)* หวัด wàt 108, 141
collar คอเสื้อ kor sêua 116
colour สี sěe 103, 111, 124, 125
colour chart ตารางสี (d)tar rarng sěe 30
colour rinse ทำสีผม tarp sěe pǒm 30
colour shampoo แชมพูยอมผม chairm poo
yórm pǒm 110
colour slide ฟิล์มสไลด์ feem sa lai 124
colourfast สีตก sěe(d)tòk 113
comb หวี wěe 110
come, to มา mar 16, 95, 137, 144, 146
comedy ละครตลก la korn (d)ta lòk 86
commission *(fee)* ค่าบริการ kâr bo ri garn
130
common *(frequent)* บ่อย bòy 155
compact disc ซีดี see dee 127
compartment *(train)* ห้องวาง nôrng wǎrng
70
compass เข็มทิศ kěhm tít 106
complaint คำร้อง (d)tòr wâr 62
concert คอนเสิร์ต korn sèrt 88
concert hall ที่แสดงดนตรี têe sa dairng
don (d)tree 81, 88
condom ถุงยางอนามัย tǔng yarng a nar
mai 108
conductor *(orchestra)* วาทยากร wârt ta
yar gorn 88
conference room ห้องประชุม hông (b)pra
chum 23
confirm, to ยืนยัน yeurn yan 66
confirmation คำยืนยัน kam yeurn yan 23
congratulation ขอแสดงความยินดีด้วย kǒr
sa dairng kwarm yin dee dûay 153
connection *(transport)* ต่อ (d)tòr 65
constipated ท้องผูก tórng pòok 140
consulate กงสุล gong sǔn 157
contact lens คอนแท็คเลนส์ korn táihk leyns
123
contagious โรคติดต่อ rôek (d)tìt (d)tòr
142
contain, to มี mee 38

contraceptive คุมกำเนิด kum gam nèrt 108

contract สัญญา săn yar 131

control ควบคุม kûap kum 16

convent คอนแวนท korn wairn 81

cookie คุกกี้ kúk gêe 64

cool box กระติกน้ำแข็ง gra (d)tik nárm kăihng 106

copper ทองแดง torng dairng 122

coral หินปะการัง hĭn (b)pa gar rang 122

corduroy ผ้าริ้ว pâr riw 113

corn (foot) ตาปลา (d)tar (b)plar 108

corn plaster พลาสเตอรสำหรับปิดตาปลา plar sa ter săm ràp (b)pìt (d)tar (b)plar 108

corner มุม mum 21, 36, 77

cost คาใชจาย kâr chái jài 131

cost, to เทาไหร tôwrài 11, 80, 133

cotton ผาฝาย pâr fâi 113

cotton wool สำลี săm lee 108

cough ไอ ai 108, 141

cough drops ยาแกไอ yar gâir ai 108

cough, to ไอ ai 142

countryside ชนบท chon a bòt 85

court house ศาล sărn 81

cousin ญาติ yârt 93

cover charge คาบริการตอหัว kâr boe ri garn (d)tòr hŭa 63

crab ปูทะเล (b)pòo ta ley 45

cramp ตะคริว (d)ta kríw 141

crayon ดินสอสี din sŏr sĕe 104

cream ครีม kreem 61

cream (toiletry) ครีม kreem 109

crease resistant กันยับ gan yáp 113

credit เครดิต krey dìt 130

credit card บัตรเครดิต bàt krey dìt 20, 31, 63, 102, 130

crepe แพรยน prair yôn 113

crockery ถวยชาม tûay charm 120

cross ไมกางเขน mái garng kĕyn 121

crossing (maritime) ขามฟาก kârm fârk 74

crossroads สี่แยก sèe yâirk 77

cruise ลองเรือ lông reua 74

crystal แกวผลึก , ควิสตัล gâiw pléuhk, krí sa (d)tan 122

cucumber แตงกวา (d)tairng gwar 53

cuisine อาหาร ar hărn 35

cup ถวย tûay 37; แกว gâiw 120

curler เครื่องมวนผม krêuang meur dàt pŏm 110

currency เงิน ngern 129

currency exchange office ที่รับแลกเงิน têe ráp lâirk ngern 19, 68, 129

current กระแสน้ำ gra săir nárm 91

curried แกง gairng 46

curtain ผามาน pâr mărn 28

customs ศุลกากร sŭn la gar gorn 17, 102

cut (wound) บาด bàrt 139

cut glass แกวเจียรไน gâiw jea ra nai 122

cut, to (with scissors) ตัด (d)tàt 30

cut off, to (interrupt) (สาย)ขาด (săi) kàrt 135

cuticle remover ที่แตงโคนเล็บ têe (d)tàihng kpen léhp 109

cutlery ชอน-สอม chórn sôm 120, 121

cycling แขงจักรยาน kàihng jàk ra yarn 90

cystitis กระเพาะปสสาวะอักเสบ gra póh (b)pàt sa wá ak sèyp 142

D

dance, to เตนรำ (d)têhn ram 88, 96

danger อันตราย an (d)ta rai 156, 157

dangerous อันตราย aŋ (d)ta rai 91

dark มืด mêurt 25; เขม kêhm 101, 111, 112

date (appointment) นัดหมาย nát măi 95; (day) วันที่ wan têe 25, 151; (fruit) อินทผาลัม in ta păr lam 56

daughter ลูกสาว lôok sŏw 93

day วัน wan 20, 24, 32, 80, 94, 151

day off วันหยุด wan yìrt 151

daylight แสงธรรมชาติ săirng tam má chârt 124

decade ทศวรรษ tótt sa wát 149

decaffeinated ชนิดไมมีคาเฟอีน chanít mâi mee kar fey een 61

December ธันวาคม tan war kom 150

decision ตัดสินใจ (d)tàt sĭn jai 25, 102

deck (ship) ดาดฟาเรือ dàrt fár reua 74

deck chair เกาอี้ผาใบ gôw êe păr bai 91, 106

declare, to (customs) แสดงรายการสิ่งของ sa dairng rai garn sìng kŏrng 17

deep ลึก léuhk 142

degree (temperature) องศา ong săr 140

delay ชา chár 69

delicious อรอย ar òy 63

deliver, to สง sòng 102

delivery การสง garn sòng 102

denim ผายีนส păr yeen 113

Denmark เดนมารก deyn mârk 146

dentist หมอฟน mŏr fan 98, 145

denture ฟนปลอม fan (b)plorm 145

deodorant ยาดับกลิ่นตัว yar dàp glìn (d)tua 109

department (museum) แผนก pa nàirk 84; (shop) ราน rárn 100

department store หางสรรพสินคา hârng sàp pá sĭn kár 99

departure ขาออก kăr òrk 66

deposit (down payment) เงินมัดจำ ngern mát jam 20; (bank) ธนาคาร ta nar karn 130

dessert ของหวาน kŏrng wărn 38, 57

diabetic โรคเบาหวาน rôek bow wǎrn 38, 141
dialling code ระหัสพื้นที่ ra hàt péurn têe 134
diamond เพชร péht 122
diaper ผ้าอ้อม pâr bôrm 110
diarrhoea ท้องร่วง tórng rûang 140
dictionary พจนานุกรม po ja nar nú grom 104
diesel ดีเซล dee seyn 75
diet อาหาร ar hǎrn 38
difficult ยาก yârk 14
difficulty ยุงยาก yûng yârk 28, 102
digital ดิจิตอล di jì (d)torn 122
dining car รถเสบียง rót sa bearng 68, 71
dining room ท้องอาหาร hôrng ar hǎrn 27
dinner อาหารเย็น ar hǎrn kǎm 35, 95
dinner, to have กินอาหารเย็น gin ar hǎrn yehn 95
direct ตรง (d)trong 65
direct, to บอก(ทาง) bòrk (tarng) 13
direction ที่ tít 76
director (theatre) ผู้กำกับ pôo gam gàp 87
directory (phone) สมุดโทรศัพท์ sa mùt toe ra sàp 134
disabled คนพิการ, kon pí garn 83
discotheque ดิสโกเธค dìt sa gôe táihk 88, 96
discount ส่วนลด sùan lót 131
disease โรค rôeg 142
dish จาน jarn 36
dishwashing detergent น้ำยาล้างจาน nárm lárng jarn 120
disinfectant ยาฆ่าเชื้อ yar kǎr chéua 108
dislocated เคลื่อน klêuan 140
display case โชว์ญ choe yòo 101
dissatisfied ไม่ชอบใจ mâi chôrp jai 103
district (of town) ย่าน yârn 81
disturb, to รบกวน róp guan 156
dizzy เวียนศีรษะ wearn sěe sa 140
doctor หมอ mǒr 79, 137, 144, 145
doctor's office คลีนิคหมอ klee ník mǒr 137
dog สุนัข su nák 156
doll ตุ๊กตา (d)túk a (d)tar 128
dollar ดอลลาร์ dorn lar 19, 102, 129
door ประตู (d)pra.(d)too 156
double bed เตียงคู่ (d)teang kôo 23
double room ห้องคู่ hôrng kôo 19, 23
down ลง long 15
downtown ในเมือง nai meuang 81
dozen โหล lǒe 149
drawing paper กระดาษวาดเขียน gra dàrt wârt kěarn 104
drawing pins เข็มหมุดสำหรับวาดเขียน kěhm mùt sǎm ràp wârt kěarn 105
dress เสื้อกระโปรงชุด sêua gra (b)proeng

chút 115
dressing gown เสื้อคลุมอาบน้ำ sêua klum àrp nárm 115
drink เครื่องดื่ม krêuang dèurm 59, 60, 61, 95
drink, to ดื่ม dèurm 36, 38
drinking water น้ำดื่ม nárm dèurm 32
drip, to หยด yòt 28
driving licence ใบขับขี่ bai kàp kèe 20, 79
drop (liquid) ยาหยอด yar yòrt 108
drugstore ร้านขายยา rárn kǎi yar 99, 107
dry แห้ง hǎirng 30, 110; (wine) ครา da rai 60
dry cleaner's ร้านซักแห้ง rárn sák hǎirng 29, 99
dry shampoo แชมพูผง chairm poo pǒng 110
duck เป็ด (b)pèht 49
dummy (baby's) จุกนม jùk nom 110
during ระหว่าง ra wàrng 15
duty (customs) ภาษีศุลกากร parsǎr sǔn la gar gorn 18
duty-free shop ร้านค้าปลอดภาษี rárn kár (b)plòrt par sěe 19
dye ยายอมผม yar yórm pǒm 30, 111

E
ear หู hǒo 138
ear drops ยาหยอดหู yar yòrt hǒo 108
earache ปวดหู (b)pùat hǒo 141
early เช้า, chów 14, 31
earring ตุ้มหู (d)tûm hǒo 121
east ที่ตะวันออก tít (d)tawan òrk 77
easy ง่าย ngâi 14
eat, to กิน gin 36, 38; ทาน tarn 144
eel ปลาไหล (b)plar lǎi 45
egg ไข่ kài 41, 64
eggplant มะเขือยาว ma kěua yow 53
eight แปด (b)pàirt 147
eighteen สิบแปด sìp (b)pàirt 147
eighth ที่แปด têe (b)pàirt 149
eighty แปดสิบ (b)pàirt sìp 148
elastic bandage ผ้าพันแผล pâr pan plǎir 108
electric(al) ไฟฟ้า fai fár 118
electrical appliance เครื่องใช้ไฟฟ้า krêuang chái fai fár 118
electrical goods shop ร้านขายเครื่องไฟฟ้า rárn kǎi krêuang fai fár 99
electricity ไฟฟ้า fai fár 32
electronic ไฟฟ้า fai fár 128
elevator ลิฟท์ líf 27, 100
eleven สิบเอ็ด sìp èht 147
embarkation point ท่าเรือ târ reua 74
embassy สถานทูต sa tǎrn tôot 157
emerald มรกต mo ra gòt 122
emergency ฉุกเฉิน chùk chěrn 157

emergency exit ทางออกฉุกเฉิน tarng òrk chùk chěrn 27, 100

emery board ตะไบเล็บ (d)tà bai léhp 109

empty ว่าง wârng 14

enamel ลงยา, เคลือบ long yar, klêuap 109

end ปลาย (b)plai 150

engaged (phone) ติด(สาย), (d)tìt (săi) 136

engagement ring แหวนหมั้น wăirn mân 122

engine (car) เครื่องยนต์ krêuang yon 78

England อังกฤษ ang grìt 134, 146

English อังกฤษ ang grìt 11, 17, 80, 82, 93, 104, 105, 126

enjoy oneself, to รู้สึกสนุก róo sèuhk sa nùk 96

enjoyable สนุก sa nùk 31

enlarge, to ขยาย ka yǎi 125

enough พอ pɒr 14

entrance ทางเข้า, tarng kôw 67, 100, 156

entrance fee ค่าผ่านประตู kâr pàrn (b)pra (d)tòo 82

envelope ซองจดหมาย sorng jot mǎi 105

equipment เครื่องมือ krêuang meur 91, 106

eraser ยางลบ yarng lóp 105

escalator บันไดเลื่อน ban dai lêuan 100

estimate (cost) ประเมิน (b)pra mern 131

Eurocheque ยูโรเช็ค yoo roe chéhk 130

Europe ยุโรป yu ròep 146

evening เย็น yehn 95, 96

evening dress ชุดราตรีสโมสร chút rar (d)tree sa mǒe sǒrn 89

evening dress (woman's) ชุดราตรี chút rar (d)tree 115

evening, in the ตอนเย็น (d)torn yehn 151; เวลาเย็น wey lar yehn 153

every ทุก túk 143

everything ทุกอย่าง túk yàrng 31, 63

exchange rate อัตราแลกเปลี่ยน a (d)tra lâirk (b)plèarn 19

excursion รายการนำเที่ยว rai garn nam têaw 80

excuse, to แก้ตัว kâir (d)tua 10

excuse me ขอโทษ kǒr tôet 154

exercise book สมุดแบบฝึกหัด sa mùt bàirp fèuhk hàt 105

exhaust pipe ท่อไอเสีย tòr ai sěar 79

exhibition นิทรรศการ ní tát sa garn 81

exit ทางออก, tarng òrk 67, 100, 156

expenses ค่าใช้จ่าย kâr chái jài 131

expensive แพง pairng 14, 19, 24, 101

exposure (photography) รูป rôop 124

exposure counter ที่บอกจำนวนรูปที่ถ่าย têe bòrk jam nuan rôop têe tài 125

express ด่วน dùan 133

expression แสดงออก sa dairng òrk 10, 100

expressway ทางด่วน tarng dùan 76

extension (phone) ต่อ (d)tòr 135

extension cord/lead สายต่อ(ไฟฟ้า) săi (d)tòr (fai fár) 118

extra เพิ่ม pêrm 27

eye ตา (d)tar 138, 139

eye drops ยาหยอดตา yar yòrt (d)tar 108

eye shadow ที่ทาตา têe tar (d)tar 109

eye specialist จักษุแพทย์ jàk sù pàirt 137

eyebrow pencil ดินสอเขียนคิ้ว din sǒr kěarn kíw 109

eyesight สายตา săi (d)tar 123

F

fabric (cloth) เนื้อผ้า néua pàr 112

face หน้า nâr 138

face pack ฟอกหน้า fôrk nâr 30

face powder แป้งผัดหน้า (b)pâirng pàt nâr 109

factory โรงงาน roeng ngarn 81

fair งานออกร้าน, ngarn òrk rárn 81

fall (autumn) ฤดูใบไม้ร่วง rí doo bai mái rûang 150

fall, to หกล้ม hòk lóm 139

family ครอบครัว krôrp krua 93, 144

fan พัดลม pát lom 28

fan belt สายพานพัดลม săi parn pát lom 76

far ไกล glai 14, 100

fare (ticket) ค่า kâr 68, 73

farm นา, ไร nar, rǎi 85

fast เร็ว rehw 124

fat (meat) มัน man 38

father พ่อ pôr 93

faucet ก๊อกน้ำ gók nárm 28

fax แฟ็กซ์ fáihk 133

February กุมภาพันธ์ gum par pan 150

fee (doctor's) ค่ารักษา kâr rák sǎr 144

feeding bottle ขวดนม kùat nárm 110

feel, to (physical state) รู้สึก róo sèuhk 140, 142

felt ผ้าสักหลาด pâr sàk làrt 113

felt-tip pen ปากกาเมจิก (b)pàrk gar meyjìk 105

ferry เรือข้ามฟาก reua kàrm fârk 74

fever ไข้ kâi 140

few น้อย nói 14

few (a few) เล็กน้อย măi gèe 14

field ทุ่ง tûng 85

fifteen สิบห้า sìp hâr 147

fifth ที่ห้า têe hâr 149

fifty ห้าสิบ hâr sìp 147

file (tool) ตะไบขัดเล็บ (d)ta bai kàt léhp 109

fill in, to กรอก gròrk 26, 144

filling (tooth) อุด ùt 145

filling station ปั๊มน้ำมัน (b)pám nám man

DICTIONARY

พจนานุกรม

75

film หนัง năng 86; , ฟิล์ม feem 124, 125
film winder ตัวขึ้นฟิล์ม (d)tua kéuhn feem 125
filter ฟีลเตอร์ ˌfil (d)ter 125
filter-tipped ก้นกรอง gôn grorng 126
find, to หา hăr 11, 12, 100
fine (OK) สบายดี sa bai dee 10, 92
fine arts วิจิตรศิลป์ wi jìt ra sĭn 83
finger นิ้ว níw 138
Finland ฟินแลนด์ fin lairn 146
fire ไฟ fai 157
first แรก rârk 68, 73, 77; ที่หนึ่ง têe nèuhng 149
first class ชั้นหนึ่ง chán nèuhng 69
first name ชื่อ, chêur 25
first-aid kit เครื่องมือปฐมพยาบาล krêuang meur (d)pa tŏm pa yar barn 108
fish ปลา (b)plar 45
fishing ตกปลา (d)tòk (b)plar 90
fishing permit ขออนุญาตตกปลา kŏr an nú yârt (d)tòk (b)plar 90
fishing tackle คันเบ็ดชนิดมีรอก kan bèht cha nít mee ĝòrk 106
fishmonger's ร้านขายปลา rárn kăi (b)plar 99
fit, to พอดี por dee 114
fitting room ห้องลอง hôrng lorng 114
five ห้า hâr 147
fix, to ปะ (b)pà 76; อุด ùt 145
fizzy (mineral water) ชนิดที่มีก๊าซ cha nít têe mee gárt 61
flannel ผ้าสักหลาดอ่อน păr sàk làrt òrn 113
flash (photography) แฟลช fláirt 125
flash attachment แป้นแฟลช (b)pâirn fláirt 125
flashlight ไฟกระพริบ fai gra príp 106
flat (apartment) แฟลต fláiht 23
flat (shoe) พื้นราบ péurn rârp 117
flat tyre ยางแบน yarng bairn 76
flight เที่ยวบิน têaw bin 65
floating market ตลาดน้ำ (d)ta làrt nárm 81
floor show ฟลอร์โชว์ ˌflor choe 89
florist's ร้านขายดอกไม้ rárn kăi dòrk mái 99
flour แป้ง (b)pâirng 38
flower ดอกไม้ dòrk mái 85
flu ไข้ háq 142
fluid (brake) น้ำมัน(เบรก) nárm man (breyk) 75; น้ำยาล้าง nárm yar lárng 123
foam rubber mattress ที่นอนยาง têe norn yarng 106
fog หมอก mòrk 94
folding chair เก้าอี้พับ gô wêe páp 106
folding table โต๊ะพับ (d)tóh páp 106

folk song เพลงพื้นบ้าน pleyng péun bârn 128
follow, to ตาม (d)tarm 77
food อาหาร ar hărn 37, 38, 62, 110
food box กล่องอาหาร glòrng ar hărn 120
food poisoning อาหารเป็นพิษ ar hărn (b)pehn pít 142
foot เท้า tów 138
foot cream ครีมทาเท้า kreem tar tów 109
football ฟุตบอล fút born 89, 90
footpath ทางเท้า tarng tów 85
for เพื่อ, สำหรับ pêua, săm ràp 15
forbidden ห้าม hârm 156
forecast พยากรณ์ pa yar gorn 94
forest ป่า (b)pàr 85
fork ส้อม sôrm 37, 62, 120,
form (document) แบบฟอร์ม bàirp form 26, 133, 144
fortnight สองอาทิตย์ sŏrng ar tít 151
fortress ป้อมปราการ (b)pôrm (b)pra garn 81
forty สี่สิบ sèe sìp 147
foundation cream ครีมรองพื้น kreem rorng péurn 109
fountain น้ำพุ nárm pú 81
fountain pen ปากกาหมึกซึม (b)pàrk gar mèuhk suhm 105
four สี่ sèe 147
fourteen สิบสี่ sìp sèe 147
fourth ที่สี่ têe sèe 149
frame (glasses) กรอบ(แว่น) gròrp (wăirn) 123
France ฝรั่งเศส fa ràng sèyt 146
free ว่าง wârng 14, 80, 96, 155
fresh สด sòt 56, 62
Friday วันศุกร์ wan sùk 151
fried egg ไข่ดาว kài dow 41
friend เพื่อน pêuan 95
fringe ผมม้า pŏm márt 30
from จาก jàrk 15
front ด้านหน้า (d)ârn nâr 76
frost น้ำค้างแข็ง nárm kárng kăihng 94
fruit ผลไม้ pŏn la mái 56,
fruit cocktail ค็อกเทลผลไม้ kók teyn pŏn la mái 56,
fruit juice น้ำผลไม้ nárm pŏn la mái 41, 61
frying pan กะทะ ga tá 120
full เต็ม (d)tehm 14
full board รวมอาหารทุกมื้อ ruam ar hărn túk méur 24
full insurance ประกันเต็มที่ (b)pra gan (d)tehm têe 20

G
gabardine ผ้าลายสองหน้าเดียว păr lai sôrng năr deaw 113

gallery หอศิลป์ hŏr sĭn 81, 98
game เกม geym 128
garage โรงรถ roeng rót 26
garden สวน sŭan 85
gardens สวน sŭan 81
gas แก๊ส gárt 157
gasoline เบนซิน beyn sin 76; น้ำมัน námman 78
gastritis โรคกระเพาะอักเสบ rôeg gra póh àk sèyp 142
gauze ผ้าก๊อซ păr górt 108
gem เพชรพลอย péht ploy 121
general ทั่วไป tûa (b)pai 27, 100, 137
general delivery ส่งทั่วไป sòng tûa (b)pai 133
general practitioner หมอ mŏr 137
genitals อวัยวะเพศ a way a wá pêyt 138
gentleman สุภาพบุรุษ su pàrp bù rút 156
geology ธรณีวิทยา to ra nee wít ta yar 83
Germany เยอรมันนี yer ra man nee 146
get, to หา hăr 11, 32; เรียก rêark 19, 21, 31; ซื้อ séur 108
get off, to ลง(รถ) long (rót) 73
get past, to ผ่านไป (b)pàrn (b)pai 70
get to, to ไป (b)pai 19, 76, 100
get up, to ลุก lúi 144
gift ของฝาก kŏrng fàrk 17
gin จิน jin 60
gin and tonic จินโทนิค jin toe ník 60
ginger ขิง kĭng 55
girdle เข็มขัด, ผ้าคาดเอว kĕhm kàt, păr kârt ew 115
girl เด็กหญิง dèhk yĭng 111, 112, 128
girlfriend แฟนสาว fairn sŏw 93
give, to ให้ hăi 13
give way, to (traffic) ให้ทาง hăi tarng 79
gland ต่อม (d)tòrm 138
glass แก้ว, gâiw 37, 60, 62, 143
glasses แว่นตา wâirn (d)tar 123
gloomy หน้าเศร้า năr sôw 84
glove ถุงมือ tŭng meur 115
glue กาว gow 105
go, to ไป (b)pai,21, 72, 77, 96
go away! ไปให้พ้น (b)pai hăi pón 157
go back, to กลับไป glàp (b)pai 77
go out, to ไปข้างนอก (b)pai kârng nôrk 96
gold ทอง torng 121, 122
gold plate ชุบทอง chúp torng 122
golden สีทอง see torng 112
golf กอล์ฟ gorf 89
golf course สนามกอล์ฟ sa nărm gorf 89
good ดี dee 14, 86, 101
good afternoon สวัสดี sa wàt dee 10
good evening สวัสดี sa wàt dee 10
good morning สวัสดี sa wàt dee 10
good night ราตรีสวัสดี rar tree sa sàt 10
goodbye สวัสดี sa wàt dee 10

goose ห่าน hàrn 49
gram กรัม gram 120
grammar ไวยากรณ์ wai ya gorn 160
grammar book หนังสือไวยากรณ์ náng sĕur wai ya gorn 105
grape องุ่น a ngùn 56, 64
gray สีเทา sĕe tow 112
graze แผลถลอก plăir ta lòrk 139
greasy มัน man 30, 111
great (excellent) ดีมาก dee mârk 95
Great Britain สหราชอาณาจักร sa har rârt ar nar jàk 146
Greece กรีก grèek 146
green สีเขียว sĕe kĕaw 112
greeting ทักทาย ták tai 10, 153
grey สีเทา sĕe tow 112
grilled ปิ้ง, ย่าง (b)píng, yârng 46, 47
grocer's ร้านขายของชำ rárn kăi kŏrng cham 99, 119
groundsheet ผ้ายางปูพื้น păr yarng (b)poo péurn 106
group กลุ่ม glùm 82
guesthouse เกสต์เฮาส์ géyt hówt 20, 23
guide ไกด์ gai 80
guidebook หนังสือคู่มือ náng sĕur kôo meur 82, 104, 105
guinea fowl ไก่ตอก gài (d)tók 49
gum (teeth) เหงือก ngèuak 145
gynaecologist นรีแพทย์ na ree pâirt 137

H
hair ผม pŏm 30, 111
hair dryer เครื่องเป่าผม krêuang (b)pòw pŏm 118
hair gel เยลใส่ผม yehl sài pŏm 30, 111
hair lotion โลชั่นใส่ผม loe chăn sài pŏm 110
hair spray สเปรย์ฉีดผม sa (b)prey chèet pŏm 30, 111
hairbrush หวีแปรงผม wĕe (b)prairng pŏm 110
haircut ตัดผม, (d)tàt pŏm 30
hairdresser ร้านทำผม rárn tam pŏm 30, 99
hairgrip กิ๊บติดผม gíp (d)tìt pŏm 110
hairpin ปิ่นปักผม (b)pìn (b)pàk pŏm 110
half ครึ่ง krêuhng,149
half an hour ครึ่งชั่วโมง krêuhng chûa moeng 155
half price ครึ่งราคา krêuhng rar kar 69
hall porter พนักงานยกกระเป๋า pa nák ngarn yók gra (b)păo 26
ham แฮม hairm 41, 64
ham and eggs แฮมกับไข่ดาว hairm gàp kài dow 41
hammer ฆ้อน kórn 120
hammock เปลญวน (b)pley yuan 106

DICTIONARY

hand มือ meur 138
hand cream ครีมทามือ kreem tar meur 109
hand washable ซักด้วยมือ sák dûay meur 113
handbag กระเป๋ามือถือ gra (b)pŏw meur tĕur 115, 157
handicrafts งานฝีมือ ngarn fĕe meur 83
handkerchief ผ้าเช็ดหน้า pắr chéht nắr 115
handmade ทำด้วยมือ tam dûay meur 112
hanger ไม้แขวนเสื้อ mái kwǎirn sêua 27
happy สุขสันต์ sùk sǎn 153
harbour ท่าจอดเรือ tǎr jòrt reua 74, 81
hard ฮาร์ด(เลนส์) härt 123
hard-boiled (egg) ไข่ต้มสุกๆ kài tôm sùk sùk 41
hardware store ร้านขายเครื่องโลหะ rárn kǎi krêuang loe hà 99
hat หมวก mùak 115
have to, to (must) ต้อง (d)tôrng 18, 69, 77, 95
hay fever โรคแพ้อากาศ rôek páir ar gàrt 108, 141
head หัว hǔa 138, 139
head waiter หัวหน้าบอย hǔa nắr bŏy 62
headache ปวดหัว (b)pùat hǔa 141
headphones หูฟัง hǒo fang 118
health insurance form แบบฟอร์มประกันสุขภาพ bàirp form (b)pra gan sùk ka pàrp 144
heart หัวใจ hǔa jai 138
heating เครื่องทำความร้อน krêuang tam kwarm rórn 28
heavy หนัก nàk 139
heel ส้น sôn 117
helicopter เฮลิคอปเตอร์ hey li kòrp (d)ter 75
hello สวัสดี sa wàt dee 10, 135
help ช่วย chûay 157
help! ช่วยด้วย chûay dûay 157
help, to ช่วย chûay 12, 71, 100, 134
help, to (oneself) ช่วย(ตัวเอง) chûay ((d)tua eyng) 119
herb tea ชาสมุนไพร char sa mǔn prai 61
herbs สมุนไพร sa mǔn prai 55
here ที่นี่ têe nêe 14
hi สวัสดี sa wàt dee 10
high สูง sŏong 141
high season ฤดูท่องเที่ยว ri doo tông têaw 150
high tide น้ำขึ้น nárm kéuhn 91
hill เนินเขา nern kŏw 85
hire เช่า chôw 20, 74
hire, to เช่า chôw 19, 20, 74, 90, 91, 118, 156
history ประวัติศาสตร์ (b)pra wàt tí sàrt 83
hitchhike, to โบกรถ bòek rót 75

hold on! (phone) รอสักครู่ ror sák krôo 136
hole รู roo 30
holiday(s) วันหยุดพักผ่อน wan yúk pák pòrn 151, 153
home บ้าน bârn 96
home address ที่อยู่ têe yòo 31
home town บ้านเกิด bârn gèrt 25
honey น้ำผึ้ง nárm pêuhng 41
hope, to หวัง wǎng 96
horse racing แข่งม้า kàihng már 90
horseback riding ขี่ม้า kèe már 90
hospital โรงพยาบาล roeng pa yar barn 99, 142, 144
hot ร้อน rórn 14, 25, 94
hot (spicy) รสจัด rót jàt 37
hot water น้ำร้อน nárm rórn 24, 28
hot-water bottle ถุงน้ำร้อน tǔng nárm rórn 27
hotel โรงแรม roeng rairm 19, 21, 22, 26, 80, 102
hotel directory/guide สมุดรายชื่อโรงแรม sa mùt rai chêur roen grairm 19
hotel reservation ของโรงแรม jorng roengrairm 19
hour ชั่วโมง chûa moeng 80, 143
house บ้าน bârn 85
household article ของใช้ในบ้าน kŏrng chái nai bârn 120
how ยังไง yang ngay 11
how far ไกลไหม glai mái 11, 76, 85
how long นานไหม narn mái 11, 24
how many เท่าไหร่ tôw rài 11
how much เท่าไหร่ tôw rài 11, 24
hundred ร้อย róy 148
hungry หิว hǐw 13, 36
hurt, to เจ็บ jèhp 139, 140, 142
husband สามี sǎr mee 93

I
ice cream ไอศกรีม ai sa kreem 57
ice cube น้ำแข็ง nárm kǎihng 27
ice pack น้ำแข็ง nárm kǎihng 106
iced tea ชาเย็น char yehn 61
if ถ้า târ 143
ill ไม่สบาย mâi sa bay 140
illness เจ็บป่วย jèhp (b)pùay 140
important สำคัญ sǎm kan 13
imported นำเข้า nam kôw 112
impressive น่าประทับใจ nǎr (b)pra táp jai 84
in ใน nai 15
include, to รวม ruam 24, 31, 32
included บวก bùak 20; ruam 31, 32
India อินเดีย jn dear 146
indigestion ท้องผูก tórng pòok 141
Indonesia อินโดนีเซีย in doe nee sear 146

indoor ในร่ม nai rôm 90
inexpensive ไม่แพง mâi pairng 36, 124
infected ติดเชื้อ (d)tìt chéua 140
infection ติดเชื้อ (d)tìt chéua 141
inflammation อักเสบ àk sèyp 142
inflation rate อัตราเงินเฟ้อ a (d)tra ngern fér 131
information ข้อมูล kôr moon 67, 156
injection ฉีดยา chèet yar 142, 143, 144
injured (ได้รับ)บาดเจ็บ (dâi ráp) bàrt jèhp 139
injury บาดเจ็บ bàrt jèhp 139
ink หมึก mèuhk 105
inquiry สอบถาม sòrp tărm 68
insect bite แมลงกัดต่อย ma lairng gàt (d)tòy 139
insect repellent ยากันแมลง yar gan ma lairng 108
insect spray ยาฉีดกันยุง yar chèet gan yung 106
inside ข้างใน kârng nai 15
instead of แทน tairn 37
insurance ประกันภัย (b)pra gan pai 20, 144
insurance company บริษัทประกันภัย bo ri sàt (b)pra gan pai 79
interest (finance) ดอกเบี้ย dòrk bêar 131
interested, to be สนใจ sŏn jai 83, 96
interesting น่าสนใจ năr sŏn jai 84
international ระหว่างประเทศ ra wàrng (b)pra têyt 133, 134
interpreter ล่าม lârm 131
intersection สี่แยก sèe yâirk 77
introduce, to แนะนำ náih nam 92
Introduction (social) การแนะนำตัว garn náih nam (d)tua 92
investment ลงทุน long tun 131
invitation คำเชื้อเชิญ kam chéua cheurn 95
invite, to ชวน chuan 95
invoice ใบเรียกเก็บเงิน bai rêark gèhp ngern 131
iodine ไอโอดีน ai oe deen 108
Ireland ไอร์แลนด์ al lairn 146
Irish ไอริช ai rít 93
iron (for laundry) เตารีด (d)tow rêet 118
iron, to รีด rêet 29
ironmonger's ร้านขายเครื่องเหล็ก rárn kăi krêuang lèhk 99
Israel อิสราเอล ìt sa rar eyn 146
Italy อิตาลี it (d)tar lêe 146

J

jacket เสื้อแจ๊กแก๊ต sêua jáihk gáiht 115
jade หยก yòk 122
jam (preserves) แยม yairm 41
jam, to เปิดไม่ได้ (b)pèrt mâi dâi 28;

laundry (clothes)

เลื่อนไม่ไป lêuan mâi (b)pai 125
January มกราคม mok ga rar kom 150
Japan ญี่ปุ่น yêe (b)pùn 146
jar (container). ขวด kùat 119
jaundice โรคดีซ่าน rôeg dee sărn 142
jaw ขากรรไกร kăr gan grai 138
jazz แจ๊ส jáiht 128
jeans ยีนส์ yeens 115
jersey เสื้อไหมพรม sêua mâi prom 115
jewel box ตู้เครื่องเพชร (d)tôo krêuang péht 121
jeweller's ร้านขายเครื่องประดับ rárn kăi krêuang (b)pra dàp 99, 121
joint ข้อต่อ kôr (d)tòr 138
journey การเดินทาง Jar dern tarng 72
juice (fruit) น้ำ(ผลไม้) nárm (pŏn la mái) 38, 41, 61
July กรกฎาคม ga rák ga (d)tar kom 150
jumper เสื้อไหมพรม sêua mâi prom 115
June มิถุนายน mí tú nar yon 150
just (only) เท่านั้น tôw nán 16

K

keep, to เก็บ gèhp 63
kerosene น้ำมันก๊าด nám man gárt 106
key กุญแจ gun jair 27
kick boxing มวยไทย muay tai 89
kidney ไต (d)tai 138
kilo(gram) กิโล(กรัม) gi loe (gram) 119
kilometre กิโลเมตร gi loe méyt 20, 79
kind ใจดี jai dee 95
kind (type) ประเภท (b)pra pêyt 85, 140
knee เข่า kòw 138
kneesocks ถุงเท้ายาวถึงเข่า tŭng tów yow tŭng kòw 115
knife มีด mêet 37, 62, 120
knock, to เคาะ kóh 156
know, to รู้จัก róo jàk 16, 96, 114

L

label .ป้าย (b)pâi 105
lace ผ้าลูกไม้ păr lôok mái 113
lacquer ware เครื่องเขิน krêuang kěrn 127
lake ทะเลสาบ ta ley sàrp 81, 85, 90
lamb (meat) เนื้อแกะ néua gàih 47
lamp หลอดไฟ lòrt fai 29; ตะเกียง (d)ta gearng 106; โคมไฟ koem fai 118
language ภาษา par săr 104
lantern โคมไฟ koem fai 106
large ใหญ่ yài 20, 101, 130
last ที่แล้ว têe láiw 14, 149, 151; สุดท้าย sút tái 68, 73
late สาย săi 14
laugh, to หัวเราะ hŭa ró 95
launderette ร้านซักผ้า rárn sák păr 99
laundry (clothes) ซักรีด sák rêet 29

laundry *(place)* ร้านซักรีด rárn sák păr 29, 99

laundry service บริการซักรีด bo ri garn sák rêet 24

laxative ยาระบาย yar ra bai 108

lead *(metal)* ตะกั่ว (d)ta gùa 75

lead *(theatre)* (ดารา)นำ (dar rar) nam 87

leap year ปีอธิกสุรทิน (b)pèe ar tí kà sù ra tin 149

leather หนัง năng 113, 117

leave, to ออก(จาก) òrk (jàrk) 31, 69

leave, to *(deposit)* ฝาก fàrk 26; *(leave behind)* ทิ้ง tíng 29

left ซาย sái 21, 69, 77

left-luggage office ตรวจกระเป๋า (d)trùat gra (b)pŏw 68, 71

leg ขา kăr 138

lemon มะนาว ma now 37, 41, 56, 61

lemonade เล็มมะเนด lehm ma nèyd 61

lens *(camera)* เลนส์ leyns 125

lens *(glasses)* เลนส์ leyns 123

lentils ถั่วแขก tùa kàirk 53

less น้อยกว่า nóy gwàr 14

let, to *(hire out)* ให้เช่า hăi chôw 156

letter จดหมาย jòt măi 132

letter box ตู้จดหมาย (d)tôo jòt măi 132

letter of credit แอลซี airl see 130

lettuce ผักสลัด pàk sa làt 53

library หองสมุด hŏrng sa mùt 81, 99

licence *(driving)* ใบขับขี่ bai kàp kèe 20, 79

lie down, to นอนราบ norn rârp 142

life belt เข็มขัดนิรภัย kĕhm kàt ni rá pai 74

life boat เรือชูชีพ reua choo chêep 74

life belt เข็มขัดนิรภัย kĕhm kàt ni rá pai 74

life boat เรือชูชีพ reua choo chêep 74

life guard *(beach)* ยาม yarm 91

lift *(elevator)* ลิฟท์ líft 27, 100

light *(weight)* เบา bow 14, 101

light ไฟฟ้า fai fár 28; แสง săirng 124

light *(colour)* ออน òrn 101, 111, 112

light *(for cigarette)* ไฟ fai 95

light meter เครื่องวัดแสง krêuang wát săirng 125

lighter ไฟแช็ก fai chéhk 126

lightning ฟ้าแลบ fár lâirp 94

like เหมือนกับ mĕuan gàp 111

like, to อยาก(ได้) yàrk (dâi) 96, 103, 112

like, to *(please)* ชอบ chôrp 25, 93, 102

linen *(cloth)* ลินิน li nin 113

lip ริมฝีปาก rim fĕe (b)pàrk 138

lipsalve ขี้ผึ้งทาปาก kêe pêuhng tar (b)pàrk 109

lipstick ลิปสติก líp sa (d)tìk 109

liqueur เหล้าชนิดหวาน lôw cha nít wărn 60

litre ลิตร lít 75, 119

little *(a little)* น้อย nóy 14

liver ตับ (d)tàp 138

lobster ลอบสเตอร์ lób sa (d)têr 45

local พื้นบ้าน péurn bârn 37

long ยาว yow 115

long-sighted สายตายาว sǎi (d)tar yow 123

look for, to หา hăr 13

look out! ระวัง ra wang 157

look, to ดู doo 100, 123, 139

loose *(clothes)* หลวม lŭam 114

lose, to หาย hăi 123, 157

loss ขาดทุน kàrt tun 131

lost หลงทาง lŏng tarng 13

lost and found office/lost property office ฝ่ายจัดการเรื่องของหาย fǎi jàk ra yarn rêuang kŏrng hăi 157

lot *(a lot)* มาก mârk 14

lotion โลชั่น loe chăn 110

loud *(voice)* ดัง dang 135

love, to อยาก(ไป) yàrk 95

low ต่ำ (d)tàm 141

low season นอกฤดูทองเที่ยว nôrk ri doo tôrng têaw 150

low tide น้ำลง nárm long 90

lower ชั้นล่าง chán lârng 70, 71

luck โชค chôek 153

luggage กระเป๋า gra (b)pŏw 18, 26, 31, 71

luggage locker ตู้เก็บของ (d)tôo gèhp kŏrng 68, 71

luggage trolley รถเข็นกระเป๋า rót kĕhn gra (b)pŏw 18, 71

luggage/baggage กระเป๋า gra (b)pŏw 18, 26, 31, 71

lump *(bump)* บวม, โน buam, noe 139

lunch อาหารเที่ยง/กลางวัน ar hărn glarng wan 35, 80, 95

lung ปอด (b)pòrt 138

lychee ลิ้นจี่ lín jèe 56

M

machine *(washable)* (ซัก)เครื่อง(ได้) (sák) krêuang (dûay) 113

mackerel ปลาทู (b)plar too 45

magazine วารสาร wa ra sărn 105

magnificent งดงามมาก ngót ngarm mârk 84

maid พนักงานดูแลห้องพัก sŏw chái 26

mail จดหมาย jòt măi 28, 133

mail, to *(post)* ส่ง(จดหมาย) sòng (jòt măi) 28

mailbox ตู้จดหมาย (d)tôo jòt măi 132

main สำคัญ săm kan 100

make, to *(photocopies)* ถาย(เอกสาร) tài (èyk ga sărn) 131

make-up เครื่องสำอางค์ krêuang să marng 109

make-up remover pad แผ่นเช็ดเครื่องสำอางค์ pǎihn chéhk

krêuang sǎm arng 109
mallet ฆ้อนไม้ kórn mái 106
manager ผู้จัดการ pôo jàt garn 26
mango มะม่วง ma mûang 56
manicure แต่งเล็บ (d)tàirng léhp 30
many หลาย lǎi 14
map แผนที่ pǎirn tée 77, 105
March มีนาคม mee nar kom 150
market ตลาด (d)ta làrt 81, 99
marmalade แยมเปลือกส้ม yairm (b)plèuak sôm 41
married แต่งงาน (d)tàihng ngarn 94
masked drama โขน kǒen 87
mass *(church)* คนชั่วไป kon tûa (b)pai 84
mat/matt *(finish)* ด้าน dârn 125
match *(matchstick)* ไม้แขงขืน nát kàirng kán 106; ไม้ขีด mái kèet 126
match, to *(colour)* เขากับ... kôw gàp 111
matinée รอบกลางวัน rôrp glarng wan 87
mattress ที่นอน têe norn 106
May พฤษภาคม prút sa pǎr kom 150
may *(can)* ขอ kǒr 12
meadow ทุ่งหญ้า tûng yâr 85
meal อาหาร ar hǎrn 24, 35, 142
mean, to มีความหมายว่า mee kwarm mǎi wâr 11, 26
means วิธี wi tee 75
measles โรคหัด rôek hàt 142
measure, to วัดตัว wát (d)tua 113
meat เนื้อ néua 38, 47, 48, 62
meatball ลูกชิ้น lôok chín 47
mechanic ช่าง chârng 78
mechanical pencil ดินสอกด din sǒr gòt 105, 121
medical certificate ใบรับรองแพทย์ bai ráp rorng pǎirt 144
medicine เวชกรรม, การแพทย์ wêyt cha gam, garn pǎirt 83
medicine *(drug)* ยา yar 143
medium *(meat)* สุกปานกลาง sùk (b)parn glarng 47
medium-sized ขนาดกลาง ka nàrt glarng 20
melon แตงไทย (d)tairng tai 56
memorial อนุสรณ์สถาน ar nú sǒrn sa tǎrn 81
mend, to ปะ(ยาง) (b)pà (yarng) 76
mend, to *(clothes)* ซ่อม sôrm 29
menthol *(cigarettes)* รสเมนทอล rót meyn torl 126
menu รายการอาหาร rai garn ar hǎrn 37, 39, 40
merry สุขสันต์ sùk sǎn 153
mesh screen มุ้งลวด múng lûat 28
message ข้อความ kôr kwarm 28, 136
metre เมตร mèyt 111
mezzanine *(theatre)* ชั้นลอย chán loy 87, 88

middle ตรงกลาง (d)trong glarng 69, 150
midnight เที่ยงคืน têarng keurn 154
mild *(light)* รสอ่อน rót òrn 126
mileage ระยะทาง rá yá tarng 20
milk นม nom 41, 61, 64
milkshake มิลค์เชค milk chéyk 61
million ล้าน lárn 148
mineral water น้ำแร่ nárm rǎir 61
minister *(religion)* พระ pÁra 84
mint สะระแหน่ sà rá nàir 55
minute นาที nar tee 21, 69, 154
mirror กระจก gra jòk 114, 123
miscellaneous เบ็ดเตล็ด bèht (d)talèht 127
miss, to หาย hǎi 18, 30
mistake ผิดพลาด pìt plârt 62, 63
moisturizing cream ครีมบำรุงผิว kreem bam rung pǐw 109
moment สักครู่ sák krôo 12, 136
monastery วัด wát 81
Monday วันจันทร์ wan jan 151
money เงิน ngern 18, 130
money order ธนาณัติ ta nar nát 133
monsoon มรสุม mora sǔm 94
month เดือน deuan 16, 150
monument อนุสาวรีย์ ar nú sǒw a ree 81
more มากกว่า mârk gwàr 14
morning, in the ในตอนเช้า nai (d)torn chów 143, 153; เวลาเช้า wey lar chów 151
mortgage จำนอง jam norng 131
mosquito net มุ้ง múng 106
motel โรงแรม roen grairm 22
mother แม่ mǎir 93
motorbike จักรยานยนต์ jàk ra yarn 74
motorboat เรือยนต์ reua yon 91
motorway ทางด่วน tarng dùan 76
mountain ภูเขา poo kǒw 85
mountaineering ปีนเขา (b)peen kǒw 90
moustache หนวด nùat 31
mouth ปาก (b)pàrk 138, 142
mouthwash น้ำยาล้างปาก nárm yar lárng (b)pàrk 108
move, to ขยับ ka yàp 139
movie หนัง nǎng 86
movie camera กล้องถ่ายหนัง glông tài nǎng 124
movies หนัง nǎng 86
much มาก mârk 14
mug เหยือก yèuak 120
muscle กล้าม glârm 138
museum พิพิธภัณฑ์ pi pít ta pan 81
mushroom เห็ด hèht 53
music ดนตรี don (d)tree 83, 128
musical เพลง pleyng 87
mussel หอยแมงภู่ hǒy mairng pôo 45
must *(have to)* ต้อง (d)tôrng 38, 95, 142
mustard มัสตาร์ด mát sa tàrt 55, 64

myself ผม(ดิฉัน)เอง pŏm (di chán) eyng 119

N

nail *(human)* เล็บ léhp 109
nail brush แปรงขัดเล็บ (b)prairng kàt léhp 109
nail clippers กรรไกรขลิบเล็บ gan grai klíp léhp 109
nail file ตะไบขัดเล็บ (d)tà bai kàt léhp 109
nail polish ยาทาเล็บ yar tar léhp 109
nail polish remover น้ำยาลางเล็บ nám yar lárng léhp 109
nail scissors กรรไกรตัดเล็บ gan grai (d)tàt léhp 109
name ชื่อ chêur 23, 25, 79, 92, 131
name *(surname)* นามสกุล narm 25
napkin กระดาษเช็ดปาก gra dàrt chét (b)pàak 37, 105
nappy ผ้าอ้อม pâr ôrm 110
narrow แคบ kâirp 117
nationality สัญชาติ sǎn chârt 25, 93
natural ธรรมชาติ tam ma hârt 83
natural history ธรรมชาติวิทยา tam ma hârt wít ta yar 83
nauseous คลื่นไส้ klêuhn sâi 140
near ใกล้ glâi 14, 15
near(by) ใกล้ๆแถวนี้ glâi glâi tǎew née 32, 78
nearest ใกล้ที่สุด glâi têe sùt 75, 78, 98
neat *(drink)* เพียว peaw 60
neck คอ kor 30, 138
necklace สรอยคอ sôy kor 121
need, to ตองการ (d)tôrng garn 90
needle เข็ม kěhm 27
negative ฟิลมลางแลว feem lárng láiw 124
nephew หลานชาย lǎrn chay 93
nerve เสนประสาท sêhn (b)pra sàrt 138
Netherlands เนเธอรแลนด ney ter lairn 146
never ไมเคย mâi koei 15
new ใหม mài 14
New Year ปใหม (b)pee mài 152
New Zealand นิวซีแลนด niw see lairn 146
newspaper หนังสือพิมพ náng sěur pim 104, 105
newsstand แผงขายหนังสือพิมพ pǎirng kǎi náng sěur pim 19, 67, 99, 104
next หนา nâr 14, 76, 149, 151; ตอไป (d)tòr (b)pai 65, 68, 73
next time คราวหนา krow nâr 95
next to ติดกับ (d)tìt gàp 15, 77
nice *(beautiful)* ดี dee 94
niece หลานสาว lǎrn sǒw 93
niello ware เครื่องถม krêuang tŏm 127

night กลางคืน glarng keurn 151
night, at เวลากลางคืน wey lar glarng keurn 151
night cream ครีมบำรุงผิวตอนกลางคืน kreem bam rung pǐw (d)torn glarng keurn 109
nightclub ไนทคลับ nai klàp 88
nightdress/-gown ชุดนอน chút norn 115
nine เกา gôw 147
nineteen สิบเกา sìp gôw 147
ninety เกาสิบ gôw sìp 148
ninth ที่เกา têe gôw 149
no ไม mâi 10
noisy เสียงดัง sěarng dang 25
non-smoking หามสูบบุหรี่ hârm sòop bu rèe 36, 70
nonalcoholic ไมมีอัลกอฮอล mâi mee alkorhorl 61
none ไมเลย mâi loei 15
noodle กวยเตี๋ยว gúay tǎew 50
noon เที่ยง têarng 31, 154
normal ธรรมดา tam ma dar 30
north เหนือ něua 77
North America อเมริกาเหนือ a mey ri gar něua 146
Norway นอรเวย nor wey 146
nose จมูก ja mòok 138
nose drops ยาหยอดจมูก yar yòrt ja mòok 108
nosebleed เลือดกำเดาไหล lêuat gam dow lǎi 141
not ไม mâi 15
note paper กระดาษจดบันทึก gra dàrt jòt ban téuhk 105
notebook สมุดโนต sa mùt nóht 105
nothing ไมมีอะไร mâi mee arai 15, 17
notice *(sign)* ปาย sǎn yarn 156
notify, to แจง jâirng 144
November พฤศจิกายน prút sa jìk gar yon 150
now ตอนนี้ (d)torn née 15
number หมายเลข mǎi lêyg 26, 135, 136, 147
nurse พยาบาล pa ya barn 144
nutmeg ลูกจันทร lôok jan 55

O

o'clock โมง moeng 154
occupation *(profession)* อาชีพ archêep 25
occupied ไมวาง mâi wârng 14, 156
October ตุลาคม (d)tù lar kom 150
office ที่(ทำการ) têe (tam garn) 19, 67, 80, 99, 132
oil น้ำมัน nám man 37, 75, 110
oily *(greasy)* มัน man 30, 111
old เกา gòw 14

old town เมืองเก่า meuang gòw 81
on บน bon 15
on foot เดินไป dern (b)pai 77
on time ตรงเวลา (d)trong wey lar 68
once ครั้งหนึ่ง kráng nèuhng 149
one หนึ่ง nèuhng 147
one-way *(traffic)* วันเวย wan wey 77
one-way ticket เที่ยวเดียว têaw deaw 65, 69
onion หอมหัวใหญ่ hŏrm hŭa yài 53
only เทานั้น tôw nán 15, 88
onyx หินจำพวกโมรา hĭn jam pûak moe rar 122
open เปิด (b)pèrt 14, 156
open, to เปิด (b)pèrt 11, 18, 82, 107, 130, 132, 142
open-air กลางแจ้ง glarng jâirng 90
opera อุปรากร ù (b)pa rar gorn 88
operation ผาตัด pàr (d)tàt 144
operator โอเปอเรเตอร์ oe (b)per rey (d)ter 134
operetta ละครร้องขนาดสั้น la korn rórng ka nàrt sân,88
opposite ตรงข้าม, (d)trong kǎrm 77
optician ร้านตัดแว่น rárn (d)tàt wǎihn 99, 123
or หรือ rěua 15
orange ส้ม sôm 56, 64
orange *(colour)* (สี)ส้ม sěe sôm 112
orange juice น้ำส้ม nárm sôm 41, 61
orchestra ออเคสตรา or,key sa trâr 88
orchestra *(seats)* ที่นั่งชั้นหน้าเวที têe nâng chán dée wey tee 87
order, to *(goods, meal)* สั่ง sàng 62, 102, 103
ornithology ปักษีวิทยา (b)pàk sěe wít ta yar 83
other อื่นๆ èurn èurn 75, 101
out of order เสีย sěar 156
out of stock ไม่มีของเหลือ mǎi mee kŏrng lĕua 103
outlet *(electric)* ปลั๊ก(ไฟฟ้า) (b)plàk (fai fár) 27,
outside ทางนอก tarng nôrk 15; ด้านนอก dârn nôrk 36
oval รูปไข่ rôop kài 101
overdone *(meat)* สุกเกินไป sùk gern (b)pai 62
overheat, to *(engine)* ร้อนเกินไป rórn gern (b)pai 78
oyster หอยนางรม hŏy nang rom 45

P
pacifier *(baby's)* จุกนม jùk nom 110
packet ซอง sorng 126
pail ถัง tǎng 120, 128
pain เจ็บ jèhp 140, 144; ปวด (b)pùat

painkiller ยาแก้ปวด yar gǎir (b)pùat 140
paint สี sěe 156
paint, to วาด wârt 83
paintbox กล่องสี glôrng sěe 105
painter จิตรกร jìt ra gorn 83
painting จิตรกรรม jìt ra gam 83
pair คู่ kôo 115, 117, 149
pajamas เสื้อกางเกงนอน sêua garng geyng norn 116
palace วัง wang 81
palpitations ใจสั่น jai sàn 141
panties กางเกงใน garng geyng rát rôop 116
pants *(trousers)* กางเกงขายาว garng geyng kǎr yow 116
panty girdle ถุงนอง tǔng nông 116
panty hose ถุงนอง tǔng nông 116
paper กระดาษ gra dàrt 105
paper napkin กระดาษเช็ดปาก gra dàrt chéhk (b)pàrk 105 , 120
paperback หนังสือปกอ่อน náng sěur (b)pòk òrn 105
paperclip ที่หนีบกระดาษ gíp nèep gra dàrt 105
paraffin *(fuel)* น้ำมันก๊าด nám man ụárt 106
parcel พัสดุ pát sa du 132, 133
pardon, I beg your อะไรนะ arai ná 10
parents พ่อแม่ pôr mâir 93
park สวนสาธารณะ sŭan sǎr tar ra ná 81
park, to จอดรถ jòrt rót 26, 78
parking การจอดรถ garn jòrt rót 77, 78
parliament building ตึกรัฐสภา (d)tèuhk rát ta sa par.81
parsley ผักชีฝรั่ง pàk chee far àng 55
part ส่วน sùan 138
partridge นกกระทา nók gra tar.49
party *(social gathering)* งานปาร์ตี้ ngarn (b)pàr (d)têe 95
pass *(mountain)* ช่องเขา chông kǒw 85
pass through, to แวะผ่าน wáih pàrn 16
pass, to *(driving)* (ขับ)ผ่าน (kàp) pàrn 79
passport พาสปอร์ต pàrs (b)pòrt 16, 17, 25, 26; หนังสือเดินทาง náng sěur dern tarng 156
passport photo รูปติดพาสปอร์ต rôop (d)tìt pà sa (b)pòrt 124
paste *(glue)* แป้งเปียก (b)pâirng (b)pèark 105
pastry shop ร้านขายขนม rárn kǎi ka nŏm 99
patch, to *(clothes)* ปะ (b)pà 29
path ทางเดิน tarng dern 85
patient คนไข้ kon kâi 144
patterned ลวดลาย lùat lai 112
pay, to จ่าย jài 18, 31, 102, 136
payment จ่าย jài 131

พจนานุกรม

peach ลูกท้อ lôok tór 56
peak ยอดเขา yôrt kôw 85
peanut ถั่วลิสง tùa li song 56
pear ลูกแพร lôok pair 56
pearl ไข่มุก kài múk,122
peg (tent) หมุด(ปักเตนท์) mùt ((b)pàk têyn) 106
pen ปากกา (b)pàrk gar 105
pencil ดินสอ din sŏr 105
pencil sharpener ที่เหลาดินสอ têe lŏw din sŏr 105
pendant จี้ jêe 121
penicillin เพนนิซิลิน peyn ni si lin 143
penknife มีดพับ mêet páp 120
pensioner ผู้ที่รับเงินบำนาญ pôo têe ráp ngern bam narn 82
pepper พริกไทย prík tai 37, 41, 55, 64
per cent เปอร์เซนต์ (b)per sehn 149
per day ต่อวัน (d)tòr wan 20, 32, 90
per hour ต่อชั่วโมง (d)tòr chûa moeng 78, 89
per person ต่อคน .(d)tòr kon 32
per week ต่ออาทิตย์ (d)tòr ar tít 20, 24
percentage เปอร์เซนต์ (b)per sehn 131
perfume น้ำหอม nárm hŏrm 109
perhaps บางที barng tee 15
period (monthly) ประจำเดือน (b)pra jam deuan 141
period pains ปวดประจำเดือน (b)pùat (b)pra jam deuan 141
permanent wave ดัดถาวร dàt tăr worn 30
permit อนุญาต an nú yârt 90
person คน kon 32
personal ส่วนตัว sùan (d)tua 17
personal call/person-to-person call โทรส่วนตัว toe sùan (d)tua 135
personal cheque เช็คส่วนตัว chéhk sùan (d)tua 130
petrol เบนซิน beynsin 75; น้ำมัน nám man 78
pewter พิวเตอร์ piw (d)ter 122
Philippines ฟิลิปปินส์ fi li peen 146
photo รูป rôop 124, 125
photocopy ถ่ายเอกสาร tài èyk ga sărn 131
photographer ร้านถ่ายรูป rárn tài rôop 99
photography การถ่ายรูป garn tài rôop 124
phrase วลี wa lee 12
pick up, to (person) รับ ráp 80
picnic ปิ๊คนิค (b)pík,nik 64
picnic basket ตะกร้าปิ๊คนิค (d)ta grăr (b)pík ník 106
picture (painting) วาดภาพ wârt părp 83
picture (photo) รูป rôop 82
piece ชิ้น chín 18, 119
pig หมู mŏo 47
pigeon นกพิราบ nók pí rârp 49

pill ยาคุม yar kum 141
pillow หมอน mŏrn 27
pin เข็ม(กลัด) kĕhm (glàt) 107, 121; กิ๊บ gíp 110
pineapple สับปะรด sàp (b)pa rót 56
pink สีชมพู sĕe chom poo 112
pipe ไปป์ (b)pái 126
pipe cleaner ที่ทำความสะอาดไปป์ têe tam kwarm sa àrt (b)pái 126
pipe tobacco ยาเส้นสำหรับไปป์ yar sêhn săm ràp (b)pái 126
place สถานที่ sa tărn têe 25
place of birth สถานที่เกิด sa tărn têe gért 25
plain (colour) สีเรียบ sĕe rêarp 112
plane เครื่องบิน krêuang bin 65
planetarium ท้องฟ้าจำลอง tórng fár jam lorng 81
plaster เฝือก fèuak 140
plastic พลาสติก plar sa (d)tìk 120
plastic bag ถุงพลาสติก tŭng plar sa (d)tìk 120
plate จาน jarn 37, 62, 120
platform (station) ชานชาลา charn cha lar 67, 68, 69, 70
platinum แพลตตินัม plàirt (d)ti năm 122
play (theatre) เล่น(ละคร) (b)pêhn (la korn) 86
play, to เล่น lêhn 87, 88, 94; แข่ง kàihng 89
playground สนามวิ่งเล่น sa nărm wîng lêhn 32
playing card ไพ่ păi 105, 128
please กรุณา ga rú na 10
plimsolls รองเท้าผ้าใบ rorng tów păr bai 117
plug (electric) ปลั๊กไฟ (b)plàk fai 29, 118
plum ลูกพลัม lôok plam 56
pneumonia ปอดบวม (b)pòrt buam 142
pocket กระเป๋า gra (b)pŏw 116
pocket watch นาฬิกาพก na lí gar pók 121
point of interest (sight) สถานที่น่าสนใจ sa tărn têe têe năr sŏn jai 80
point, to ชี้ chée 12
poison ยาพิษ yar pít 109, 157
poisoning (อาหาร)เป็นพิษ (ar hărn) (b)pehn pít 142
pole (tent) เสา(เตนท์) sŏw ((d)têhn) 106
police ตำรวจ (d)tam rùat 79, 156, 157
police station สถานีตำรวจ sa tărn têe (d)tam rùat 99, 156, 157
pond บ่อน้ำ bòr nárm 85
poplin ผ้าแพรป๊อปลิน păr prair (b)pŏhp lin 113
pork เนื้อหมู néua mŏo 47
port ท่าเรือ tăr reua 74
portable กระเป๋าหิ้ว gar (b)pŏw hîw 118

porter คนยกกระเป๋า kon yók gra (b)pŏw 18, 26, 71
portion ที่ têe 38, 57, 62
Portugal โปรตุเกส (b)pòer (d)tu gèyt 146
post *(mail)* จดหมาย jòt măi 28, 133
post office ที่ทำการไปรษณีย์ têe tam garn (b)prai.sa nee 99, 132
post, to ส่ง(จดหมาย) sòng (jòt măi) 28
postage ค่าแสตมป์ kâr.sa 132
postage stamp แสตมป์ sa (d)tairm 28, 126, 132, 133
postcard ไปรษณียบัตร (b)pòe sa gàrt 105, 126, 132
poste restante ส่งทั่วไป sòng tûa (b)pai 133
pottery เครื่องปั้นดินเผา kr̂euang (b)pân din pŏw 83
poultry เป็ดไก่ (b)pèht gài 49
pound *(เงิน)*ปอนด์ (ngern) (b)porn 19, 102, 129
powder แป้ง (b)pâirng 109
powder compact ตลับแป้ง (d)ta làp (b)pâirng 121
powder puff แป้งพลัฟ (b)pâirng pláp 109
prawn กุ้ง gûng 45
pregnant ตั้งท้อง (d)tâng tórpg 141
premium *(gasoline)* ซุปเปอร์(เบนซิน) súp per (beynsin) 75
prescribe, to สั่ง(ยา) sàng (yar) 143
prescription ใบสั่งยา bai sàng yar 108, 143
press stud แป๊ะติดเสื้อ (b)páih (d)tit sêua 116
pressure ลม(ยางรถ) lom (yarng rót) 76; ความดัน kwarm dan 141
pretty น่ารักดี nâr rák dee 84
price ราคา rar kar 24
private ส่วนตัว sùan (d)tua 24, 81, 91, 156
process, to *(film)* ล้าง(รูป) lárng (rôop) 125
processing *(photo)* การล้างรูป garn lárng rôop 125
profession อาชีพ ar chêep 25
profit กำไร gam rai 131
programme สูจิบัตร sôo ji bàt 87
pronounce, to ออกเสียง òrk sĕarng 12
pronunciation การออกเสียง garn òrk sĕarng 6
propelling pencil ดินสอกด din sŏr gòt 105, 121
Protestant โปรเตสแตนท์ (b)proe tairt sa tairn 84
provide, to จัดหา jàt hăr 131
prune ลูกพรุน lôok prun 56
pub ผับ pàp 34
public holiday วันหยุดประจำปี wan yùt (b)pra jam (b)pee 152

pull, to ดึง deuhng 156
pull, to *(tooth)* ถอน tŏrn 145
pullover เสื้อไหมพรม sêua măi prom 115
pump ที่สูบลม têe sòop lom 106
puncture ยางรั่ว yarng rûa 76
purchase ซื้อ séur 131
pure แท้ táir 113
purple สีม่วง sĕe mûang 112
push, to ผลัก plàk 156
put, to ใส่ sài 24
pyjamas เสื้อกางเกงนอน sêua garng geyng norn 116

Q

quality คุณภาพ kun la pârp 103, 112, 113
quantity ปริมาณ (b)pa rị marn 14, 103
quarter of an hour สิบห้านาที sìp hâr nar tee 155
quartz ควอทซ์ kwòrt 122
question คำถาม kam tǎrm 11
quick(ly) เร็ว rehw 14, 79
quiet เงียบ ngêarp 23, 25

R

race แข่ง kàihng 90
race course/track ลู่วิ่ง lôo wîng 90
racket *(sport)* ไม้แร็กเก็ต mái ráihk gèht 90
radio วิทยุ wít ta yú 24, 28, 118
raft แพ pair 23
railway station สถานีรถไฟ sa tǎr nee rót fai 19, 21, 67
rain ฝน fŏn 94
rain, to ฝนตก fŏn (d)tòk 94
raincoat เสื้อกันฝน sêua gan fŏn 116
raisin ลูกเกด lôok gèyt 56
rangefinder เครื่องวัดระยะ krêuang wát ra yá 125
rare *(meat)* ไม่ค่อยสุก măi ow sùk 48
rash เป็นผื่นคัน (b)pehn pĕurn kan 139
rate *(inflation)* อัตรา(เงินเฟ้อ) a (d)tra (ngern fér) 131
rate *(price)* ราคา rar kar 20
rate *(of exchange)* อัตรา(แลกเปลี่ยน) a (d)tra (lâirk (b)plèarn) 19
razor มีดโกน mêet goen 109
razor blades ใบมีดโกน bai mêet goen 109
read, to อ่าน àrn 40
reading lamp โคมไฟหัวเตียง koem fai hŭa (d)teang 27
ready เสร็จ sèht 29, 117, 123, 125, 145
real *(genuine)* แท้ táir 117
rear ท้าย tái 69; หลัง lǎng 75
receipt ใบเสร็จรับเงิน bai sèht ráp ngern 103, 144
reception แผนกต้อนรับ pa nàirk (d)tôrn ráp 23

DICTIONARY

พจนานุกรม

receptionist พนักงานต้อนรับ pa nák ngarn (d)tôrn ráp 26

recommend, to แนะนำ náih nam 80, 86, 88, 137, 145

record (disc) แผ่นเสียง pàihn sĕarng 128, 129

record player เครื่องเล่นเทป krêuang lêhn téyp 118

recorder เครื่องอัดเทป krêuang àt téyp 118

rectangular สี่เหลี่ยมผืนผ้า sèe lèarm pĕurn pâr 101

red สีแดง sĕe daîrng 105, 112

red (wine) (ไวน์)แดง (wai) daîrng 59, 60

reduction ส่วนลด sùan lót 24

refill (pen) หมึก mèuhk 105

refund (to get a) ขอเงินคืน kŏr ngern keurn 103

regards คิดถึง, เคารพ kit tĕuhng, kow róp 153

register, to (luggage) ฝาก(กระเป๋า) fàrk (gra (b)pŏw) 71

registered mail จดหมายลงทะเบียน jòt măi long ta bearn 133

registration ลงทะเบียน long tabearn 25

registration form แบบฟอร์มลงทะเบียน bàirp form long ta bearn 25, 26

regular (petrol) ธรรมดา tam ma dar 75

religion ศาสนา sàrt sa nàr 83

religious service สวดมนต์ sùat mon 84

rent, to เช่า chôw 19, 20, 90, 91

rental เช่า chôw 20

repair ซ่อม sórm 125

repair, to ซ่อม sórm 29, 117, 118, 121, 123, 125, 145

repeat, to พูดอีกที pôot èek tee 12

report, to (a theft) แจ้งความ jâirng kwarm 157

required ต้อง (d)tôrng 89

requirement ความต้องการ kwarm (d)tôrng garn 27

reservation การจอง garn jorng 19, 23, 66, 69

reservations office แผนกสำรองที่นั่งล่วงหน้า pa nàirk săm rorng têe năng lûang năr 67

reserve, to จอง jorng 19, 23, 36, 87

reserved จอง jorng 156

rest ที่เหลือ têe lĕua 130

restaurant ร้านอาหาร rárn ar hărn 32, 34, 68; ภัตตาคาร, ภัต (d)ta karn 36

return ticket ตั๋วไปกลับ tŭa (b)pai glàp 65, 69

return, to (come back) กลับ glàp 80

return, to (give back) คืน keurn 103

rheumatism โรคปวดตามข้อ rôeg (b)pùat nai kôr 141

rib ซี่โครง sèe kroeng 138

ribbon ผ้าเทป pàr téyp 105

rice ข้าว kôw 50

right (correct) ถูก (t)òok 14

right (direction) ขวา kwar 21, 69, 77

ring (jewellery) แหวน wăirn 122

ring, to (doorbell) กดกระดิ่ง gòt gra dìng 156

river แม่น้ำ mâir nárm 85, 90

river cruise ลองแม่น้ำ lông mâir nárm 74

road ถนน ta nŏn 76, 77, 85

road assistance ความช่วยเหลือบนถนน kwarm chûay lĕua bon tanŏn 78

road map แผนที่ถนน păirn têe ta nŏn 105

road sign ป้ายจราจร (b)păi ja rar jorn 79

roasted อบ,ย àp 47

roll ขนมปังกอน ka nŏm (b)pang gôn 41, 64

roll film ฟิล์มม้วน feem múan 124

roller skate สเก็ต da gèht 128

room ห้อง hôrng 19, 23, 24, 25, 27, 29

room number หมายเลขห้อง măi lêyg hôrng 26

room service บริการรูมเซอร์วิส bo ri garn room ser wít 24

rope เชือก chêuak 106

rosary ลูกประคำ lôok (b)pra kam 122

rouge รูจ rôot 109

round กลม glom 101

round (golf) ยอบ rôrp 90

round up, to รวมทั้งหมด ruam táng mòt 63

round-neck คอกลม kor glom 116

round-trip ticket ตั๋วไปกลับ tŭa (b)pai glàp 65, 69

rowing boat เรือพาย reua pai 91

royal พระราช pra rârt 81

rubber (eraser) ยางลบ yarng lóp 105

rubber (material) ยาง yarng 117

ruby ทับทิม, táp tim 122

rucksack เป้หลัง (b)pêy lăng 106

ruin โบราณสถาน boe raṇ sa tărn 81

ruler (for measuring) ไม้บรรทัด mái ban tát 105

rum เหล้ารัม lôw ram 60

running water น้ำประปา nárm (b)pra (b)par 24

Russia รัสเซีย rát sear 146

S

safe ตู้เซฟ (d)tôo séyf 26

safe (free from danger) ปลอดภัย (b)plòrt pai 91

safety pin เข็มกลัด kĕhm glàt 109

saffron หญ้าฝรั่น yàr fa ràn 55

sailing boat เรือใบ reua bai 91

sale ขาย kăi 131

sale (bargains) ลดราคา lót rarkar 100

salt เกลือ gleua 37, 41, 64
salty เค็ม kehm 62
same แบบเดียวกัน bàirp deaw gan 117
sand ทราย sai 90
sandal รองเท้าแตะ rorng tów (d)tàih 117
sandwich แซนด์วิช saipn wít 64
sanitary napkin/towel ผ้าอนามัย păr a nar mai 108
sapphire ไพลิน, บุษราคัม pai lin, bùt rar kam 122
satin ผ้าซาติน păr sar(d)tin 113
Saturday วันเสาร์ wan sŏw 151
sauce ซอส, น้ำจิ้ม sórt, nárm jîm 52
saucepan หม้อ ,môr 120
saucer จานรองถ้วย jarn rorng tûay 120
sausage ไส้กรอก sâi gròrk 47, 64
scalded ลวก lûak 46
scalded eggs ไข่ลวก kài lûak 41
scarf ผ้าพันคอ păr pan kor 116
scarlet สีแดงเข้ม sĕe lĕuat mŏo 112
scissors กรรไกร, gang rai 109, 120
scooter สกูตเตอร์ sa góot têr 75
Scotland สก็อตแลนด์ sa gót lairn 146
scrambled eggs ไข่คน kài kon 41
screwdriver ไขควง kăi duang 120
sculptor ประติมากร (b)pra (d)tì mar gorn 83
sculpture ประติมากรรม (b)pra (d)tì mar gam 83
sea ทะเล ta ley 85, 91
seafood อาหารทะเล ar hărn ta ley 45
season ฤดู, ฤกาล rí doo, năr 150
seasoning เครื่องปรุง krêuang (b)prung 37
seat ที่นั่ง têe nâng 65, 70, 87
second ที่สอง têe sŏrng 149; วินาที wi nar tee 155
second class ชั้นสอง chán sŏrng 69
second hand (on watch) มือสอง meur sŏrng 122
secretary เลขานุการ ley kă rnú garn 27, 131
section แผนก pa nàirk 104
see, to ดู doo 25, 26, 89, 121
sell, to ขาย kăi 100
send, to ส่ง sòng 78, 102, 103, 132, 133
sentence ประโยค (b)pra yòek 12
separately แยกกัน yâirk gan 63
September กันยายน kan yar yon 150
seriously รุนแรง rái rairng 139
service บริการ bo rí garn 24, 63, 98, 100
service (church) สวดมนต์ sùat mon 84
serviette กระดาษเช็ดปาก gra dàrt chét (b)pàak 37
set (hair) เซ็ท séht 30
set menu อาหารชุด ar hărn chút 37
setting lotion น้ำยาเซ็ทผม náim yar séht pom 30; โลชั่นสำหรับเซ็ทผม loe chăn săm ràp séht pŏm 111

seven เจ็ด jèht 147
seventeen สิบเจ็ด sìp jèht 147
seventh ที่เจ็ด têe jèht 149
seventy เจ็ดสิบ jèht sìp 148
sew, to เย็บ yéhp 29
shade (colour) สี sĕe 111
shampoo แชมพู chairm poo 30, 111
shampoo and set สระเซ็ท sà séht 30
shape รูปร่าง rôop rârng 103
share (finance) หุ้น hûn 131
sharp (pain) แปลบ (b)plàirp 140
shave โกนหนวด goen nùat 31
shaver เครื่องโกนหนวดไฟฟ้า krêuang goen nùat fai fár 27, 118
shaving brush แปรงสำหรับโกนหนวด (b)prairng săm ràp goen nùat 109
shaving cream ครีมสำหรับโกนหนวด kreem săm ràp goen nùat 109
shelf ชั้น chán 119
ship เรือกำปั่น, เรือทะเล reua gam (b)pàn, reua ta ley 74
shirt เสื้อเชิร์ต ,sêua chért 116
shivery หนาวสั่น nŏw sàn 140
shoe รองเท้า rorng tów 117
shoe polish ยาขัดรองเท้า yarng kàt rorng tów 117
shoe shop ร้านขายรองเท้า rárn kăi rorng tów 99
shoelace เชือกผูกรองเท้า chêuak pòok rorng tów 1.17
shoemaker's ร้านซ่อมรองเท้า rárn sôrm rorng tów 99
shop ร้านค้า rárn kár 98
shop window ตู้โชว์ (d)tôo choe 101, 112
shopping ช็อปปิ้ง chóp (b)ping 97
shopping area ย่านช็อปปิ้ง yârn chóp (b)ping 82; ย่านการค้า yârn garn kár 100
shopping centre ศูนย์การค้า sŏon garn kár 99
shopping facilities/mall ที่ช็อปปิ้ง, รานขายของ têe chórp (b)ping, rárn kăi kŏrng 32
short สั้น sân 30, 115
short-sighted สายตาสั้น săi (d)tar sân 123
shorts กางเกงขาสั้น garng geyng kàr sân 116
shoulder ไหล่ lài 138
shovel พลั่ว plûa 128
show การแสดง garn sa dairng 87
show, to บอก bùrk 12, 13, 103; (แสดง)ให้ดู (sa dairng) hâi doo 118
shower ฝักบัว fàk bua 23, 32
shrink, to หด hòt 113
shut ปิด (b)pit 14
shutter (camera) ชัตเตอร์ chát (d)têr 125
shutter (window) หน้าต่างบานเกล็ด nàr (d)tàrng barn glèht 29

DICTIONARY

sick *(ill)* ไม่สบาย mǎi sabay 140

sickness *(illness)* เจ็บปวด jèhp (b)pùay 140,

side ด้านข้าง dârn kârng 30

sideboards/-burns จอน jorn 31

sightseeing เที่ยวชมเมือง têaw chom meuang 80

sightseeing tour ทัวร์นำเที่ยว tûa nam têaw 80

sign *(notice)* ป้าย (b)pâi 77, 79, 155

sign, to เซ็นชื่อ sehn cheur 26, 130

signature ลายมือชื่อ lai meur cheur 25

signet ring แหวนฐน wǎirn rûn 122

silk ผ้าไหม pâr mǎi 113

silver เงิน ngern 121, 122

silver *(colour)* สีเงิน sěe ngern 112

silver plate ชุบเงิน chúp ngern 122

silverware เครื่องเงิน krêuang ngern 122, 127

simple แบบธรรมดา bàirp tam ma dar 124

since ตั้งแต่ (d)tâng (d)tàir 15, 150

sing, to ร้อง(เพลง) rórng (pleyng) 88

single *(ticket)* เที่ยวเดียว têaw deaw 65, 69

single *(unmarried)* เป็นโสด (b)pehn sòet 94

single cabin ห้องนอนเดียว(ในเรือ) hông norn dèaw (nai reua) 74

single room ห้องเดียว hôrng dèaw 19, 23

sister พี่(น้อง)สาว pêe (nórng) sǒw 93

six หก hòk 147

sixteen สิบหก sìp hòk 147

sixth ที่หก têe hòk 149

sixty หกสิบ hòk sìp 148

size ขนาด ka nàrt 124

size *(clothes)* ขนาด, เบอร์ ka nàrt, ber 113

size *(shoes)* ขนาด ka nàrt 117

skiing สกี sa gee 90

skin ผิวหนัง pǐw nǎng 138

skin-diving ดำน้ำ dam nárm 91

skirt กระโปรง gra (b)proeng 116

sleep, to นอน norn 144

sleeping bag ถุงนอน tǔng norn 106

sleeping car ตู้นอน rót norn 66, 69, 70

sleeping pill ยานอนหลับ yar norn làp 109, 143

sleeve แขน(เสื้อ) kǎirn (sêua) 115, 142

sleeves, without ไม่มีแขน mǎi mee kǎirn 116

slice แผ่น pàihn 119

slide *(photo)* ฟิล์มสไลด์ feem sa lai 124

slip *(underwear)* กางเกงยาบบาวน้ำผู้หญิง garng geyng àrp párm pôo chai 116

slipper รองเท้าแตะ rorng tów (d)tàih 117

slow(ly) ช้า chár 14, 135

small เล็ก léhk 14, 20, 25, 101, 118

smoke, to สูบบุหรี่ sòop bu rèe 95

smoked รมควัน rom kwan 46

smoker สูบบุหรี่ได้ sòop bu rèe dâi 70

snack อาหารว่าง ar hǎrn wârng 64

snap fastener แปะติดเสื้อ (b)páih (d)tit sêua 116

sneaker รองเท้าผ้าใบ rorng tów păr bai 117

snorkel ท่อดำน้ำ tôr dam nárm 128

snuff ยานัดถุ์ yar nát 126

soap สบู่ sa bòo 27, 111

soccer ฟุตบอล fút born 89, 90

sock ถุงเท้า tǔng tów 116

socket *(electric)* ปลั๊กไฟฟ้า (b)plàk fai fár 27

soft ซ้อฟ(เลนส) sóf (leyn) 123

soft-boiled *(egg)* ไข่ตมไมสุกมาก Kì (d)tôm mǎi sùk mârk 41

sold out ขายหมด kǎi mòt 87

sole *(shoe)* พื้น(รองเท้า) péurn (rorng tów) 117

soloist เดี่ยว dèaw 88

some บาง barng 14

someone ใคร krai 94

something อะไร arai 36, 57, 139; (อัน)ที่ (an) têe 113

somewhere ที่ têe 88

son ลูกชาย lôok chai 93

song เพลง pleyng 128

soon ในไมช้า nai mǎi chár 15

sore *(painful)* ปวด (b)pùat 145

sore throat เจ็บคอ jèhp kor 141

sorry ขอโทษ kǒr tôet 10, 17, 88, 103

sort *(kind)* แบบ bàirp 119

soup ซุป súp 43

south ทิศใต้ tít (d)tâi 77

South Africa อาฟริกาใต้ ar fri gar (d)tâi 146

South America อเมริกาใต้ a mey ri gar (d)tâi 146

souvenir ของที่ระลึก kǒrng têe raléuk 127

souvenir shop ร้านขายของที่ระลึก rárn kǎi kǒrng têe ra léuk 99

spade พลั่ว plûa 128

Spain สเปน sa (b)peyn 146

spare tyre ยางสำรอง yarng sǎm rorng 76

spark(ing) plug หัวเทียน hǔa tearn 76

sparkling *(wine)* สปารกลิ้ง sa (b)par gîng 60

speak, to พูด pôot 11, 16, 135

speaker *(loudspeaker)* ลำโพง lam poeng 118

special พิเศษ pi sèyt 20,

special delivery ไปรษณีย์ด่วน (b)prai sa nee dùan 133

specimen *(medical)* ตัวอย่าง (d)tua yàrng 142

spectacle case ซองใส่แว่น sorng sài wǎihn 123

DICTIONARY

spell, to สะกด sa gòt 12

spend, to จ่าย jài 102

spice เครื่องเทศ krêuang téyp 53

spicy รสจัด rót yàt 37

spinach ผักขม pàk kŏm 53

spine กระดูกสันหลัง gra dùk săn lăng 138

sponge ฟองน้ำขัดตัว forng nárm kàt (d)tua 110

spoon ช้อน chórn 37, 62, 120

sport กีฬา gee lar 89

sporting goods shop ร้านขายเครื่องกีฬา rárn kăi krêuang gee lar 99

sprained เคล็ด klèht 140

spring (season) ฤดูใบไม้ผลิ ri doo bai mái plì 150

spring (water) บ่อน้ำแร่ bor nárm ràir 85

square สี่เหลี่ยมจัตุรัส sèe lèarm jàt(d)tù rát 101

square (town) จัตุรัส jàt (d)tù rát 82

squid ปลาหมึก (b)plar mèuhk 45

stadium สนามกีฬา sa nărm gee lar 82

staff (personnel) พนักงาน pa nák ngarn 26

stain รอยคราบ roy kràrp 29

stainless steel สแตนเลส สa (d)tairn léyt 122

stalls (theatre) ที่นั่งชั้นดีหน้าเวที têe nâng chán dee nâr wey tee 87

stamp (postage) แสตมป์ sa (d)tairm 28, 126, 132, 133

staple ที่เย็บกระดาษ têe yéhp gra dàrt 105

start, to (begin) เริ่ม rêrm,80, 87

starter (meal) อาหารเรียกน้ำย่อย ar hărn rêark nárm yôi 42

station (railway) สถานี(รถไฟ) sa tăr nee (rót fai) 19, 21, 67

stationer's ร้านขายเครื่องเขียน rárn kăi krêuang kěarn 99, 104

statue รูปปั้น rôop (d)pân 82

stay อยู่ yòo 31, 93

stay, to อยู่ yòo 16, 24, 26, 142

steal, to ขโมย ka moey 157

steamed นึ่ง nêuhng 46

stewed ตุ๋น (d)tŭn 47

sticky rice ข้าวเหนียว kôw něaw 50

stiff neck คอแข็ง kor kăihng 141

still (mineral water) ชนิดไม่มีก๊าซ cha nít mâi mee gárt 61

sting ถูกแมลงต่อย tòok ma lairng (d)tòy 139

sting, to แมลงต่อย ma lairng (d)tòy 139

stitch, to เย็บ sòy 29

stock exchange ตลาดหุ้น (d)ta làrt hûn 82

stocking ถุงน่อง tŭng nôrng 116

stomach ท้อง tórng 138

stomach ache ปวดท้อง (b)pùat tórng 141

stools อุจจาระ ùt jar rá 142

stop (bus) ป้าย (b)pâi (rót mey) 73

stop, to จอด jòrt 21, 70, 72; หยุด yùt 69

stop! หยุด yùt 157

store (shop) ร้านค้า rárn kár 98

straight (drink) เพียว peaw 59, 64

straight ahead ตรงไป (d)trong (b)pai 21, 77

strange แปลก (b)plàirk 84

strawberry สตรอเบอร์รี sa (d)tror ber rêe 56

street ถนน ta nŏn 25, 77

street map แผนที่ถนน pàirn têe ta nŏn 20, 105

string เข็มเย็บกระดาษ kĕhm yéhp gra dàrt 105

strong (รส)จัด (rót) jàt 126

student นักศึกษา nák sèuhk săr 82, 94

study, to ศึกษา sèuhk săr 94

stuffed ยัดไส้ yát sâi 42

sturdy แข็งแรงทนทาน kăihng rairng ton tarn 101

suede ชูนังกลับ năng glàp 113, 117

sugar น้ำตาล nárm (d)tarn 37, 64

suit (man's) ชุดสากล chút săr gon 116

suit (woman's) ชุดสากล chút săr gon 116

suitcase กระเป๋า gra (b)pŏw 18

summer ฤดูร้อน ri doo rórn 150

sun-tan cream ครีมกันแดด kreem gan dàirt 110

sun-tan oil น้ำมันกันแดด nám man gan dàirt 110

sunburn แดดเผา dàirt pŏw 107

Sunday วันอาทิตย์ wan ar tít 151

sunglasses แว่นตาดำ wăirn (d)tar dam 123

sunshade (beach) ร่มกันแดด rôm gan dàirt 91

sunstroke (เป็น)ลมแดด ((b)pehn)lom dàirt 141

superb เยี่ยมมาก yêarm mârk 84

supermarket ซุปเปอร์มาร์เกต súp (b)per mar géht 99

suppository ยาเหน็บทวาร yar nèhp ta warn 108

surgery (consulting room) คลีนิคหมอ kleeník mŏr 137

surname นามสกุล narm sagun 25

suspenders (Am.) สายแขวนกางเกง săi kwăirn garng geyng 116

swallow, to กลืน kleurn 143

sweater เสื้อไหมพรม sêua măi prom 116

sweatshirt เสื้อคอกลมแขนยาว sêua geelar kor glom kăirn yow 116

Sweden สวีเดน sa wee deyn 146

sweet หวาน wărn 60; (wine) สวีท sa wèet 62

sweet (confectionery) ลูกกวาด lôok gwàrt 126

sweet corn ข้าวโพด kôw pôet 53

sweet shop ร้านขายขนมหวาน rárn kǎi ka nǒm wǎrn 99

sweetener น้ำตาลเทียม nárm (d)tarn team 38

swelling บวม buam 139

swim, to ว่ายน้ำ wǎi nárm 90

swimming ว่ายน้ำ wǎi nárm 90, 91

swimming pool สระว่ายน้ำ sà wǎi nárm 32, 90

swimming trunks กางเกงว่ายน้ำ garng geyng wǎi nárm 116

swimsuit ชุดว่ายน้ำ chút wǎi nárm 116

switch *(electric)* สวิตช์ไฟ sa wít faj 29

switchboard operator โอเปอเรเดอร์ oe (b)per rey (d)tềr 26

Switzerland สวิตเซอร์แลนด์ sa wít ser lairn 146

swollen บวม buam 139

synagogue สุเหร่ายิว sú,ròw yiw 84

synthetic ผ้าใยสังเคราะห์ pǎr yai sǎng kró 113

T

T-shirt เสื้อคอกลม sêua kor glom 116

table โต๊ะ (d)tóh 36, 106

tablet *(medical)* ยาเม็ด yar méht 108

tailor's ร้านตัดเสื้อ rárn (d)tàt sêua 99

take, to ยก yók 18; เอา ow 25, 102

take away, to หอไปกินบาน hòr (b)pai gin bârn 64

take pictures, to *(photograph)* ถ่ายรูป tài rôop 82

take to, to ไปส่งที่ (b)pai sòng te 21, 67

taken *(occupied)* มีคนนั่ง mee kon nǎng 70

talcum powder แป้งโรยตัว (b)pǎirng roey (d)tua 110

tampon ผ้าอนามัยชนิดแท่ง pǎr a nar mai cha nít tǎjhng 108

tangerine ส้มจีน sôm jeen 56

tap *(water)* ก๊อกน้ำ gók nárm 28

tax ภาษี par sěe 32

taxi แท็กซี่ táihk sêe 19, 21, 31, 67

taxi rank/stand ที่จอดรถแท็กซี่ têe jòrt rót táihk sêe 21

tea ชา char 41, 61, 64

team ทีม teem 89

tear, to *(muscle)* ฉีก chèek 140

teaspoon ช้อนชา chórn char 120, 143

telegram โทรเลข toe ra lêyk 133

telegraph office ที่ทำการโทรเลข têe tam garn toe ra lêyk 99

telephone โทรศัพท์ toe ra sàp 28, 79, 134

telephone booth ตู้โทรศัพท์ (d)tôo toe ra sàp 134

telephone call โทรศัพท์ toe ra sàp 136

telephone directory สมุดโทรศัพท์ sa mút toe ra sàp 134

telephone number หมายเลขโทรศัพท์ mǎi lêyk toe ra sàp 135, 136, 157

telephone, to *(call)* โทร toe 134

telephoto lens เลนส์เทเล leyn tey lêy 125

television โทรทัศน์ toe ra tát 24, 28, 118

telex เทเล็กซ์ tey léhk 133

telex, to เทเล็กซ์ tey léhk 130

tell, to บอก bòrk 73, 76

temperature อุณหภูมิ u na ha poom 90, 140, 142

temporarily ชั่วคราว chûa krow 145

ten สิบ sìp 147

tendon เอ็นในรางกาย ehn nai rǎrng gai 138

tennis เทนนิส teyn nít 90

tennis court สนามเทนนิส sa nǎrm teyn nít 90

tennis racket ไม้แร็กเก็ต mái rǎirk gèht 90

tent เต็นท์ (d)têyn 32, 106

tent peg หมุดปักเต็นท์ mùt (b)pàk (d)têhn 106

tent pole เสาเต็นท์ sǒw (d)têhn 106

tenth ที่สิบ têe sìp 149

term *(word)* เงื่อนไข ngêuan kǎi 131

terrace ระเบียง rá beang 36

terrifying น่ากลัว nâr glua 84

tetanus บาดทะยัก bàrt ta yák 140

Thai ไทย tai 11, 95, 113

Thailand ไทย tai 146

than กว่า gwàr 14

thank you ขอบคุณ kòrp kun 10

thank, to ขอบคุณ kòrp kun 10, 96

that นั่น nân 11; นั้น nán 101

theatre โรงละคร roeng la korn 82, 86, 87

theft ขโมย ka moey 157

then แล้วก็ láiw gô 15

there ที่นั่น têe nân 14

thermometer ปรอท (b)pròrt 109, 144

thigh ตนขา (d)tôn kǎr 138

thin บาง barng 112

think, to *(believe)* คิดว่า kít wâr 31, 63, 94

third ที่สาม têe sǎrm 149

thirsty , to be หิวน้ำ hǐw nárm 13, 36

thirteen สิบสาม sìp sǎrm 147

thirty สามสิบ sǎrm sìp 147

this นี่ nêe 11; อันนี้ an née 101

thousand พัน pan 148

thread ด้าย dâi 27

three สาม sǎrm 147

throat ลำคอ lam kor 138, 141

throat lozenge ยาอม yar om 108

through ผ่าน pàrn 15

through train โมเดยเปลี่ยนรถไฟ mǎi (d)tôrng plêarn rót fai 68

thumb นิ้วหัวแม่มือ níw hǔa mǎir meur 138

thumbtack เป๊กติดกระดาษ (b)péhk (d)tìt

gra dàrt 105

thunder ฟ้าร้อง fár rórng 94

thunderstorm ฝนฟ้าคะนอง fŏn fár ka norng 94

Thursday วันพฤหัสบดี wan pá rú hàt 151

ticket ตั๋ว tŭa 65, 69, 87, 89

ticket office แผนกจำหน่ายตั๋ว pa nàirk jam nài (d)tŭa 68

tie เนคไท néhk tai 116

tie clip ที่หนีบเนคไท têe nèep néhk tai 122

tie pin เข็มกลัดเนคไท kăihm glàt néhk tai 122

tight (close-fitting) คับ káp 116

tights ถุงน่อง tŭng nông 116

time เวลา wey lar 68, 80, 153

time (occasion) ครั้ง kráng 143

timetable (trains) ตารางเดินรถ (d)tar rarng dern ràt 68

tin (container) กระป๋อง gra (b)pŏrng 119

tin opener ที่เปิดกระป๋อง têe (b)pèrt gra (b)pŏrng 120

tint ย้อมผม yar yórm pŏm 110

tinted สี sĕe 123

tire (vehicle) ยาง(รถ) yarng (rót) 76

tired เหนื่อย nèuay 13

tissue (handkerchief) กระดาษทิชชู่ gra dàrt tít sôo 110

to ถึง tĕuhng 15

toast ขนมปังปิ้ง ka nŏm (b)pang (b)pîng 41

tobacco ยาเส้น yar sêhn 126

tobacconist's ร้านขายบุหรี่และยาสูบ rárn kăi burèe láih yar sòop 126

today วันนี้ wan née 29, 151

toe นิ้วเท้า níw táw 138

toilet paper กระดาษชำระ gra dàrt cham rá 110

toilet water โอดิโคโลญ oe do koe loen 110

toiletry เครื่องใช้ในห้องน้ำ krêuang chái nai hông nárm 110

toilets ห้องน้ำ hông nárm 24, 27, 32, 37, 68

tomato มะเขือเทศ ma kĕua tèyt 61

tomato juice น้ำมะเขือเทศ nárm ma kĕua tèyt 61

tomb สุสาน su sărn 82

tomorrow วันพรุ่งนี้ wan prûng née 29, 96, 151

tongue ลิ้น lín 138

tonic water โทนิค toe ník 61

tonight คืนนี้ keurn née 29, 86

tonsils ต่อมทอนซิล (d)tòrm torn sin 138

too เกินไป gern (b)pai 15

too (also) เหมือนกัน mĕuan gan 15

too much มากเกินไป mârk gern (b)pai 14

tools เครื่องมือ krêuang meur 120

tooth ฟัน fan 145

toothache ปวดฟัน (b)pùat fan 145

toothbrush แปรงสีฟัน (b)prairng sĕe fan 110, 118

toothpaste ยาสีฟัน yar sĕe fan 110

toothpick ไม้จิ้มฟัน mái jîm fan 37

top, at the ข้างบน kârng bon 30; ด้านบน dârn bon 145

torch (flashlight) ไฟฉาย fai chăi 106

torn (muscle) ฉีก chèek 140

touch, to จับ jàp 156

tough (meat) เหนียว nĕaw 62

tour เที่ยว têaw 74, 80

tourist office สำนักงานท่องเที่ยว săm nák ngarn tông têaw 80

tourist tax ภาษีนักท่องเที่ยว par sĕe nák tông têaw 32

tow truck รถลาก rót lârk 78

towards ตรงไปที่ (d)trong (b)pai têe 15

towel ผ้าขนหนู pâr kŏn nŏo 27, 111

towelling (terrycloth) ผ้าขนหนู pâr kŏn nŏo 113

town เมือง meuang 19, 77, 89

town center ใจกลางเมือง jai glarng meuang 21, 77; ในเมือง nai meuang 72

town hall ศาลากลางจังหวัด săr lar wăr garn jang wàt 82

toy ของเล่น kŏrng lêhn 128

toy shop ร้านขายของเล่น rárn kăi kŏrng lêhn 99

tracksuit ชุดวอร์ม chút worm 116

traffic light แยกไฟแดง yâirk fai dairng 77

trailer รถคาราวาน jòrt rót norm 32

train รถไฟ rót fai 66, 68, 69, 70, 153

tranquillizer ยากล่อมประสาท yar glòrm (b)pra sàrt 109, 143

transfer (finance) โอนเงิน oen ngern 131

transformer หม้อแปลงไฟฟ้า môr (b)plairng fai fár 118

translate, to แปล (b)plair 12

transport, means of การเดินทาง garn dern tarng 75

travel agency เอเยนต์ท่องเที่ยว ey yêhn tôrng têaw 99

travel guide หนังสือคู่มือ náng sĕur kôo meur 105

travel sickness เมารถเมาเรือ mow rót mow reua 107

travel, to เดินทางท่องเที่ยว dern tarng (d)tôrng têaw 94

traveller's cheque เช็คเดินทาง chéhk dern tarng 19, 63, 102, 129

travelling bag กระเป๋า(เดินทาง) gra (b)pŏw dern tarng 18

tree ต้นไม้ (d)tôn mái 85

trim, to (a beard) เล็ม lehm 31

trip เดินทาง garn dern tarng 72

trolley รถเข็น rót kĕhn 18, 71

trousers กางเกงขายาว garng keyng kăr

yow 116
try on, to ลอง lorng 114
Tuesday วันอังคาร wan ang karn 151
tuk tuk ตุ๊กๆ (d)túk (d)túk 21
tumbler ถ้วยแก้ว tûay gãiw 120
turkey ไก่งวง gài nguang 49,
turn, to *(change direction)* เลี้ยว léaw 21,
77
turquoise เทอร์คอยส์ teŗ koys 122
turquoise *(colour)* สีเทอร์คอยส์ sẽe ter
koys 112
turtleneck คอโปโล kor (b)poe loe 116
tweezers แหนบ nàirp 110
twelve สิบสอง sìp sõrng 147
twenty ยี่สิบ yêe sìp 147
twice สองครั้ง sõrng kráng 149
two สอง sõrng 147
typewriter เครื่องพิมพ์ดีด krêuang pim
dèet 27
typing paper กระดาษพิมพ์ดีด gra dàrt pim
dèet 105
tyre ยาง(รถ) yarng (rót) 76

U

ugly น่าเกลียด nâr glèart 14, 84
umbrella ร่ม rôm.116
umbrella *(beach)* ร่มกันแดด rôm gan dàirt
91
uncle ลุง lung 93
unconscious หมดสติ mòt sa(d)ti 139
under ใต้ (d)tâi 15
underpants กางเกงใน garng geyng nai
116
undershirt เสื้อยืด sêua yèurt 116
understand, to เข้าใจ kôw jai 12, 17
undress, to ถอดเสื้อ tôrt sêua 142
United States สหรัฐ sa har rát 146
university มหาวิทยาลัย ma hãr wít ta yar
lai 82
unleaded ไร้สารตะกั่ว rái sãrn (d)ta gùa
75
until กระทั่ง gra tãng 15
up ขึ้น kêun 14
upper ชั้นบน chán bon 70
upset stomach ท้องเสีย tórng sẽar 107
upstairs ชั้นบน chán bon 15
urgent ด่วน dùan 13, 145
urine ปัสสาวะ (b)pàt sãr wá 142
use ใช้ chái 108
use, to ใช้ chái 134
useful เป็นประโยชน์ (b)pehn (b)pra yòet
15
usual เป็นประจำ (b)pehn (b)pra jam 143

V

V-neck คอวี kor wee 115
vacant ว่าง wârng 14, 23, 156
vacation วันหยุดพักผ่อน wan yùt pák pòrn

151
vaccinate, to ฉีดวัคซีน chèet wák seen
140
vacuum flask กระติกสุญญากาศ gra (d)tik
sõon yar gàrt 120
valley หุบเขา hùp kõw 85
value มูลค่า moon kâr 131
vanilla วานิลา war ni lar 55
veal เนื้อลูกวัวอ่อน néua lôok wua òrn 47
vegetable ผัก pàk 53
vegetable store ร้านขายผัก rárn kãi pàk
99
vegetarian มังสวิรัติ mang sa wi rát 38
vein เส้นเลือด sêhn lêuat 138
velvet ผ้ากำมะหยี่ pâr gam ma yêe 113
velveteen ผ้ากำมะหยี่เทียม pâr gam ma
yêe tearm 113
venereal disease กามโรค garm ma rôek
142
vermouth เวอมัธ wer mát 60
very มาก mârk 15
vest เสื้อกล้าม sêua glârm 116
vest *(Am.)* เสื้อกั๊ก sêua gák 116
veterinarian สัตวแพทย์ sàt pàirt 99
video camera กล้องวีดีโอ glông wee dee
oe 124
video cassette ม้วนเทปวีดีโอ múan téyp
wee dee oe 118, 124, 127
video recorder เครื่องอัดวีดีโอ krêuang àt
wee dee oe 118
view *(panorama)* วิว wiw 23, 25
village หมู่บ้าน mòo bârn 76, 85
vinegar น้ำส้มสายชู nárm sôm sài choo
37
visit มาที่นี่ mar têe nêe 93
visit, to เยี่ยม yêarm 95
visiting hours เวลาเปิดทำการ wey lar
(b)pèrd tam garn 144
vitamin pill วิตามิน wí (d)tar min 108
vodka ว็อดกา wód gãr 60
volleyball วอลเลย์บอล worn lêy born 90
voltage โวลต์ wôel 27, 118
vomit, to อาเจียน ar jearn 140

W

waist เอว ew 142
waistcoat เสื้อกั๊ก sêua gák 116
wait, to รอ ror 21; คอย koy 107
waiter บอย bõry 26, 36; พนักงานเสิร์ฟ pa
nák ngarn sèrp.26
waiting room ห้องพักผู้โดยสาร hôrng pák
pôo dory sãrn 68
waitress พนักงานเสิร์ฟ pa nák ngarn sèrp
26; คุณ kun 36
wake, to ปลุก (b)plùk 27, 71
Wales เวลส์ weyls 146
walk, to เดิน dern 75, 85

wall กำแพง **gam pairng** 85
wallet กระเป๋าใส่เงิน **gra (b)pŏw sài ngern** 160
want, to ต้องการ **(d)tông garn** 13; อยากได้ **yàrk (dâi)** 101, 102
warm อุ่น **ùn** 94
wash, to ซัก **sák** 29, 113
washable ซักได้ **sák dûay** 113
washbasin อ่างล้างหน้า **àrng lárng nâr** 28
washing powder ผงซักฟอก **pŏng sák fôrk** 120
washing-up liquid น้ำยาล้างจาน **nárm yar lárng jarn** 120
watch นาฬิกาข้อมือ **nar lí gar kôr meur** 121, 122
watchmaker's ร้านนาฬิกา **rárn nar li gar** 121
watchstrap สายนาฬิกาข้อมือ **săi na li gar kôr meur** 122
water น้ำ **nárm** 24, 28, 32, 41, 75, 90
water flask กระติกน้ำ **gra (d)tìk nárm** 106
water melon แตงโม **(d)tairng moe** 56
water-skis สกีน้ำ **sa gee nárm** 91
waterfall น้ำตก **nárm (d)tòk** 85
waterproof กันน้ำ **gan nárm** 122
wave คลื่น **klêurn** 91
way ทาง **tarng** 76
weather อากาศ **ar gàrt** 94
weather forecast พยากรณ์อากาศ **pa yar gorn ar gàrt** 94
wedding ring แหวนแต่งงาน **wăirn (d)tàihng ngarn** 122
Wednesday, วันพุธ **wan pút** 151
week อาทิตย์ **ar tít** 16, 20, 24, 80, 92, 151
well (สบาย)ดี **(sa bai) dee** 10
well-done (meat) สุกๆ **sùk sùk** 47
west ทิศตะวันตก **tít (d)tawan (d)tòk** 77
what อะไร **arai** 11
wheel ล้อรถ **lór rót** 78
when เมื่อไหร่ **mêua rài** 11
where ที่ไหน **têe năi** 11
where from มาจากไหน **mar jàrk năi** 93, 146
which อันไหน **an năi** 11
whisky วิสกี้ **wít sa gêe** 17, 60
white สีขาว **sêe kŏw** 59, 112
who ใคร **krai** 11
whole ทั้งหมด **táng mòt** 143
why ทำไม **tam mai** 11
wick ไส้ตะเกียง **sâi (d)ta gearng** 126
wide กว้าง **gwârng** 117
wide-angle lens เลนส์มุมกว้าง **leyn mum gwârng** 125
wife ภรรยา **pan ra yar** 93
wig วิกผม **wík pŏm** 110
wild boar หมูป่า **mŏo (b)pàr** 49
wind ลม **lom** 94
window หน้าต่าง **nâr (d)tàrng** 28, 36, 65, 70

window (shop) ตู้โชว์ **(d)tôo choe** 101, 112
windscreen/shield กระจกหน้ารถยนต์ **gra jòk năr rót yon** 76
windsurfer วินด์เซิร์ฟ **win sêrf** 91
wine เหล้าไวน์ **lôw wai** 59, 62
wine list รายการเหล้าไวน์ **rai garn lôw wai** 59
winter ฤดูหนาว **rí doo nŏw** 150
wiper (car) ที่ปัดน้ำฝน **têe (b)pàt nárm fŏn** 76
wish อวยพร **uay porn** 153
with กับ, ควย **gàp, dûay** 15
withdraw, to (from account) ถอนเงิน **tŏrn ngern** 130
withdrawal ถอน **tŏrn** 130
without ไม่มี, ม่าย **mâi mee** 15
wonderful เยี่ยม **yêarm** 96
wood ป่า **(b)pàr** 85
wool ผ้าขนแกะ **păr kŏn gàih** 113
word คำ **kam** 12, 15, 133
work, to ทำงาน **tam ngarn** 28, 118
working day วันทำงาน **wan tam ngarn** 151
worse เลวกว่า **leyw gwàr** 14
worsted ไหมพรม **măi prom** 113
wound ได้รับบาดเจ็บ **dâi ráp bàrt jèhp** 139
wrap up, to ห่อ **hòr** 103
wrinkle-free กันยับ **gan yáp** 113
wristwatch นาฬิกาข้อมือ **na li gar kôr meur** 122
write, to เขียน **kĕarn** 12, 101
writing pad กระดาษเขียนหนังสือ **gra dàrt kĕarn náng sĕur** 105
writing paper กระดาษเขียนหนังสือ **gra dàrt kĕarn náng sĕur** 105
wrong ผิด **pìt** 14, 77, 135

Y
year ปี **(b)pee** 149
yellow สีเหลือง **sĕe lĕuang** 112
yes ครับ (คะ) **kráp (kâ)** 10
yesterday เมื่อวาน **mêua warn** 151
yet ยัง **yang** 15, 16, 25
yoghurt โยเกิร์ต **yoo gèrt** 41, 64
young เด็ก **dèhk** 14
youth hostel ที่พักเยาวชน **têe pák yo wa chon** 32

Z
zero ศูนย์ **sŏon** 147
zip(per) ซิป, ซิ่ป **síp** 116
zoo สวนสัตว์ **suan sàt** 82
zoology สัตววิทยา **sàt wít ta yar** 83

ดัชนีภาษาไทย